Isles of Wonder

Îles aux merveilles

London 2012 Olympic Games
Opening Ceremony
27 July 2012

Cérémonie d'ouverture des
Jeux Olympiques de Londres 2012
Le 27 juillet 2012

Please note, the Ceremony includes strobe lighting, pyrotechnics and lasers.

*Veuillez noter que la Cérémonie inclut des éclairages stroboscopiques,
des dispositifs pyrotechniques et des lasers.*

Her Majesty The Queen

It is with tremendous pride that the people of London and the United Kingdom welcome the world to the London 2012 Olympic Games.

We look forward to celebrating the uplifting spirit which distinguishes the Olympic Games, drawing on Britain's unique sporting and Olympic heritage.

Athletes from every corner of the globe speak of their enormous desire to represent their country through sport. It is at the Olympic Games that their many years of dedication and commitment are truly realised.

The athletes' endeavours and triumphs will excite and inspire people wherever they live. I look forward to memorable Games that leave a lasting legacy for London, the UK and the worldwide Olympic Movement.

C'est avec une immense fierté que les habitants de Londres et du Royaume-Uni accueillent le monde aux Jeux Olympiques de Londres 2012.

Nous avons hâte de célébrer l'esprit positif qui caractérise les Jeux Olympiques en nous appuyant sur le patrimoine sportif et olympique unique de la Grande-Bretagne.

Partout dans le monde, les athlètes évoquent leur désir immense de représenter leur pays au travers du sport. C'est aux Jeux Olympiques que se concrétisent véritablement toutes leurs années de dévouement et d'engagement.

Les efforts et les réussites des athlètes enthousiasmeront et inspireront les gens où qu'ils vivent. Je me réjouis à l'avance de ces Jeux mémorables qui laisseront un héritage durable à la fois à Londres, au Royaume-Uni et au Mouvement olympique mondial.

Jacques Rogge

President of the International Olympic Committee
Président du Comité International Olympique

Tonight's Opening Ceremony marks the official beginning of the Games of the XXX Olympiad, the moment when people around the world come together for 16 days to celebrate sport and human excellence.

For the thousands of athletes participating at London 2012, the Games represent the culmination of years of dedication, sacrifice and training. Athletes are the true heart of the Olympic Games, and this is their time to shine, to put in the performances of their lives and to inspire a generation.

For many competitors, London 2012 will be the highlight of their sporting careers. Some will of course reach the podium and set records along the way. But win or lose, it will be those athletes who compete in a spirit of excellence, friendship and respect that will set an example for us all.

I have no doubt that London will offer them ideal conditions in which to achieve their personal bests. The local organisers have done a terrific job preparing for the Games and the athletes are eager to get started turning their Olympic dreams into reality.

Sixteen days of world-class athletic performances await us, and the hosts are ready to deliver an excellent Olympic Games that will leave a positive legacy for London, the United Kingdom and the Olympic Movement for many years to come.

Like the billions of Olympic fans in London and around the world, I too will be watching and willing on the athletes. I wish each one the best of luck and an excellent and memorable Games, and to everyone in attendance tonight an enjoyable evening.

Let the Games begin!

La cérémonie d'ouverture de ce soir marque le début officiel des Jeux de la XXXᵉ Olympiade, moment où des personnes venues du monde entier se rassemblent pour célébrer pendant 16 jours l'excellence sportive et humaine.

Pour les milliers d'athlètes participant aux Jeux de 2012 à Londres, les Jeux représentent le couronnement de longues années de dévouement, de sacrifices et d'entraînement. Les athlètes sont le cœur même des Jeux Olympiques, et pour eux, c'est leur heure de briller, de livrer leurs plus belles performances et d'inspirer toute une génération.

Pour de nombreux concurrents, les Jeux de 2012 à Londres seront le temps fort de leur carrière sportive. Naturellement, certains monteront sur le podium et établiront au passage quelques records. Mais qu'ils gagnent ou qu'ils perdent, ces athlètes en quête d'excellence qui concourront dans un esprit d'amitié et de respect, seront des exemples pour nous tous.

Je ne doute pas que Londres leur offrira des conditions idéales pour livrer leurs meilleures prestations personnelles. Les organisateurs locaux ont fait un travail extraordinaire pour préparer les Jeux et les athlètes sont impatients de commencer, pour transformer leur rêve olympique en réalité.

Seize jours de performances sportives de niveau mondial nous attendent et nos hôtes sont prêts à nous offrir d'excellents Jeux Olympiques qui laisseront un héritage positif à la ville de Londres, au Royaume-Uni et au Mouvement olympique pendant de nombreuses années à venir.

Comme les milliards de passionnés des Jeux à Londres et dans le monde entier, je regarderai et encouragerai moi aussi les athlètes. À chacun je souhaite bonne chance ainsi que d'excellents et mémorables Jeux, et à tous ceux présents ici ce soir, je souhaite de vivre une agréable soirée.

Que les Jeux commencent !

Sebastian Coe

Chair, London 2012 Organising Committee
Président du Comité d'organisation de Londres 2012

Bienvenue à Londres. Welcome to London. We stand before you this evening with a deep sense of history and responsibility as we prepare to become the first city to host the Summer Olympic Games for a third occasion, following the 1908 and 1948 London Games. This is an enormous honour.

We meet in difficult and different times – in a period of adversity, but also of opportunity, to inspire a world in need of hope, and like our predecessors, we turn to sport and to the athletes to connect the world in a global celebration of achievement and inspiration.

The journey to this Opening Ceremony has included times of great social, economic and community turbulence and change, as we've planned and prepared for this moment for a decade – from the London bombings to the global financial crisis. But we are resilient and we are ready. Support has never wavered, reflecting the importance of sport in British society, and the commitment of the British people and the global community to the Games and the Olympic ideal.

We've seen great passion and enthusiasm from people across the United Kingdom for these Games, highlighted by the Olympic Torch Relay, which has united nations and regions, and placed a spotlight on the humbling heroism and courage of local Torch carriers from all cultures and walks of life. They have lifted the country's spirits, reminding us of the best we can be, and demonstrating that the Olympic values still matter in real and relevant ways in the 21st century.

These Games have been inspired by many people and many motivations, including parents who prepare breakfasts, make school lunches and drive their children to sports centres in the pre-dawn darkness; the belief of the world's most admired person, Nelson Mandela, in London as the city that can stage Games that unite the world; sporting greats who have captured our imagination and redefined the boundaries of human achievement on and off the sporting field; and athletes from every culture and country who have dedicated half their young lives for this Olympic moment in London. Young people everywhere know that something special and important is about to happen as the world gets ready for the Games.

We want London 2012 to be a beacon of hope and possibility, and to inspire a generation, as athletes from more than 200 nations – more than the United Nations – come together in tonight's Opening Ceremony, in the world's greatest peacetime gathering of countries and territories, providing a glimpse perhaps of what the world might look like as one nation or as the United Nations of Sport.

We hope you enjoy the Ceremony this evening – an extraordinary experience is about to begin. Thank you for sharing this with us.

Welcome to London. Bienvenue à Londres. Un profond sentiment d'histoire et de responsabilité nous habite ce soir alors que nous nous préparons à devenir la première ville à organiser pour la troisième fois les Jeux Olympiques d'été, après ceux de 1908 et de 1948. C'est un immense honneur.

Nous sommes réunis aujourd'hui en des temps difficiles et différents – une période d'adversité, mais aussi d'opportunités, pour inspirer un monde en attente d'espoir – et, comme nos prédécesseurs, nous nous tournons une fois encore vers le sport et les athlètes pour rassembler le monde en une célébration planétaire de la réussite et de l'inspiration.

Des attentats de Londres à la crise financière mondiale, nous avons traversé des zones de turbulences et de changements sociaux, économiques et communautaires majeurs au cours de la décennie où nous nous sommes préparés à ces Jeux. Mais nous sommes endurants et tenaces, et nous sommes prêts. Le soutien n'a jamais faibli, reflétant l'importance du sport dans la société britannique ainsi que

l'attachement du peuple britannique et de la communauté internationale à ces Jeux et à l'idéal olympique.

Nous avons vu une formidable passion et un immense enthousiasme pour ces Jeux chez les habitants de tout le Royaume-Uni à l'occasion du relais de la Flamme olympique, un relais qui a uni nations et régions et braqué les projecteurs sur l'héroïsme impressionnant et le courage des porteurs locaux de la Flamme, issus de toutes les cultures et tous les horizons. Ils ont réchauffé le cœur de la nation, nous ont montré le meilleur de ce que nous pouvons être et nous ont prouvé que les valeurs olympiques sont toujours présentes et d'actualité au XXIe siècle.

Nombreuses sont les personnes et les motivations à avoir inspiré ces Jeux : les parents qui font le petit déjeuner, préparent les sandwiches et conduisent en voiture leurs enfants au centre sportif avant les premières lueurs de l'aube ; la foi de Nelson Mandela, l'homme le plus admiré de la Terre, en Londres et en sa capacité à organiser des Jeux qui unissent le monde ; les grands du sport, qui ont captivé notre imagination et ont conduit à réévaluer ce dont l'Homme est capable sur un terrain de sport et ailleurs ; les athlètes de toutes les cultures et tous les pays qui ont dédié la moitié de leur jeune vie à ce moment olympique à Londres. Partout dans le monde, alors que la planète tout entière se prépare à ces Jeux, les jeunes savent que quelque chose de spécial et d'important est sur le point de se produire.

À l'heure où la cérémonie d'ouverture de ce soir réunit les athlètes de plus de 200 nations – plus qu'aux Nations Unies – au sein du plus grand rassemblement de pays et territoires en temps de paix, offrant peut-être un aperçu de ce que pourrait être le monde uni en une seule nation ou en Nations Unies du Sport, nous voulons que Londres 2012 soit un flambeau d'espérance et de potentialités et l'inspiration d'une génération.

Nous espérons que vous aimerez la cérémonie de ce soir : une expérience extraordinaire commence. Merci d'être avec nous pour la partager.

Rt Hon David Cameron MP

Prime Minister
Premier ministre

After years of planning, months of build-up and weeks of fevered anticipation, this is it: the Olympic Games 2012 have arrived.

This is a great moment for London; a chance to show our bustling, dynamic capital city at its very best. And this is a great moment for the whole of the United Kingdom. Many thousands of people from all over our country have worked to make this happen, excavating tonnes of soil, planting countless trees, building huge new sports grounds. Now the stage is set – and the Games can begin.

We want these to be the most spectacular and enjoyable Olympics the world has ever seen. Above all, we want these Games to inspire people around the world. On a monument right in the heart of the Olympic Village, the words of the British poet Tennyson have been engraved: 'To strive, to seek, to find, and not to yield.' It's that spirit – that relentless pursuit of glory and greatness – that makes the Olympic Games so special. And it is that spirit that will go out from London to inspire the world.

I want to warmly welcome you to the Olympic Games 2012 – and I hope you enjoy the greatest show on earth.

Après des années de préparation, des mois de montée en puissance et des semaines d'attente fiévreuse, les Jeux Olympiques de 2012 sont enfin là.

C'est un moment historique pour Londres, l'occasion de montrer notre capitale vivante et dynamique sous son meilleur jour. Et c'est un moment historique pour le Royaume-Uni tout entier. Partout dans notre pays, des milliers de personnes ont œuvré pour rendre cet événement possible, excavant des tonnes de terre, plantant d'innombrables arbres, bâtissant des terrains de sport gigantesques. Aujourd'hui, la scène est prête et les Jeux peuvent commencer.

Ces Olympiades, nous les voulons les plus spectaculaires et les plus agréables que le monde ait jamais vues. Surtout, nous voulons que ces Jeux inspirent les gens partout dans le monde. Sur un monument au cœur du village olympique ont été gravés les mots du poète britannique Alfred Tennyson : « To strive, to seek, to find, and not to yield » (Lutter, chercher, trouver et ne pas céder). C'est cet esprit, cette recherche sans relâche de la gloire et de l'excellence, qui fait des Jeux Olympiques un événement si spécial. Et c'est cet esprit qui, de Londres, inspirera le reste du monde.

Je tiens à vous souhaiter de tout cœur la bienvenue aux Jeux Olympiques de 2012 et j'espère que vous apprécierez le plus grand spectacle du monde.

Boris Johnson

Mayor of London
Maire de Londres

Today London becomes the first city in history to stage a third Summer Olympic Games. I am delighted to welcome you to tonight's event, where we gather to mark this thrilling and humbling moment in our city's history.

This evening's Ceremony celebrates the best of London's past, present and future. After centuries as a global centre for culture and commerce, London enjoys a diversity unrivalled anywhere in the world. This diversity – of culture, language, cuisine, thought, belief and imagination – is now thoroughly twined into London's DNA, both cause and effect of its phenomenal success and much-envied reputation.

It also makes this year's Games unique, and uniquely enjoyable. Almost every team competing this year will find a ready-made home crowd to cheer them on. Meanwhile, for those athletes, officials and spectators who can tear themselves away from the sport for even a moment, London offers a mouth-watering selection of things to see and do – and we've pulled out all the stops to make this summer's menu even richer and spicier than usual.

But the Games are not just celebrating what London has to offer – they have helped to shape it. The Stadium in which you sit is at the centre of a transformational renaissance for east London, with investment in the Games providing much-needed homes, jobs and green space for Londoners and infrastructure that is already attracting investment to the area from all over the world.

I hope you will treasure your memories of tonight's celebration for as long as Londoners treasure their own Olympic legacy.

Aujourd'hui, Londres devient la première ville de l'histoire à accueillir pour la troisième fois les Jeux Olympiques d'été. Je suis ravi de vous souhaiter la bienvenue à l'événement qui nous rassemble ce soir pour marquer ce moment à la fois excitant et synonyme d'humilité dans l'histoire de notre ville.

La cérémonie de ce soir célèbre ce que Londres a de meilleur dans son passé, son présent et son futur. Centre culturel et commercial du monde pendant des siècles, Londres bénéficie aujourd'hui d'une diversité unique sur la planète. Cette diversité culturelle, linguistique, gastronomique, intellectuelle, cultuelle et imaginative est maintenant inscrite au cœur-même de l'ADN londonien, à la fois cause et effet de la réussite éblouissante et de la réputation ô combien convoitée de la ville.

Cette diversité fait aussi des Jeux de cette année des Jeux uniques, offrant un plaisir à nul autre pareil. Presque toutes les équipes en compétition trouveront cette année sur place une foule de supporters nationaux pour les encourager. Pour les athlètes, dignitaires et spectateurs qui, l'espace d'un instant, parviendront à s'arracher au sport, Londres offre une alléchante sélection d'attractions et de sites à visiter. Et nous n'avons pas ménagé nos efforts pour donner au menu de cet été une tonalité plus riche et plus épicée encore qu'à l'accoutumée.

Mais les Jeux ne sont pas simplement une célébration de ce que Londres a à offrir. Ils ont aussi contribué à façonner cette ville. Le stade où vous êtes assis est au cœur-même d'une véritable transformation qui fait souffler un vent de renouveau sur l'est de Londres. Les investissements réalisés dans les Jeux ont apporté logements, emplois et espaces verts à des Londoniens qui en avaient bien besoin, ainsi que des infrastructures qui attirent déjà dans le secteur des investissements des quatre coins du monde.

J'espère que vous garderez en souvenir et chérirez les célébrations de ce soir aussi longtemps que les Londoniens chériront leur héritage olympique.

Rt Hon Jeremy Hunt MP

Secretary of State for Culture, Olympics, Media and Sport
Secrétaire d'État à la culture, aux Jeux Olympiques, aux médias et au sport

This will be a summer like no other for the UK – a unique sporting and cultural celebration to which the whole world is invited. But it won't stop there.

From the start, London 2012 was designed as much around what will happen in the years after the Games as what happens in 2012 itself.

In east London, we're creating a brand-new quarter that will benefit local communities for decades to come, served by world-class transport links, facilities and services.

Across the UK, we're building on the excitement of the Torch Relay and the London 2012 Festival – not to mention the Queen's Diamond Jubilee – to bring people together and foster a new culture of volunteering.

For our economy, we're seizing the opportunity to fire up our businesses, showcase our incredible tourism offer, and attract new investment.

And most importantly, we're using the power of London 2012 to reinvigorate our country's sporting culture and inspire more young people to choose sport for life.

This is a golden moment for the UK, and we are determined to make the most of it – so that the coming weeks leave not only lasting memories, but a lasting legacy in this country and beyond.

Cet été sera un été à nul autre pareil pour le Royaume-Uni. Une célébration sportive et culturelle unique, à laquelle le monde entier est invité. Mais ce n'est pas tout.

Dès le début, Londres 2012 a été conçu autant autour de ce qui se passera après les Jeux qu'autour de ce qui se passera en 2012.

Dans l'est londonien, un quartier entièrement neuf est en cours de création. Un quartier dont profiteront les communautés locales pendant des décennies et doté de transports, d'infrastructures et de services de tout premier plan.

Dans tout le Royaume-Uni, nous profitons de l'enthousiasme généré par le relais de la flamme et le festival de Londres 2012 (sans oublier le Jubilé de diamant de la Reine) pour rapprocher les communautés et encourager le développement d'une nouvelle culture du volontariat.

Pour notre économie, nous mettons à profit l'événement pour stimuler nos entreprises, mettre en avant notre offre touristique incroyable et attirer de nouveaux investissements.

Enfin, et c'est peut-être le plus important, nous profitons de Londres 2012 pour revigorer la culture sportive de notre pays et inspirer davantage de jeunes à s'engager dans le sport.

C'est une période dorée pour le Royaume-Uni et nous sommes déterminés à en profiter au maximum, pour que les semaines qui viennent laissent derrière elles non seulement des souvenirs durables, mais aussi un héritage durable, dans ce pays et ailleurs.

Rt Hon Tessa Jowell MP

Shadow Minister for London and the Olympics
Porte-parole de l'opposition pour Londres et les Jeux Olympiques

Seven years ago, this Olympic Park was a derelict, contaminated wasteland, with old fridges and debris piled high where the Stadium and other venues now stand. Now it is the largest new urban park in Europe for 150 years – set to become a cultural, sporting and commercial centre. It is a legacy that will create opportunities for all the communities of the Olympic boroughs.

Those of us in Government and Mayor Ken Livingstone wanted 2012 to be the year that changed east London forever. And it has – with this park, new jobs, new infrastructure and a renewed sense of local pride. All that, and the greatest athletes in the world competing to the limits of possibility.

For young people watching them, it's a chance to see that ambition is worth having, that dreams are worth pursuing and that bars should be set high and leapt over.

I am so proud to have been a part of this for the last 10 years. Proud, too, that over those years we politicians have set London 2012 above party politics and acted together to bring it to fruition.

We are, all of us, proud to say to you: welcome to London.

Rt Hon Sir Menzies Campbell MP

Liberal Democrat spokesman for London 2012 and former Olympian
Porte-parole du parti libéral-démocrate pour Londres 2012 et ancien athlète olympique

Rt Hon Don Foster MP

Liberal Democrat spokesman for London 2012
Porte-parole du parti libéral-démocrate pour Londres 2012

Il y a sept ans, ce Parc olympique n'était qu'un terrain vague pollué où s'entassaient vieux réfrigérateurs et détritus là où se trouvent maintenant le Stade et d'autres sites. C'est aujourd'hui le plus grand parc urbain nouvellement créé en Europe depuis 150 ans, promis à un avenir de centre culturel, sportif et commercial. C'est un héritage qui sera source d'opportunités pour toutes les communautés des districts olympiques.

Ceux d'entre nous alors au gouvernement et le maire Ken Livingstone voulaient que 2012 soit l'année qui changerait l'est de Londres pour toujours. Et c'est le cas avec ce parc, de nouveaux emplois et équipements, avec ce regain de fierté locale. Sans oublier les plus grands athlètes du monde, venus concourir aux limites de l'impossible.

Pour les jeunes qui les regardent, c'est l'occasion de voir qu'il vaut la peine d'avoir de l'ambition, que les rêves méritent d'être poursuivis et que la barre doit être placée haut et dépassée.

Je suis très fière de faire partie de tout cela depuis 10 ans. Fière également que, pendant ces années, nous, politiques, ayons placé Londres 2012 au-dessus des clivages partisans et agi ensemble pour mener à bien ce projet.

C'est avec fierté que nous vous disons tous Bienvenue à Londres.

For many, London 2012 began back in 2005 when we won the bid to stage the Olympic Games.

Since then thousands have worked tirelessly, the length and breadth of the country, to prepare, not just in London but throughout the UK – from Weymouth and Portland to Hampden Park in Glasgow. The whole country has been involved in designing and constructing the Olympic Park and venues, and tonight we will see entertainment and talent drawn together from across the UK.

We will be transported, stewarded and protected by thousands of people, including volunteers who have given their time and service to deliver the Games.

London 2012 has already inspired many young people to take up sport, with some of the best performing at the Schools Games in this Stadium earlier this year.

And tonight we will see athletes from across the globe who themselves were schoolchildren only a few years ago.

The Games will inspire us to achieve our goals. Using true British style and humour, tonight will be a celebration of the Olympic ethos that combines values of friendship, excellence and respect.

We salute the athletes you will be privileged to see over the coming days for their dedication, determination and spirit.

Pour beaucoup, Londres 2012 a commencé en 2005, lorsque nous avons été désignés ville organisatrice des Jeux.

Des milliers de personnes ont depuis travaillé sans relâche, pas seulement à Londres, mais aux quatre coins du Royaume-Uni, de Weymouth à Portland en passant par Hampden Park à Glasgow, pour préparer l'événement. Le pays tout entier s'est impliqué dans la conception et la construction du Parc et des sites olympiques et nous verrons ce soir des spectacles et talents issus de tout le Royaume-Uni.

Nous serons transportés, accueillis et protégés par des milliers de personnes, dont des bénévoles qui ont donné de leur temps et de leurs services pour permettre la réalisation de ces Jeux.

Londres 2012 a déjà poussé de nombreux jeunes à se mettre au sport. Quelques-uns des meilleurs se sont d'ailleurs retrouvés dans ce Stade au début de l'année pour les School Games.

Et nous verrons ce soir, venus du monde entier, des athlètes qui n'étaient encore eux-mêmes qu'écoliers il y a quelques années.

Les Jeux vont nous inspirer à atteindre nos objectifs. Avec un style et un humour tout britanniques, cette soirée va célébrer la philosophie olympique qui rassemble des valeurs d'amitié, d'excellence et de respect.

Nous saluons les athlètes que vous aurez le privilège de voir ces prochains jours pour leur dévouement, leur détermination et leur fougue.

Welcome to the Isles of Wonder

*Bienvenue
dans les
Îles aux merveilles*

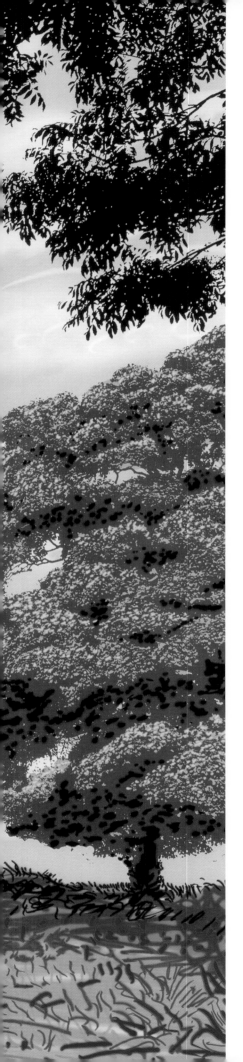

David Hockney came to prominence as part of *Young Contemporaries*, the exhibition that kick-started Pop Art in 1961. Fifty years on, he's as innovative and surprising as ever – his *A Bigger Picture* at the Royal Academy earlier this year was a sensation. He's constantly pushing the boundaries of technique. The brilliant colours and swirling rhythms of this traditional landscape, 'Summer Sky', for example, were produced on a computer graphic tablet and inkjet printer in 2008.

David Hockney s'est fait connaître en participant à Young Contemporaries, l'exposition qui lança le Pop Art en 1961. Cinquante ans plus tard, il continue à innover et à étonner comme au premier jour, comme en témoigne son exposition A Bigger Picture, qui a fait sensation à la Royal Academy au début de cette année. Il repousse sans cesse les limites de la technique. Les couleurs vives et les ondulations de ce paysage traditionnel, Summer Sky, par exemple, ont été créées en 2008 sur tablette graphique informatique et imprimante à jet d'encre.

Running Order

Countdown
Green and Pleasant Land
Pandemonium
Happy & Glorious
Second to the right, and straight on till morning
Interlude
frankie & june say... Thanks Tim
Abide With Me
Welcome
Bike a.m.
Let the Games Begin
There is a Light That Never Goes Out
And in the end...

Ordre de passage

Compte à rebours
Douces terres verdoyantes
Pandémonium
Rayonnante et glorieuse
Deuxième étoile à droite et tout droit jusqu'au matin
Interlude
frankie et june disent... Merci Tim
Reste avec moi
Bienvenue
Vélo a.m.
Que les Jeux commencent
Une lueur qui ne s'éteint jamais...
Et au final...

Danny Boyle

Artistic Director, London 2012 Olympic Games Opening Ceremony
Directeur artistique de la cérémonie d'ouverture des Jeux Olympiques de 2012 à Londres

At some point in their histories, most nations experience a revolution that changes everything about them. The United Kingdom had a revolution that changed the whole of human existence.

In 1709 Abraham Darby smelted iron in a blast furnace, using coke. And so began the Industrial Revolution. Out of Abraham's Shropshire furnace flowed molten metal. Out of his genius flowed the mills, looms, engines, weapons, railways, ships, cities, conflicts and prosperity that built the world we live in.

In November 1990 another Briton sparked another revolution – equally far-reaching – a revolution we're still experiencing. The digital revolution was sparked by Tim Berners-Lee's amazing gift to the world – the World Wide Web. This, he said, is for everyone.

We welcome you to an Olympic Opening Ceremony for everyone. A ceremony that celebrates the creativity, eccentricity, daring and openness of the British genius by harnessing the genius, creativity, eccentricity, daring and openness of modern London.

You'll hear the words of our great poets – Shakespeare, Blake and Milton. You'll hear the glorious noise of our unrivalled pop culture. You'll see characters from our great children's literature – Peter Pan and Captain Hook, Mary Poppins, Voldemort, Cruella de Vil. You'll see ordinary families and extraordinary athletes. Dancing nurses, singing children and amazing special effects.

But we hope too that through all the noise and excitement you'll glimpse a single golden thread of purpose – the idea of Jerusalem – of the better world, the world of real freedom and true equality, a world that can be built through the prosperity of industry, through the caring nation that built the welfare state, through the joyous energy of popular culture, through the dream of universal communication. A belief that we can build Jerusalem. And that it will be for everyone.

À un moment de leur histoire, la plupart des nations vivent une révolution qui les change du tout au tout. Le Royaume-Uni, lui, a connu une révolution qui a bouleversé l'humanité tout entière.

En 1709, Abraham Darby fit fondre du charbon dans un haut fourneau à l'aide de coke. Ainsi naquit la Révolution industrielle. Du fourneau d'Abraham dans le Shropshire jaillit le métal fondu et de son génie jaillirent les moulins, les métiers à tisser, les moteurs, les armes, les voies de chemin de fer, les bateaux, les villes, les conflits et la prospérité qui bâtirent le monde dans lequel nous vivons.

En novembre 1990, un autre Britannique initia une autre révolution. Une révolution aux conséquences tout aussi fondamentales, et que nous vivons encore aujourd'hui. La révolution numérique fut initiée par le cadeau extraordinaire que fit au monde Tim Berners-Lee : le World Wide Web. Ceci, disait-il, est pour tout le monde.

Nous vous souhaitons la bienvenue dans une cérémonie d'ouverture olympique destinée à tout le monde. Une cérémonie qui célèbre la créativité, l'excentricité, l'audace et l'ouverture du génie britannique en mettant à profit le génie, la créativité, l'excentricité, l'audace et l'ouverture du Londres moderne.

Vous entendrez les mots de nos grands poètes, Shakespeare, Blake et Milton. Vous entendrez le son glorieux de la culture pop sans équivalent qui est la nôtre. Vous verrez des personnages issus de notre fabuleuse littérature enfantine : Peter Pan et le Capitaine Crochet, Mary Poppins, Voldemort, Cruella d'Enfer. Vous verrez des familles ordinaires et des athlètes extraordinaires. Des infirmières qui dansent, des enfants qui chantent et des effets spéciaux à couper le souffle.

Mais nous espérons aussi que, dans tout ce bruit et cette excitation, vous discernerez un seul et unique fil directeur, tissé d'or, celui de Jérusalem, du monde meilleur, le monde de la vraie liberté et de la véritable égalité, un monde pouvant être construit grâce à la prospérité de l'industrie, à la nation attentionnée qui bâtit l'État-providence, à l'énergie joyeuse de la culture populaire, au rêve d'une communication universelle. La conviction que nous pouvons construire Jérusalem. Et qu'elle sera pour tout le monde.

11

Countdown
5,4,3,2,1

Compte à rebours 5,4,3,2,1

Bells ring out the changes of our days. They call us to wake, to pray, to work, to arms, to feast and, in times of crisis, to come together. Almost everyone in Britain lives within a sonic parish. Anyone born within hearing of the bells of St Mary-le-Bow in Cheapside, London, has the right to call themselves 'cockney'.

The art of ringing bells in complex mathematical patterns is called 'change ringing'. The sheets on which the changes are worked out are said to be the first computer programmes.

Tonight you'll hear the sound of the largest harmonically tuned bell in the world – the Olympic Bell.

Above all, bells are the sound of freedom and peace. Throughout World War II all of Britain's bell towers were stilled, to be rung only in case of emergency. They hung in dusty silence until the day came when they could ring in the peace.

The Olympic Bell was made by Whitechapel Bell Foundry, whose workshop is just a few miles from the Stadium, and measures two metres by three metres. Founded in 1570, during the reign of Elizabeth I, it's probably the oldest manufacturing company in the world. The Foundry also created the Liberty Bell (in 1752) and Big Ben (1858). The Olympic Bell will hang in the Olympic Park for the next 200 years. Why only 200? Because then it will have to be taken back to Whitechapel to be retuned. It's already in their diary.

Par leurs tintements, les cloches rythment les changements quotidiens de nos vies. Elles sonnent l'heure du réveil, de la prière, du travail, du combat, de la fête et, en temps du crise, du rassemblement. Presque tous les habitants de Grande-Bretagne vivent dans une paroisse dotée d'un clocher. Toute personne née assez près de l'église de St Mary-le-Bow, dans le quartier londonien de Cheapside, pour entendre résonner ses cloches peut se considérer comme un « cockney ».

L'art de sonner les cloches selon des formules mathématiques complexes s'appelle le « change ringing ». Les feuilles sur lesquelles étaient élaborés les « changements » inhérents à cette méthode seraient dit-on les premiers programmes informatiques.

Ce soir, vous allez entendre le son de la plus grand cloche accordée du monde, la cloche olympique.

Le son des cloches est avant tout son de liberté et de paix. Pendant la Seconde Guerre mondiale, tous les clochers de Grande-Bretagne restèrent silencieux, leurs tintements réservés aux cas d'urgence. Les cloches restèrent en sommeil, nimbées d'un silence poussiéreux, jusqu'au jour où elles purent sonner en paix.

La cloche olympique a été fabriquée par la Whitechapel Bell Foundry, dont l'atelier se trouve à quelques kilomètres du Stade, et ses dimensions sont de deux mètres sur trois. Fondée en 1570, sous le règne d'Elizabeth I, la fonderie est probablement la plus ancienne manufacture du monde. Elle a également créé la Liberty Bell (1752) et Big Ben (1858). La cloche olympique restera suspendue dans le Parc olympique pendant les 200 prochaines années. Pourquoi seulement 200 ? Parce qu'il lui faudra alors retourner à Whitechapel pour être réaccordée. La date est déjà dans leur agenda.

Some days, although we cannot pray, a prayer
utters itself. So, a woman will lift
her head from the sieve of her hands and stare
at the minims sung by a tree, a sudden gift.

Some nights, although we are faithless, the truth
enters our hearts, that small familiar pain;
then a man will stand stock-still, hearing his youth
in the distant Latin chanting of a train.

Pray for us now. Grade 1 piano scales
console the lodger looking out across
a Midlands town. Then dusk, and someone calls
a child's name as though they named their loss.

Darkness outside. Inside, the radio's prayer –
Rockall. Malin. Dogger. Finisterre.

Prayer, *Carol Ann Duffy*

The Shipping Forecast is broadcast four times
a day on BBC Radio. Designed to be useful for
sailors, it has a strange poetry of its own and
has become a kind of national litany. As we wake
or as we're about to sleep, it walks us name by
name around the limits of our islands.

*Il y a des jours où, bien qu'on ne prie pas, une prière
monte d'elle-même. Une femme alors
relève la tête, qu'elle tenait entre ses mains, et contemple
les notes chantées par un arbre, cadeau soudain.*

*Il y a des nuits où, bien qu'on n'ait pas la foi, la vérité
perce notre cœur, petite douleur familière,
et un homme se fige en statue, en entendant sa jeunesse
dans le chant grégorien lointain d'un train.*

*Priez pour nous maintenant. Les gammes au piano du débutant
réchauffent le cœur du locataire des Midlands
qui regarde par la fenêtre. Au crépuscule, quelqu'un appelle
un nom d'enfant, comme s'il venait de disparaître.*

*L'obscurité dehors. Dedans, la prière à la radio :
Rockall. Malin. Dogger. Finisterre.*

Prayer, *Carol Ann Duffy*

*La météo marine est diffusée quatre fois par jour sur
BBC Radio. Conçue pour assister les navigateurs,
elle exhale une poésie étrange toute particulière
et est devenue une sorte de litanie nationale.
Au réveil ou au coucher, elle nous entraîne nom
après nom le long des limites de nos côtes.*

The cock is crowing
The stream is flowing
The small birds twitter
The lake doth glitter
The green field sleeps in the sun

Written in March, William Wordsworth

Le coq chante
La rivière coule
Les petits oiseaux gazouillent
Le lac, vraiment, scintille
Le champ vert dort au soleil

Écrit en mars, William Wordsworth

Principal Performers / *Artistes principaux*
Dockhead Choir

Choreographer / *Chorégraphe*
Toby Sedgwick

Green and Pleasant Land

Douces terres verdoyantes

Somewhere there's a meadow, where it's always summer and there's a picnic waiting with lashings of ginger beer. There's a river stuffed with sticklebacks and tadpoles, and a bridge where you can play Poohsticks. Over the water is the Hundred Acre Wood, where Winnie the Pooh and Piglet are hunting for Heffalumps. Upstream, Ratty and Mole are launching their rowing boat because 'there is nothing, simply nothing half so much fun as simply messing about in boats'.

You can't find it on a map but we carry it in our hearts. A reminder and a promise of a once and future better life.

The tradition of dancing around a maypole goes back to the middle ages. It was banned by Oliver Cromwell's government, but when Charles II was crowned king, a huge maypole, 134 foot high, was set up at St Mary le Strand where it stayed for 50 years until Isaac Newton took it to support his 'great telescope'.

Il est quelque part une prairie où l'été ne cesse jamais et où vous attend un pique-nique généreusement pourvu de bière au gingembre. Une rivière coule, chargée d'épinoches et de têtards, enjambée d'un pont où l'on peut jouer, tel Winnie l'Ourson, à qui fera réapparaître le premier le bâton jeté de l'autre côté du pont. Près de l'eau s'étend la Forêt des rêves bleus, où Winnie et Porcinet chassent les Éfélants. En amont, Rat et Taupe mettent à flot leur canot, puisqu'il « n'est rien de plus amusant, mais vraiment rien, que de simplement traînasser dans une barque. »

Cette prairie, on ne la trouve sur aucune carte, mais elle est dans nos cœurs, souvenir et promesse d'une vie meilleure.

La coutume de danser autour de l'Arbre de mai remonte au Moyen-Âge. Elle fut interdite par le gouvernement d'Oliver Cromwell, mais à l'accession au trône de Charles II, un gigantesque Arbre de mai de plus de 4 mètres de haut fut érigé à St Mary-le-Strand, où il resta pendant 50 ans jusqu'à ce qu'Isaac Newton en fasse le mât de son « grand télescope ».

Traditional songs representing the four nations of the United Kingdom

England
And did those feet in ancient time
Walk upon England's mountains green?
And was the holy Lamb of God
On England's pleasant pastures seen?
And did the Countenance Divine
Shine forth upon our clouded hills?
And was Jerusalem builded here
Among these dark Satanic Mills?

Northern Ireland
Oh Danny boy, the pipes, the pipes are calling
From glen to glen, and down the mountain side
The summer's gone, and all the flowers are dying
'Tis you, 'tis you must go and I must bide.
But come ye back when summer's in the meadow
Or when the valley's hushed and white with snow
'Tis I'll be here in sunshine or in shadow
Oh Danny boy, oh Danny boy, I love you so.

Scotland
O flower of Scotland,
When will we see your like again
That fought and died for
Your wee bit hill and glen.
And stood against him,
Proud Edward's army,
And sent him homeward
Tae think again.

Wales
Arglwydd, arwain trwy'r anialwch,
Fi, bererin gwael ei wedd,
Nad oes ynof nerth na bywyd
Fel yn gorwedd yn y bedd:
Hollalluog, Hollalluog,
Ydyw'r Un a'm cwyd i'r lan;
Ydyw'r Un a'm cwyd i'r lan.

Guide me, O thou great redeemer,
Pilgrim through this barren land;
I am weak, but thou art mighty,
Hold me with thy powerful hand;
Bread of heaven, bread of heaven
Feed me till I want no more;
Feed me till I want no more.

Chants traditionnels représentant les quatre nations du Royaume-Uni

Angleterre
Et ces pieds ont-ils, aux temps anciens,
Foulé les vertes montagnes d'Angleterre ?
Et a-t-on vu l'Agneau sacré de Dieu
Sur les doux pâturages d'Angleterre ?
Et la Divine Figure a-t-elle brillé
Sur nos collines embrumées ?
Et Jérusalem fut-elle construite
Au milieu de ces noires usines d'Enfer ?

Irlande du Nord
Oh Danny boy, la cornemuse, la cornemuse appelle
De vallée en vallée et à flanc de montagne
L'été s'en est allé et toutes les fleurs se meurent
C'est toi, c'est toi qui dois partir et je dois rester.
Mais reviens donc quand l'été sera dans la prairie
Ou quand la vallée silencieuse sera blanche de neige
Je serai là dans le soleil ou dans l'ombre
Oh Danny boy, oh Danny boy, je t'aime tant.

Écosse
Ô fine fleur d'Écosse
Quand reverrons-nous tes semblables
Ceux qui ont combattu et sont tombés
Pour tes petites collines et vallées
Et se sont dressés contre lui,
Le fier Édouard et son armée,
Le renvoyant dans ses pénates
Pour y réfléchir à deux fois.

Pays de Galles
Guide-moi, ô grand rédempteur
Pèlerin errant sur une terre stérile ;
Je suis faible, mais tu es fort,
Soutiens-moi de ta main puissante :
Pain céleste, pain céleste
Nourris-moi jusqu'à ce que je sois repu ;
Nourris-moi jusqu'à ce que je sois repu.

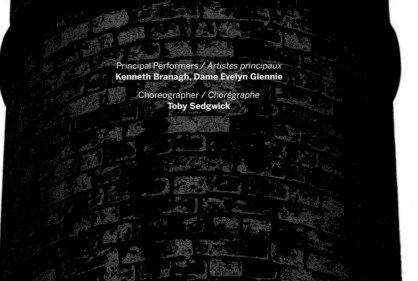

Principal Performers / *Artistes principaux*
Kenneth Branagh, Dame Evelyn Glennie

Choreographer / *Chorégraphe*
Toby Sedgwick

Pandemonium

Pandémonium

The word 'pandemonium' was invented by John Milton as the
name of the capital city of Hell in his epic poem
Paradise Lost...
**There stood a hill not far, whose griesly top
Belched fire and rowling smoke; the rest entire
Shown with a glossy scurf, undoubted sign
That in his womb was hid metallic ore,
The work of sulphur.**

*Le mot pandémonium a été inventé par John Milton pour
désigner la capitale des enfers dans son poème épique
Le Paradis perdu...*
***Non loin de là était une montagne dont le sommet affreux
Vomissait des tourbillons de flamme et de fumée ;
le reste de la montagne
Brillait d'une croûte jaunâtre, témoin assuré du riche métal
que le soufre avait formé dans ses flancs.***

In 1709 Abraham Darby used coal to smelt iron in a small blast furnace in Coalbrookdale. This is the beginning of the Industrial Revolution – an outburst of invention and innovation unparalleled in the history of the world.

Within a few years of Darby's experiment, work that had for thousands of years been done by hand was being done by machines. New sources of power, new means of transport, new forms of politics were all needed and all created. Cities grew as people poured into them in search of prosperity. For the first time in history, working people could dream of improving their lives – a dream that suffragettes, Chartists and trade unionists made reality through political struggle.

It's a pattern that is being repeated – with all its pain and all its excitement, its farewells and its heroes – across the world as developing countries experience their own industrial revolutions.

But it wasn't only work that was mechanised. Mass manufacturing meant that the luxuries of life were no longer only for the rich. The mass manufacture of weapons meant that war was no longer only for the soldier. We remember those who marched away.

Ex Terra Lucem
(out of the ground came light)
Motto of the town of St Helens,
Lancashire.

Ex Terra Lucem
(de la terre vint la lumière)
Devise de la ville de St Helens, dans
le Lancashire.

Never such innocence,
Never before or since,
As changed itself to past
Without a word – the men
Leaving the gardens tidy,
The thousands of marriages
Lasting a little while longer:
Never such innocence again.

MCMXIV, **Philip Larkin**

Jamais telle innocence
Ni autrefois, ni depuis,
N'a soudain disparu
Sans un mot – les hommes
Délaissant leurs jardins ordonnés,
Les mariages par milliers
Subsistant quelque temps encore :
Jamais telle innocence ne reviendra.

MCMXIV, *Philip Larkin*

En 1709, dans un modeste haut fourneau
de Coalbrookdale, Abraham Darby utilisa
du charbon pour fondre du fer. Ce fut
le début de la révolution industrielle,
explosion d'inventions et d'innovations
sans équivalent dans l'histoire du monde.

Dans les années qui suivirent l'expérience
de Darby, des travaux accomplis à la main
par les hommes depuis des millénaires
furent désormais réalisés par des
machines. De nouvelles sources d'énergie,
de nouveaux moyens de transport, de
nouvelles formes de politique furent
inventés pour répondre aux nouveaux
besoins apparus. Les villes grandirent,
gonflées par l'afflux d'une population en
quête de prospérité. Pour la première
fois de l'histoire, les travailleurs pouvaient
faire un rêve, celui d'améliorer leur vie.
Un rêve devenu réalité grâce au combat
politique des suffragettes, des chartistes
et des syndicalistes.

Ce modèle se retrouve aujourd'hui,
avec toute sa douleur, son excitation, ses
adieux et ses héros, à l'heure où les pays en
développement de toute la planète vivent
leurs propres révolutions industrielles.

Mais le travail ne fut pas seul à être
mécanisé. La fabrication en masse permit
d'étendre au plus grand nombre les plaisirs
de la vie naguère réservés aux riches.
Et, production en masse des armes aidant,
la guerre ne fut bientôt plus l'apanage
du soldat. Nous nous souvenons de nos
frères partis au combat.

17

Her Majesty The Queen
Head of State
and
Jacques Rogge
President of the
International Olympic
Committee
enter the Stadium

Sa Majesté la Reine
Chef de l'État
et
Jacques Rogge
Président du Comité
International
Olympique
font leur entrée dans
le Stade

Principal Performers /
Artistes principaux
The Kaos Signing Choir for
Deaf & Hearing Children

God save our gracious Queen!
Long live our noble Queen!
God save the Queen!
Send her victorious,
Happy and glorious,
Long to reign over us,
God save the Queen.

Thy choicest gifts in store
On her be pleased to pour,
Long may she reign.
May she defend our laws,
And ever give us cause,
To sing with heart and voice,
God save the Queen.

*The British National Anthem was first
performed publicly in London in 1745,
though the words and tune are anonymous
and may date back to the 17th century. In
total, around 140 composers – including
Beethoven, Haydn and Brahms – have used
the tune in their compositions.*

Que Dieu protège notre gracieuse Reine,
Longue vie à notre noble Reine,
Que Dieu protège la Reine !
Rends-la victorieuse,
Rayonnante et glorieuse,
Que soit long son règne sur nous,
Que Dieu protège la Reine !

Qu'il Te plaise de lui accorder
Tes bienfaits les plus rares ;
Puisse-t-elle régner longuement ;
Puisse-t-elle défendre nos lois
Et nous donner toujours raison
De chanter avec cœur et à pleine voix :
Que Dieu protège la Reine !

*L'hymne national britannique fut joué pour
la première fois en public à Londres, en 1745.
Les paroles et la mélodie, dont l'auteur reste
inconnu, pourraient toutefois dater du XVIIe
siècle. Au total, environ 140 compositeurs,
parmi lesquels Beethoven, Haydn et Brahms,
ont utilisé la mélodie dans leurs œuvres.*

Happy & Glorious

Rayonnante et glorieuse

Her Majesty Queen Elizabeth II is celebrating her Diamond Jubilee this year – marking the 60th year of her reign. She's the second-longest-serving monarch in British history.

Her presence today connects us in a direct and human way to the 16 countries of which she is the constitutional monarch.

She is a living link to our shared history – to the Second World War in which she served as a driver and mechanic, to the creation of the Commonwealth of which she is the head, and to other Olympic Games – the Montreal Games of 1976, which she also opened, and the London Games of 1948 opened by her father, George VI.

Beyond that, her role connects us to the long struggle to create a constitutional monarchy – in which the monarch is the head of state but the law is made by Parliament. The story of how this balance was achieved stretches back to Magna Carta (1215), includes a civil war and a revolution. It was finally resolved by the Act of Settlement of 1701 and has lasted to this day.

Sa Majesté la Reine Elizabeth II célèbre cette année son Jubilé de diamant, marquant la 60ᵉ année de son règne. Elle est le deuxième monarque ayant servi le plus longtemps dans l'histoire de la Grande-Bretagne.

Sa présence aujourd'hui nous relie de façon directe et humaine aux 16 pays dont elle est le monarque constitutionnel.

Elle est un lien vivant avec l'histoire que nous partageons. Avec la Seconde Guerre mondiale, où elle servit comme chauffeur et mécanicienne ; avec la création du Commonwealth, dont elle est le chef ; avec d'autres Jeux Olympiques, les Jeux de Montréal en 1976, qu'elle a également ouverts, et les Jeux de Londres de 1948, ouverts par son père, George VI.

Plus que cela, sa fonction nous relie au long combat mené pour instaurer une monarchie constitutionnelle, dans laquelle le monarque est chef de l'État mais où les lois sont faites par le Parlement. L'histoire de la gestation de cet équilibre remonte à la Magna Carta de 1215, en passant par une guerre civile et une révolution, avant l'aboutissement grâce à l'Acte d'Établissement de 1701 toujours en vigueur aujourd'hui.

Second to the right, and straight on till morning

Peter Pan, JM Barrie

Deuxième étoile à droite et tout droit jusqu'au matin

Almost all the volunteer dancers in this segment work for the National Health Service. They include doctors, pharmacists, managers, nurses, radiographers, midwives and social workers.

The National Health Service is the institution which more than any other unites our nation. It was founded just after the Second World War on Aneurin Bevan's famous principle, 'No society can legitimately call itself civilised if a sick person is denied medical aid because of lack of means.'

One of its most-loved hospitals is Great Ormond Street Children's Hospital, to which JM Barrie bequeathed all the royalties from his masterpiece, *Peter Pan*.

British writers of children's books have created characters who are known and loved all over the world. But the roots of their stories are every bit as global as their current success.

They draw on fairy stories from the Black Forest, Norse myths, Chinese and African folk tales. In cinemas and bestsellers they return to the world the gift that was given by word of mouth for a thousand generations.

La plupart des danseurs bénévoles de ce spectacle travaillent pour le National Health Service, le service national de santé britannique. Ils sont médecins, pharmaciens, responsables, infirmiers, manipulateurs en radiologie, sages-femmes et travailleurs sociaux.

De toutes les institutions, le National Health Service est celle qui, plus que toute autre, unit notre nation. Elle fut fondée juste après la Seconde Guerre mondiale, sur le célèbre principe édicté par Aneurin Bevan selon lequel « aucune société ne peut se prétendre civilisée si un malade ne peut bénéficier d'une aide médicale faute de moyens ».

L'un de ses hôpitaux les plus aimés est l'hôpital pour enfants de Great Ormond Street, auquel JM Barrie a légué tous les droits d'auteur de son chef-d'œuvre, Peter Pan.

Les écrivains pour enfants britanniques ont créé des personnages connus et adorés partout dans le monde. Mais leurs histoires ont des origines tout aussi internationales que leur succès actuel.

Ils puisent leur inspiration dans les contes de fées de la Forêt-Noire, la mythologie scandinave ou les contes folkloriques chinois et africains. Au cinéma et dans leurs best-sellers, ils offrent au monde en retour un peu de ce cadeau qui, pendant des milliers de générations, s'est transmis de bouche à oreille.

Principal Performers / *Artistes principaux*
Mike Oldfield, JK Rowling

Choreographer / *Chorégraphe*
Temujin Gill

Co-Choreographer / *Chorégraphe associé*
Sunanda Biswas

Interlude

A special performance of 'Chariots of Fire'

Interlude

Une représentation spéciale des Chariots de feu

Principal Performer / *Artiste principal*
Sir Simon Rattle

From Charlie Chaplin and Stan Laurel to James Bond and Harry Potter, British cinema has produced more than its fair share of great names. Throughout this evening you'll glimpse moments from some of the best-loved British movies – *A Matter of Life and Death*, *Gregory's Girl*, *Four Weddings and a Funeral*, *Mr Bean's Holiday*. To celebrate Britain's cinematic tradition, however, we've chosen to honour its most Olympic film – *Chariots of Fire*.

I believe God made me for a purpose, but he also made me fast. And when I run I feel His pleasure.
Eric Liddell

The film tells the stories of two very different athletes – Eric Liddell, a devout Scottish Christian who runs for the glory of God, and the great Jewish sprinter, Harold Abrahams, who uses his prowess to confront prejudice. The film won four Academy Awards, prompting its writer Colin Welland to say in his acceptance speech, 'The British are coming!'

If I can't win, I won't run!
Harold Abrahams

The famous scene where the athletes train on the beach was shot at West Sands in St Andrews, Scotland.

If you don't run, you can't win.
Sybil Gordon, Abrahams' girlfriend

De Charlie Chaplin à Stan Laurel en passant par James Bond et Harry Potter, le cinéma britannique a produit un nombre non négligeable de grands noms. Vous verrez tout au long de cette soirée plusieurs brefs extraits de quelques-uns des films britanniques les plus appréciés : Une question de vie ou de mort, Une fille pour Gregory, Quatre mariages et un enterrement, Les Vacances de Mr. Bean. Pour célébrer la tradition cinématographique de la Grande-Bretagne, c'est toutefois son film le plus olympique que nous avons choisi de mettre à l'honneur : Les Chariots de feu.

Je crois que Dieu m'a créé dans un but, mais il a aussi fait que je coure vite. Et quand je cours, je sens Son plaisir.
Eric Liddell

Le film retrace l'histoire de deux athlètes très différents : Eric Liddell, fervent chrétien écossais courant pour la gloire de Dieu, et Harold Abrahams, grand sprinter juif utilisant son talent pour combattre les préjugés. Le film remporta quatre Academy Awards, ce qui fit dire à son scénariste Colin Welland dans son discours d'acceptation : « Les Britanniques arrivent ! »

Si je ne gagne pas, je ne courrai plus !
Harold Abrahams

La célèbre scène où l'on voit les athlètes s'entraîner sur la plage fut filmée à West Sands, dans la ville de St Andrews, en Écosse.

Si tu ne cours pas, tu ne peux pas gagner.
Sybil Gordon, Petite amie d'Abrahams

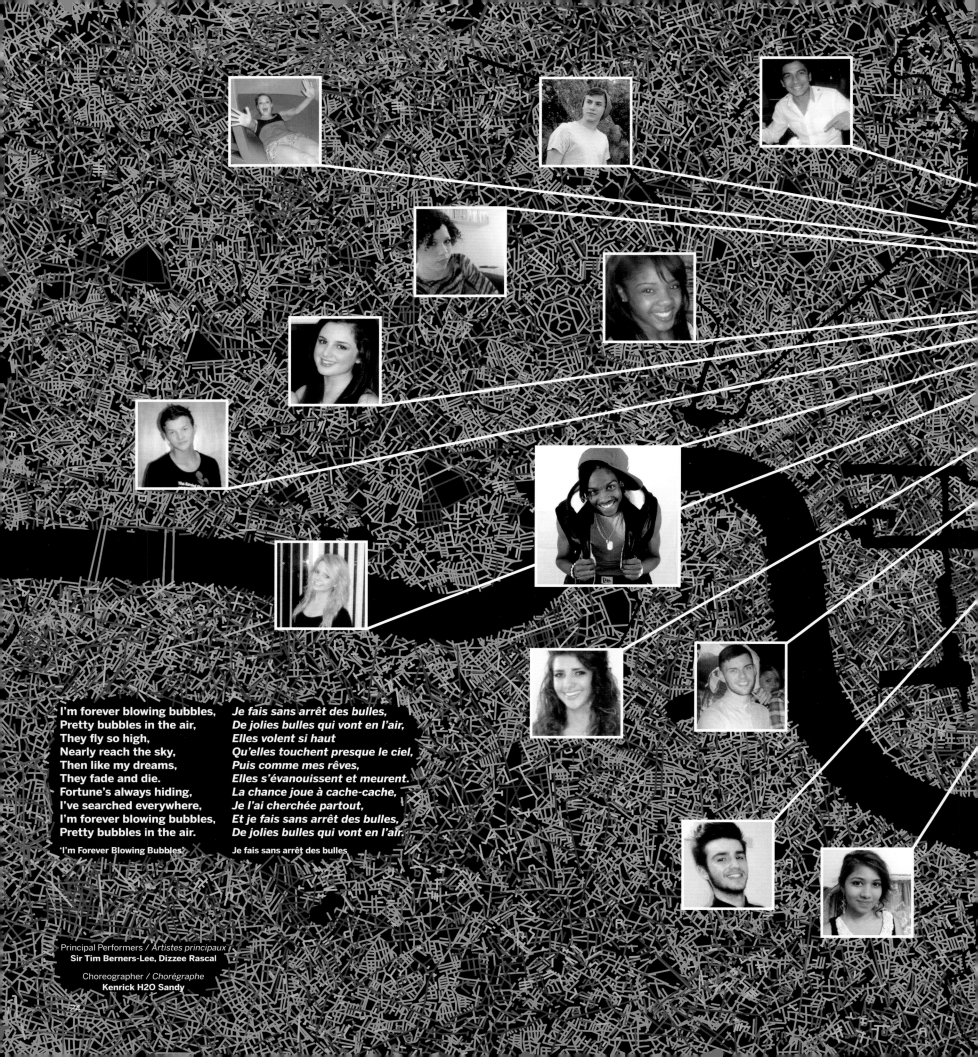

I'm forever blowing bubbles,
Pretty bubbles in the air,
They fly so high,
Nearly reach the sky,
Then like my dreams,
They fade and die.
Fortune's always hiding,
I've searched everywhere,
I'm forever blowing bubbles,
Pretty bubbles in the air.

'I'm Forever Blowing Bubbles'

Je fais sans arrêt des bulles,
De jolies bulles qui vont en l'air,
Elles volent si haut
Qu'elles touchent presque le ciel,
Puis comme mes rêves,
Elles s'évanouissent et meurent.
La chance joue à cache-cache,
Je l'ai cherchée partout,
Et je fais sans arrêt des bulles,
De jolies bulles qui vont en l'air.

Je fais sans arrêt des bulles

Principal Performers / *Artistes principaux*
Sir Tim Berners-Lee, Dizzee Rascal

Choreographer / *Chorégraphe*
Kenrick H2O Sandy

24

frankie & june say...

Thanks Tim

frankie et june disent... Merci Tim

Grandma and Grandad met in a dance hall where a real live band were playing. Mum and Dad had their first kiss at a disco, dancing to 10cc's 'I'm Not in Love'. Dad bought her a copy for their first anniversary.

By the time June was born, they were allowed to take a mix-tape cassette into the labour ward. Now that June's a teenager, she can have music wherever she goes. From her phone, through her headphones, live music streaming from a concert, retro-music downloaded from the archives.

What if she and Frankie get together forever tonight? How will they listen to 'their song' when they're 64? Will they be able to summon it just by thinking of it? Or will we have gone the other way, and they'll be singing it together round the family piano?

Music connects us with each other and with the most important moments in our lives. One of the things that makes those connections possible is the World Wide Web – invented in 1989 by the British scientist, Tim Berners-Lee, who went on to build the world's first website the following year. For changing the way we live, he sought no personal gain. He's the origin of the theme of this Ceremony, 'this is for everyone'.

Papy et Mamie se sont rencontrés dans un bal où jouait un vrai orchestre. Papa et Maman ont échangé leur premier baiser en boîte, en dansant sur I'm Not in Love de 10cc. Pour leur premier anniversaire de rencontre, Papa a offert le disque à Maman.

À la naissance de June, ils ont pu emmener une cassette de compilations en salle d'accouchement. June est maintenant adolescente et elle peut écouter de la musique partout où elle va. Sur son téléphone, avec ses écouteurs, en retransmission sur Internet en direct d'un concert, en téléchargement depuis des archives rétro.

Et si ce soir était, pour Frankie et elle, le début d'une vie à deux ? Comment écouteront-ils « leur chanson » à 64 ans ? Pourront-ils la faire retentir juste par la force de la pensée ? Ou alors, si nous prenons le chemin inverse, la chanteront-ils ensemble, réunis autour du piano familial ?

La musique nous relie les uns aux autres et aux moments les plus importants de notre vie. Si ces liens sont aujourd'hui possibles, c'est entre autres grâce au World Wide Web, inventé en 1989 par le scientifique britannique Tim Berners-Lee, concepteur l'année suivante du premier site internet du monde. Il a changé notre façon de vivre et n'a pas cherché à en tirer le moindre enrichissement personnel. Il est à l'origine du thème de cette cérémonie, « Ceci est pour tout le monde ».

London 2212

London 1666
Samuel Pepys, *The Diary of Samuel Pepys*

I made myself ready presently, and walked to the Tower… and there I did see the houses at that end of the bridge all on fire… Everybody endeavouring to remove their goods, and flinging into the river or bringing them into lighters that layoff; poor people staying in their houses as long as till the very fire touched them, and then running into boats, or clambering from one pair of stairs by the waterside to another. And among other things, the poor pigeons, I perceive, were loth to leave their houses, but hovered about the windows and balconies till they were some of them burned, their wings, and fell down.

London 1777
Samuel Johnson

There is in London all that life can afford.

London 1852
Charles Dickens, *Bleak House*

Fog everywhere. Fog up the river, where it flows among green aits and meadows; fog down the river, where it rolls defiled among the tiers of shipping and the waterside pollutions of a great (and dirty) city. Fog on the Essex marshes, fog on the Kentish heights. Fog creeping into the cabooses of collier-brigs; fog lying out on the yards, and hovering in the rigging of great ships; fog drooping on the gunwales of barges and small boats. Fog in the eyes and throats of ancient Greenwich pensioners, wheezing by the firesides of their wards; fog in the stem and bowl of the afternoon pipe of the wrathful skipper, down in his close cabin; fog cruelly pinching the toes and fingers of his shivering little 'prentice boy on deck.

London 1948
Andrea Levy, *Small Island*

You see most of the boys were looking upwards… it was wonder that lifted their eyes. They finally arrive in London town. And let me tell you, the Mother Country – this thought-I-knew-you place – was bewildering these Jamaican boys. See them pointing at the train that rumbles across the bridge. They looked shocked when billowing black smoke puffed its way around the white washing hung on drying lines – the sheets, the pants, the babies' bonnets… even the sunshine can find no colour but grey.

London 2012
Jo Shapcott, *Wild Swimmer*

Backstroke through the past
and remember how Alfred the Great
dug the Channelsea to keep out Danes
and how the mill streams powered on
through centuries. Waterworks were King.
Swoop underwater through the Prescott Channel,
touching pieces of the lost Euston Arch as you go
and break surface among reeds, oak, willow, ash.
Shoot under the stadium itself,
where the little Pudding Mill River runs:
at last, dive up into a building shaped like a wave
and swim your heart out, for you are all gold.

London Always
Benjamin Zephaniah, *The London Breed*

I love dis great polluted place
Where pop stars come to live their dreams
Here ravers come for drum and bass
And politicians plan their schemes
The music of the world is here
Dis city can play any song
They came to here from everywhere
Tis they that made dis city strong.

Two hundred years from today, a master bell-maker will set out from Whitechapel, with instructions to retune the great Olympic Bell. The bell-maker has never seen the bell, but she knows it will still be there. There are some objects that history tiptoes round, and leaves undisturbed, rocks in the river of change.

The bell-maker will stroll through leafy London. The mad roads and high-density housing are gone now, all overgrown. London 2212 is mostly trees. No one really builds things any more, not since we learnt to manipulate vegetable DNA. Why build a house when you can grow one? A house that grows as your family grows. A house you can prune when it gets too big. A house that grows food on the kitchen wall. A house that breathes oxygen.

The biggest breakthrough came when we learnt to grow computers – computers that climb up from the patio and pull information down from the cloud like sunshine. The bell-maker, for instance, is following a trail of smartleaves that rustle directions as she strolls through the Forest of Bow.

There, in a clearing, its wooden gantry covered in creepers, she'll find the bell. The size of it surprises her. She had no idea it would be this big. It takes all her strength to get the clapper to swing hard enough to strike a note from the huge metal dome. And what a note – vast, rich and complex. Its tones and overtones and half tones unfolding like petals as it breezes through the forest. Every cell in her body vibrates.

When the sound passes through the cloud, it will activate all the memories that were stored there on the day the bell was first rung – the ancient Facebook likes and recommends, the digital photo, blog entries, texts – and these will be downloaded to the bell-maker's memory in a shower of smartpollen. When she breathes in, she'll inhale the rhythm of drums, the flash of fireworks, the happy screams of children, the waves of the athletes and the lyrics of songs.

But what will she make of those lyrics? Will she wonder who, apart from tigers, had tiger feet? Was it a good thing? And what is tiger light? Does it burn bright in the forests of the night?

Will she try to figure out what exactly that Starman was waiting for in the sky?

Will scholars try to work out who Scaramouche was and whether he ever did do the fandango? And what Galileo and Figaro have to do with it? And why everyone was shouting about it?

Or will she already know that the best pop lyrics are often nonsense. Even the lyrics of the greatest, and the most important pop songs.

'Wopbopaloobop a whop bam boo' for instance. Or 'Na, na, na, na-na-na naaaa'. 'Hey Jude' – possibly the Beatles' biggest-selling single – ends with almost four minutes of 'na na nas'. Anyone who has ever stood in a vast crowd and na na na'd along with it, knows that meaning doesn't matter. The important thing is the way that chorus allows us to karaoke ourselves into the moment. It binds us together, both as members of the crowd and as part of the ongoing reverberation of that summer afternoon in Twickenham in 1968 when four young men first recorded it.

Because the lyrics are a handle – a way of holding onto the song, keeping it in your memory, bedding it into your hard drive. In a way, the more meaningless they are, the more power the song has. The less it said, the less there is to disagree with. Clever people have often tried to prove that pop music is important by showing us how deep and meaningful the lyrics can be. But we don't want meaning from a pop song really. Pop isn't important for what it says. It's important for what it does. Or what it lets us do. It lets us play and when we play we do amazing things. Popular music and technological innovation are brother and sister. The first computer programmes were the cards which bell ringers made to help them remember the order of ringing. Ever since then music and computers have walked together. Bands like Pink Floyd and musicians like Mike Oldfield and Brian Eno searching for new sounds and new ways to create music had a massive impact on the development of computers. File sharing and downloading were the catalysts of social networking. And in recent years – in the Arab Spring, for instance – they've been agents for social change. Like the bells that first inspired them, they are part of the story of liberty.

What's the point of playing if you don't share? We play best when we're together. Maybe that's what we really want from all public art – not insight or knowledge but an excuse to get together in a state of pleasant perplexity, to be part of each other's lives. Because, in the end, what matters most to us is each other.

Frank Cottrell Boyce

'House' (1993) by Rachel Whiteread is a concrete cast of the interior of a real East End terraced house – 193 Grove Road. It was exhibited in the space that the original house had occupied, after all the houses in the road had been demolished. An eerie memorial to a vanished community, it won the Turner Prize in 1993 and was itself demolished a year later.

Londres 2212

Dans deux cents ans à compter de ce jour, une campanologue chevronnée – une spécialiste des cloches – aura pour mission de se rendre à Whitechapel pour y réaccorder la grande cloche olympique. Elle n'a jamais vu cette cloche, mais elle sait qu'elle doit se trouver là. C'est l'un de ces objets que l'histoire n'ose bousculer, un rocher dans le lit de la rivière du temps.

Notre campanologue parcourt à pied un Londres très vert. Les routes encombrées et les maisons surpeuplées ont disparu dans la verdure. Le Londres de 2212 a des allures de parc boisé. Depuis que l'on a appris à manipuler l'ADN des plantes, plus personne ne construit d'immeubles. Il est en effet bien plus facile de faire pousser une maison végétale, une maison qui peut s'agrandir à volonté, une maison où les denrées poussent à même les murs de la cuisine et qui émet de l'oxygène.

L'avancée la plus étonnante est sans doute l'invention de l'informatique végétale : les ordinateurs poussent dans le jardin et tirent leurs données du « nuage informatique » ambiant. Notre campanologue trouve d'ailleurs son chemin dans la forêt de Bow grâce à une piste d'animafeuilles qui lui indiquent le bon chemin par un frétillement.

Soudain, dans une clairière, elle découvre la cloche, soutenue par une structure en bois couverte de lierre. Sa taille est impressionnante. Pour faire bouger le battant et à parvenir à tirer une note de l'énorme dôme de métal, elle doit utiliser toutes ses forces. Mais quelle note ! Un son ample, riche et complexe. Ses harmoniques profondes se développent en se réverbérant dans la forêt. Toutes les cellules de son corps vibrent à l'unisson.

En atteignant le nuage informatique, ce son réactivera les mémoires enregistrées le jour où cette cloche a sonné pour la première fois : les « j'aime » postés sur l'antique Facebook, les photos numériques, les textes et les blogs. Tous ces souvenirs seront téléchargés dans l'esprit de la campanologue par un nuage d'animapollen :

House de Rachel Whiteread (1993) est un moulage en béton de l'intérieur d'une véritable maison anglaise située dans l'East End, au 193 Grove Road, et exposé dans l'espace du modèle après la destruction de toutes les maisons de la rue. Hommage étrange à une communauté disparue, la sculpture a remporté le Prix Turner en 1993, avant d'être démolie l'année suivante.

en inhalant ce dernier, elle revivra le battement des tambours, les feux d'artifice et les cris de joie des enfants, le salut des athlètes et les paroles des chansons.

Notre fondeuse de cloches sera peut-être déroutée par les paroles de ces chansons. Comprendra-t-elle qui a des « pieds de tigre » dans la chanson Tiger feet ?

Se demandera-t-elle ce que l'homme des étoiles attend dans la chanson Starman ?

Essaiera-t-elle de deviner qui était le Scaramouche de Bohemian Rhapsody ? Et pourquoi ce dernier devait danser le fandango ? Et qui diable était le fameux Galileo Figaro ?

Ou comprendra-t-elle qu'en matière de musique pop, les paroles des chansons sont souvent fantaisistes et n'importent guère ?

Prenons « Wopbopaloobop a whop bam boo ». Ou encore, « Na, na, na, na-na-na-na naaaa »... Hey Jude, qui est peut-être la chanson des Beatles la plus célèbre, se termine par quatre bonnes minutes de « na na na naaa ». Tous ceux qui ont un jour chanté ces paroles durant un concert savent que leur sens importe peu. Cette chanson nous rapproche, nous fait communier et nous renvoie à cet après-midi de l'été 1968, lorsque les Fab Four l'ont enregistrée à Twickenham.

En fait, les paroles des chansons tiennent presque de l'astuce mnémotechnique, un truc qui fait que l'on retient un air. On pourrait même affirmer que plus les paroles sont dénuées de sens, plus la chanson fait mouche. Et moins l'on en dit, moins on prête le flanc à la critique. L'intelligentsia essaye souvent de valider l'importance de la musique pop en soulignant la profondeur et le message véhiculés par les paroles. Mais nous nous moquons bien du message : la pop vaut par ce qu'elle suscite en nous, pas par ce qu'elle raconte. La musique populaire est joueuse et lorsque nous jouons avec elle, nous inventons des choses passionnantes. Le premier programme informatique a été inventé par les carillonneurs pour les aider à sonner leurs cloches dans l'ordre voulu ; depuis, informatique et musique sont inséparables. En recherchant de nouvelles sonorités, des groupes comme Pink Floyd ou des musiciens tels que Mike Oldfield ou Brian Eno ont énormément poussé au développement de l'informatique. Le partage de la musique en ligne a plus tard été le catalyseur des réseaux sociaux, dont on a pu mesurer le rôle lors d'événements tels que le Printemps arabe. La pop est donc un facteur de changement social et, comme les cloches, son chant est celui de la liberté.

Jouer de la musique, c'est avant tout communier et d'ailleurs, on joue bien mieux quand on est à l'unisson. C'est peut-être ce que nous attendons de l'art populaire : pas tant une vision ou un savoir, mais une occasion de nous rassembler, plaisamment bluffés, et de communier. Être tous ensemble, c'est ce qui compte le plus.

Frank Cottrell Boyce

Londres 1666
Samuel Pepys, Le journal de Samuel Pepys

Je me préparai sur le champ et me rendis à la Tour de Londres... Là, de ce côté du pont, je vis toutes les maisons en feu... Tout le monde essayait de sauver ses possessions en les jetant à la rivière ou dans les barges amarrées ; les pauvres gens restaient dans leur logis jusqu'au moment où les flammes venaient les lécher et ils fuyaient alors vers les bateaux ou bien tâchaient péniblement de passer d'un escalier en bordure de rive à un autre. À mon sens, même les pauvres pigeons détestaient l'idée de devoir quitter leur logis ; certains planaient au-dessus des fenêtres et des balcons et tombaient, les ailes brûlées.

Londres 1777
Samuel Johnson

Londres dispose de tout ce que la vie peut offrir.

Londres 1852
Charles Dickens, La maison d'Âpre-Vent

Le brouillard omniprésent. Le brouillard en amont, qui enrobe les îlots et les verts pâturages ; le brouillard en aval, qui se déroule, souillé par les bateaux à quai et les miasmes déversés dans la rivière par la grande ville. Le brouillard qui nappe les marais de l'Essex, le brouillard sur les hauteurs du Kent. Brouillard qui pénètre dans les cambuses des navires charbonniers ; brouillard pesant sur les chantiers navals et sur le gréement des navires ; brouillard sur le plat-bord des chalands et des petits bateaux. Brouillard dans l'œil des antiques retraités de Greenwich dont la respiration siffle à côté de la cheminée ; brouillard dans le fourneau et la tige de la pipe du capitaine colérique, enfermé dans sa cabine ; brouillard qui mord les orteils et les doigts du jeune mousse tremblant de froid.

Londres 1948
Andrea Levy, Hortense et Queenie

La plupart des gars avaient le nez en l'air... Après des journées en mer, ils avaient le tournis. Tout ce qui les entourait les émerveillait. Ils arrivaient enfin à Londres, la capitale de la Mère Patrie. Il fallait les voir pointer du doigt un train qui traversait avec fracas un pont. Ils paraissaient choqués quand une épaisse fumée noire s'approchait du linge blanc en train de sécher. Des draps, des caleçons ou des bonnets pour bébés. ... Même le soleil ne prenait pas d'autres couleurs que le gris.

Londres 2012
Jo Shapcott, Wild Swimmer

Remonte la rivière du temps
et rappelle-toi Alfred le Grand
qui creusa la Channelsea pour repousser les Danois
et les biefs qui alimentèrent les moulins
pendant les siècles. Les eaux de la Waterworks étaient reines.
Glisse vers le fond du canal Prescott
frôlant au passage les pierres de l'arc perdu d'Euston Arch
puis refais surface parmi les roseaux, chênes, saules et frênes.
Plonge sous le stade lui-même,
où coule la petite Pudding Mill River :
enfin, émerge dans un bâtiment en forme de vague
et nage de tout ton cœur, car tu es tout or.

Londres l'éternelle
Benjamin Zephaniah, The London Breed

J'aime cette grande ville polluée
Où les stars de la pop vivent leur transe
Où les fêtards vibrent au son du djembé
Où les politiciens manigancent
Toutes les mélodies du monde s'y jouent
Cette ville connaît toutes les musiques
Ses habitants viennent de partout
Et ce sont eux qui la rendent épique.

Abide With Me

Reste avec moi

Choreographer and Principal Performer / *Chorégraphe et artiste principal*
Akram Khan

Principal Performer / *Artiste principal*
Emeli Sandé

Abide with me; fast falls the eventide;
The darkness deepens; Lord with me abide.
When other helpers fail and comforts flee,
Help of the helpless, O abide with me.

Swift to its close ebbs out life's little day;
Earth's joys grow dim; its glories pass away;
Change and decay in all around I see;
O Thou who changest not, abide with me.

I need Thy presence every passing hour.
What but Thy grace can foil the tempter's power?
Who, like Thyself, my guide and stay can be?
Through cloud and sunshine, Lord, abide with me.

I fear no foe, with Thee at hand to bless;
Ills have no weight, and tears no bitterness.
Where is death's sting? Where, grave, thy victory?
I triumph still, if Thou abide with me.

Hold Thou Thy cross before my closing eyes;
Shine through the gloom and point me to the skies.
Heaven's morning breaks, and earth's vain shadows flee;
In life, in death, O Lord, abide with me.

Reste avec moi, Seigneur, le jour décline,
La nuit s'approche et me menace ;
J'implore ta présence divine :
Reste avec moi, Seigneur, reste avec moi.

Les vains bonheurs de ce monde infidèle
N'enfantent rien que regrets ou dégoûts ;
J'ai soif d'une joie éternelle ;
Reste avec moi, Seigneur, reste avec moi.

Dans mes combats si ta main me délaisse,
Satan vainqueur me tiendra sous ses coups ;
Que ta puissance arme ma faiblesse ;
Reste avec moi, Seigneur, reste avec moi.

Sous ton regard la joie est sainte et bonne,
Près de ton cœur les pleurs mêmes sont doux ;
Soit que ta main me frappe ou me couronne,
Reste avec moi, Seigneur, reste avec moi.

Et quand, au bout de ce pèlerinage,
Je partirai pour le grand rendez-vous,
Pour me guider dans ce dernier passage,
Reste avec moi, Seigneur, reste avec moi.

This hymn was written by Henry Francis
Lyte in 1847 on his deathbed. He passed
away three weeks after finishing it.
Its honest expression of the fear of
approaching death has made it popular
with people of all religions and none. It
was Mahatma Gandhi's favourite hymn
and it was the hymn that the band was
playing on the Titanic when it sank. It
has an indelible association with sport.
It has been sung by tens of thousands of
spectators at every FA Cup Final since
1927 and every Rugby Challenge Cup
Final since 1929.

*Cet hymne fut écrit en 1847 par Henry
Francis Lyte sur son lit de mort. Lyte
succomba trois semaines après l'avoir
terminé. Sa description sans fard de la
peur éprouvée à l'approche de la mort en
a fait un chant populaire dans toutes les
religions. Reste avec moi était l'hymne
préféré du Mahatma Gandhi et c'est celui
que jouait l'orchestre du Titanic lors de
son naufrage. Irrémédiablement associé
au sport, il a été chanté par des milliers de
spectateurs à chaque finale de la Coupe
d'Angleterre de football depuis 1927 et
chaque finale de la Challenge Cup de
rugby depuis 1929.*

Welcome *Bienvenue*

Afio Mai, Akwaaba, Alii, Bem Vindos, Benvenuto, Benvinguts, Bienvenidos, Bienvenue, Bula vinaka, Bun venit, Dobrodošli, Ekamawir omo, Fáilte, Fanlathalom, Hoan nghênh, Kaaraki, Karibu, Kia Ora, Kia Orana, Laipni ļudzem, Mauya, Meřhba, Mirë se vjen, 'Oku talitali lelei koe, Selamat datang, Soo dhowow, Sveiki atvykę, Tere tulemast, Tervetuloa, Üdvözlet, Välkommen, Velkomin, Velkommen, Vitajte, Welcome, Welkam, Willkommen, Witam Cię, Xush kelibsiz, Вітаем, Добро Пожаловать, Добродошли, Қош келдіңіз!, Ласкаво просимо, Тавтай морилогтун, კეთილი იყოს თქვენი, ようこそ, أهلا وسهلا, پخير, خوش آمدید, 歓迎, 歡迎光臨, 환영합니다, መርሓባ, स्वागत, स्वागतम्, স্বাগতম, ආයුබෝවන්, ยินดีต้อนรับ, ຍິນດີຕ້ອນຮັບ, ស្វាគមន៍

At every Games, the Athletes' Parade is led by Greece to honour the birthplace of the Olympics. They're followed by teams from the rest of the world in alphabetical order, with the exception of the Host Nation who conclude the Parade. So this evening, that's Team GB. For the 10,490 athletes from more than 200 nations this is the moment when the years of training are behind them and the excitement of the Games ahead – 26 sports, 34 venues and 302 medal events.

À chaque Olympiade, le défilé des athlètes débute par la Grèce, en hommage à la patrie des Jeux Olympiques. Viennent ensuite les équipes du reste du monde classées par ordre alphabétique, à l'exception de la nation organisatrice qui clôture le défilé. Ce soir, ce sera donc l'équipe britannique. Pour les 10 490 athlètes venus de plus de 200 pays, c'est le moment où les années d'entraînement sont derrière et où ne reste que l'excitation des Jeux à venir : 26 sports, 34 sites et 302 remises de médailles.

Greece > Afghanistan > Albania > Algeria > American Samoa > Andorra > Angola > Antigua and Barbuda > Argentina > Armenia > Aruba > Australia > Austria >

Grèce > Afghanistan > Albanie > Algérie > Samoa américaines > Andorre > Angola > Antigua-et-Barbuda > Argentine > Arménie > Aruba > Australie > Autriche >

Azerbaijan > Bahamas > Bahrain > Bangladesh > Barbados > Belarus > Belgium > Belize > Benin > Bermuda > Bhutan > Bolivia > Bosnia and Herzegovina >

Azerbaïdjan > Bahamas > Bahreïn > Bangladesh > Barbade > Bélarus > Belgique > Belize > Bénin > Bermudes > Bhoutan > Bolivie > Bosnie-Herzégovine >

Botswana > Brazil > British Virgin Islands > Brunei Darussalam > Bulgaria > Burkina Faso > Burundi > Cambodia > Cameroon > Canada > Cape Verde >

Botswana > Brésil > Îles Vierges britanniques > Brunéi Darussalam > Bulgarie > Burkina Faso > Burundi > Cambodge > Cameroun > Canada > Cap-Vert >

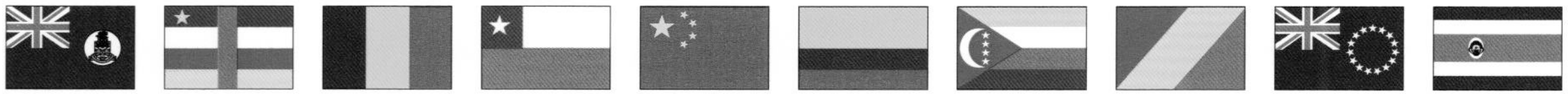

Cayman Islands > Central African Republic > Chad > Chile > People's Republic of China > Colombia > Comoros > Congo > Cook Islands > Costa Rica >

Îles Caïmans > République centrafricaine > Tchad > Chili > République populaire de Chine > Colombie > Comores > Congo > Îles Cook > Costa Rica >

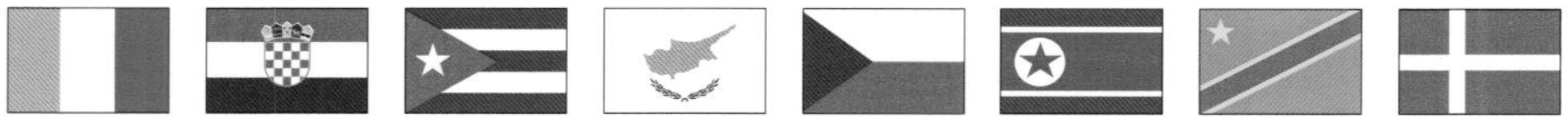

Côte d'Ivoire > Croatia > Cuba > Cyprus > Czech Republic > Democratic People's Republic of Korea > Democratic Republic of the Congo > Denmark >

Côte d'Ivoire > Croatie > Cuba > Chypre > République tchèque > République populaire démocratique de Corée > République démocratique du Congo > Danemark >

Djibouti > Dominica > Dominican Republic > Ecuador > Egypt > El Salvador > Equatorial Guinea > Eritrea > Estonia > Ethiopia > Fiji > Finland >

Djibouti > Dominique > République dominicaine > Équateur > Égypte > El Salvador > Guinée équatoriale > Érythrée > Estonie > Éthiopie > Fidji > Finlande >

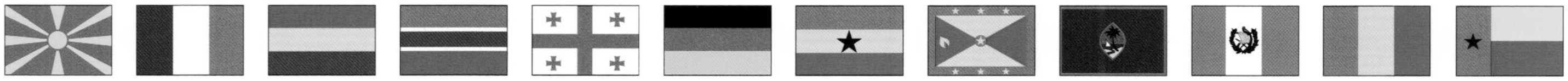

Former Yugoslav Republic of Macedonia > France > Gabon > Gambia > Georgia > Germany > Ghana > Grenada > Guam > Guatemala > Guinea > Guinea-Bissau >

Ex-République yougoslave de Macédoine > France > Gabon > Gambie > Géorgie > Allemagne > Ghana > Grenade > Guam > Guatemala > Guinée > Guinée-Bissau >

Guyana > Haiti > Honduras > Hong Kong, China > Hungary > Iceland > Independent Olympic Athletes > India > Indonesia > Islamic Republic of Iran > Iraq >
Guyana > Haïti > Honduras > Hong Kong, Chine > Hongrie > Islande > Athlètes olympiques indépendants > Inde > Indonésie > République islamique d'Iran > Iraq >

Ireland > Israel > Italy > Jamaica > Japan > Jordan > Kazakhstan > Kenya > Kiribati > Republic of Korea > Kuwait > Kyrgyzstan > Lao People's Democratic Republic >
Irlande > Israël > Italie > Jamaïque > Japon > Jordanie > Kazakhstan > Kenya > Kiribati > République de Corée > Koweït > Kirghizistan > République démocratique populaire lao >

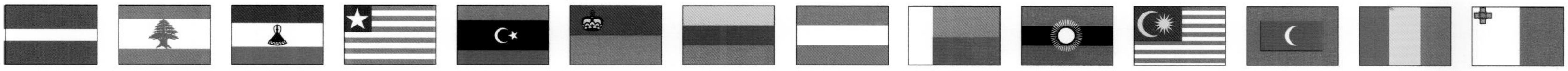

Latvia > Lebanon > Lesotho > Liberia > Libya > Liechtenstein > Lithuania > Luxembourg > Madagascar > Malawi > Malaysia > Maldives > Mali > Malta >
Lettonie > Liban > Lesotho > Libéria > Libye > Liechtenstein > Lituanie > Luxembourg > Madagascar > Malawi > Malaisie > Maldives > Mali > Malte >

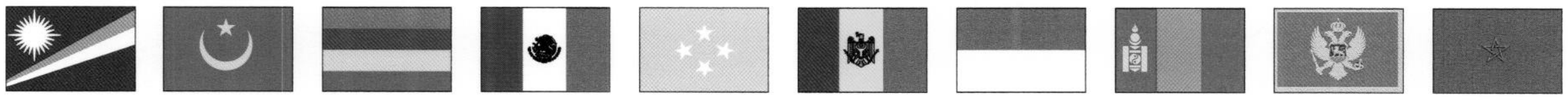

Marshall Islands > Mauritania > Mauritius > Mexico > Federated States of Micronesia > Republic of Moldova > Monaco > Mongolia > Montenegro > Morocco >
Îles Marshall > Mauritanie > Maurice > Mexique > États fédérés de Micronésie > République de Moldova > Monaco > Mongolie > Monténégro > Maroc >

Mozambique > Myanmar > Namibia > Nauru > Nepal > Netherlands > New Zealand > Nicaragua > Niger > Nigeria > Norway > Oman > Pakistan > Palau >
Mozambique > Myanmar > Namibie > Nauru > Népal > Pays-Bas > Nouvelle-Zélande > Nicaragua > Niger > Nigéria > Norvège > Oman > Pakistan > Palau >

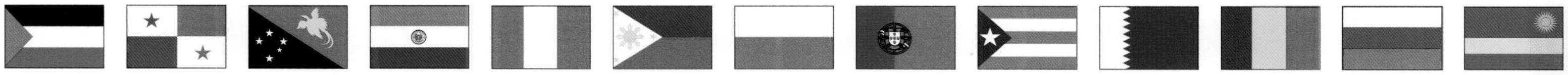

Palestine > Panama > Papua New Guinea > Paraguay > Peru > Philippines > Poland > Portugal > Puerto Rico > Qatar > Romania > Russian Federation > Rwanda >
Palestine > Panama > Papouasie-Nouvelle-Guinée > Paraguay > Pérou > Philippines > Pologne > Portugal > Porto Rico > Qatar > Roumanie > Fédération de Russie > Rwanda >

Saint Kitts and Nevis > Saint Lucia > Saint Vincent and the Grenadines > Samoa > San Marino > Sao Tome and Principe > Saudi Arabia > Senegal > Serbia >
Saint-Kitts-et-Nevis > Sainte-Lucie > Saint-Vincent-et-les-Grenadines > Samoa > Saint-Marin > Sao Tomé-et-Principe > Arabie Saoudite > Sénégal > Serbie >

Seychelles > Sierra Leone > Singapore > Slovakia > Slovenia > Solomon Islands > Somalia > South Africa > Spain > Sri Lanka > Sudan > Suriname > Swaziland >
Seychelles > Sierra Leone > Singapour > Slovaquie > Slovénie > Îles Salomon > Somalie > Afrique du Sud > Espagne > Sri Lanka > Soudan > Suriname > Swaziland >

Sweden > Switzerland > Syrian Arab Republic > Chinese Taipei > Tajikistan > United Republic of Tanzania > Thailand >
Suède > Suisse > République arabe syrienne > Chinese Taipei > Tadjikistan > République-Unie de Tanzanie > Thaïlande >

Timor-Leste > Togo > Tonga > Trinidad and Tobago > Tunisia > Turkey > Turkmenistan > Tuvalu > Uganda > Ukraine > United Arab Emirates >
Timor-Leste > Togo > Tonga > Trinité-et-Tobago > Tunisie > Turquie > Turkménistan > Tuvalu > Ouganda > Ukraine > Émirats arabes unis >

United States of America > Uruguay > Uzbekistan > Vanuatu > Venezuela > Vietnam > Virgin Islands > Yemen > Zambia > Zimbabwe > Great Britain
États-Unis d'Amérique > Uruguay > Ouzbékistan > Vanuatu > Venezuela > Vietnam > Îles Vierges des États-Unis > Yémen > Zambie > Zimbabwe > Grande-Bretagne

Bike a.m.

Vélo a.m.

Kirkpatrick Macmillan, a blacksmith, built the world's first mechanically propelled bicycle at his forge in Keir, Dumfries. Described in a newspaper report of the time as 'a velocipede of ingenious design', it had iron wheels and a wooden frame. Macmillan was also the first cyclist to be prosecuted for a traffic offence, after he ran down a pedestrian in Glasgow in 1842. A plaque on the smithy wall reads, 'He builded better than he knew'.

In ancient Greece, each team competing in the Olympics brought with them a homing dove. These were released at the end of the Games so that they could fly back to the athletes' city, with messages tied to their legs warning the families to prepare a victor's welcome. Or not. Since long before classical times – since a dove returned to Noah's Ark carrying an olive twig as proof that land was nearby – doves have been associated with peace. The story of mass communication that brought us to the internet and the mobile phone, and which includes the postman and the paperboy on their bicycles, begins on the wings of a dove.

Kirkpatrick Macmillan, forgeron de son état, a construit la première bicyclette à propulsion mécanique dans sa forge de Keir, dans la région de Dumfries. Qualifiée de « vélocipède de conception ingénieuse » dans un journal de l'époque, elle était pourvue de roues en fer et d'un cadre en bois. Macmillan fut aussi le premier cycliste poursuivi pour infraction au code de la route après avoir renversé un piéton à Glasgow en 1842. Sur une plaque apposée au mur de sa forge on peut lire ces mots : « Il construisait mieux qu'il ne le savait. »

Dans la Grèce antique, chaque équipe participant aux Jeux Olympiques apportait avec elle une colombe voyageuse. Les oiseaux étaient lâchés à la fin des Jeux pour qu'ils regagnent la cité des athlètes avec, à la patte,

un message prévenant les familles de se préparer ou non à accueillir un vainqueur. Les colombes symbolisaient la paix bien avant l'époque classique, depuis le retour sur l'arche de Noé d'une colombe qui, tenant dans son bec un rameau d'olivier, témoigna de la proximité d'une terre. L'histoire de la communication de masse, qui nous a menés à Internet et au téléphone portable en passant par le facteur et le distributeur de journaux à vélo, commence sur les ailes d'une colombe.

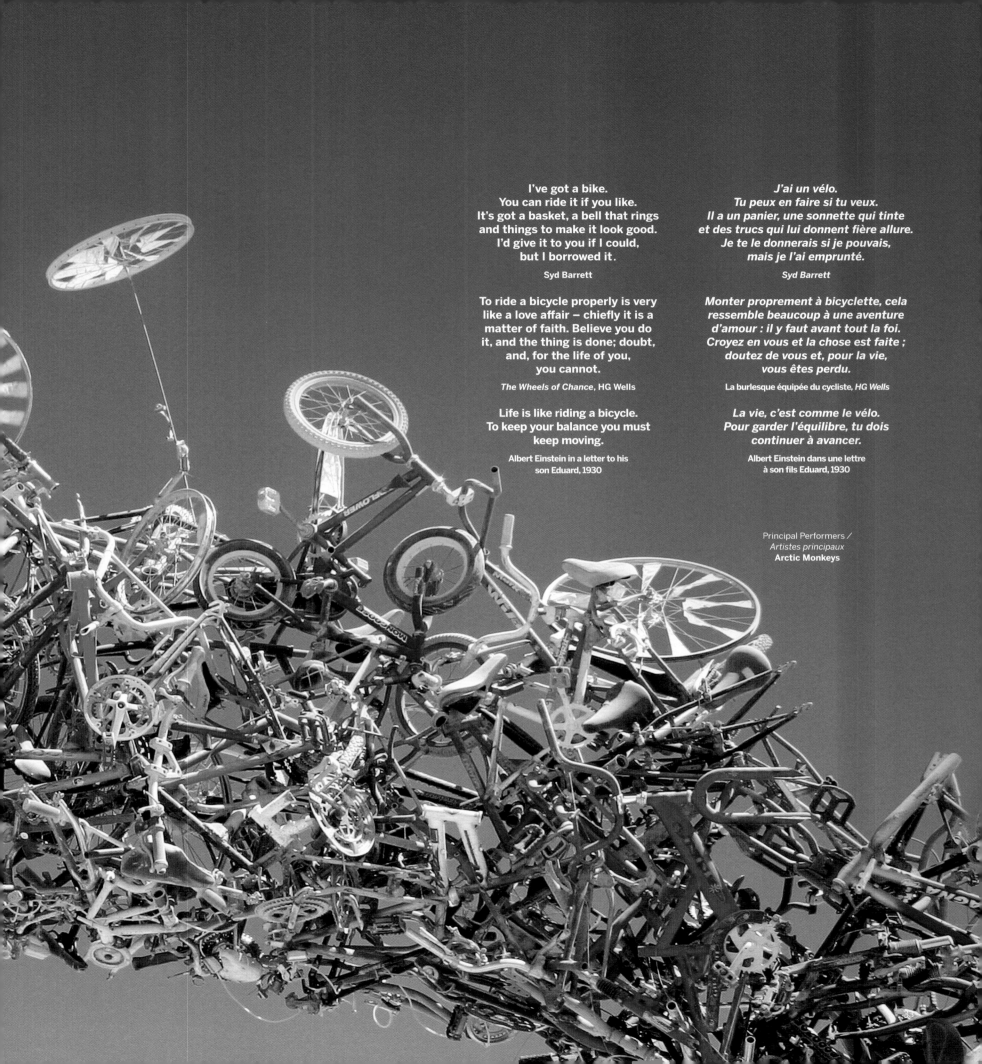

I've got a bike.
You can ride it if you like.
It's got a basket, a bell that rings
and things to make it look good.
I'd give it to you if I could,
but I borrowed it.

Syd Barrett

To ride a bicycle properly is very
like a love affair – chiefly it is a
matter of faith. Believe you do
it, and the thing is done; doubt,
and, for the life of you,
you cannot.

The Wheels of Chance, HG Wells

Life is like riding a bicycle.
To keep your balance you must
keep moving.

Albert Einstein in a letter to his
son Eduard, 1930

J'ai un vélo.
Tu peux en faire si tu veux.
Il a un panier, une sonnette qui tinte
et des trucs qui lui donnent fière allure.
Je te le donnerais si je pouvais,
mais je l'ai emprunté.

Syd Barrett

Monter proprement à bicyclette, cela
ressemble beaucoup à une aventure
d'amour : il y faut avant tout la foi.
Croyez en vous et la chose est faite ;
doutez de vous et, pour la vie,
vous êtes perdu.

La burlesque équipée du cycliste, *HG Wells*

La vie, c'est comme le vélo.
Pour garder l'équilibre, tu dois
continuer à avancer.

Albert Einstein dans une lettre
à son fils Eduard, 1930

Principal Performers /
Artistes principaux
Arctic Monkeys

The flags you can see waving in the mosh pit were all created by British children whose schools are involved in the London 2012 education programme, Get Set, which encourages them to learn about the more than 200 countries taking part in the Games. The flags are designed to express the Olympic ideals of peace and friendship and to welcome the world's athletes to this world city.

Les drapeaux que vous voyez flotter dans la fosse ont tous été créés par de petits Britanniques des écoles participant au programme éducatif de Londres 2012. Baptisé Get Set, il encourage les enfants à découvrir les plus de 200 pays participant aux Jeux. Ces drapeaux sont conçus pour exprimer les idéaux olympiques de paix et d'amitié et souhaiter la bienvenue aux athlètes du monde dans cette ville mondiale.

**History says, Don't hope
on this side of the grave.
But then, once in a lifetime
the longed-for tidal wave
of justice can rise up,
and hope and history rhyme.**

The Cure at Troy, Seamus Heaney

***L'Histoire nous dit
De ne pas espérer ici-bas
Mais un beau jour
La lame de fond de la justice
Vient tout emporter
Et espoir et histoire faire rimer***

The Cure at Troy, *Seamus Heaney*

Speeches

Sebastian Coe
Chair, London 2012
Organising Committee

An authentic Olympic giant, Seb Coe won two gold and two silver medals over successive Games – 1980 and 1984. In 1979 he broke three different world records in 41 days and his rivalry with fellow middle-distance runner Steve Ovett is one of the great Olympic stories.

Jacques Rogge
President of the International Olympic Committee

Jacques Rogge competed as a yachtsman over three Olympics – 1968, 1972 and 1976. This is his final Games as President of the IOC, a position he's held since 2001.

Discours

Sebastian Coe
Président du Comité d'organisation de Londres 2012

Véritable monument olympique, Seb Coe a remporté deux médailles d'or et deux médailles d'argent à deux Olympiades successives, en 1980 et 1984. En 1979, il a battu trois records du monde différents en 41 jours et sa rivalité avec Steve Ovett, autre coureur de demi-fond, fait partie des grandes sagas olympiques.

Jacques Rogge
Président du Comité International Olympique

Jacques Rogge a participé aux épreuves de voile de trois Jeux Olympiques : 1968, 1972 et 1976. Ces Jeux sont ses derniers en tant que président du CIO, poste qu'il occupe depuis 2001.

Let the Games Begin

Que les Jeux commencent

Olympic Truce

In Ancient Greece, the Olympic Truce traditionally lasted up to three months, before and during the Games, allowing warring city states to set aside conflict, celebrate togetherness and experience peace inspired by sport.

In 1999, the International Olympic Truce Foundation was set up to offer an opportunity for dialogue, encouraging and inspiring mankind to imagine peace. Its symbols are a dove of peace, representing the IOC's ambition to build a peaceful and better world through sport, and a flame, signifying warm friendship and global togetherness.

In 2011, the UK's Truce Resolution was submitted to the United Nations General Assembly. It referred to the main themes of the London 2012 Games – including helping to promote more inclusive and peaceful communities, urban regeneration, changing attitudes to disability and inspiring young people – and received an unprecedented show of support from all 193 member states.

Olympic Flag

The Olympic Flag was first flown at the Antwerp Games in 1920. The five interlocking rings – designed by Pierre de Coubertin, founder of the modern Olympic Games – represent the bringing together of the world's five inhabited continents.

Olympic Anthem

The Olympic Anthem was written for the first modern Games in 1896, by composer Spirou Samara and poet Kostis Palamas. It's been the official anthem since 1958 and included in every Opening Ceremony since 1960.

Olympic Oaths

An athlete first swore an oath on behalf of his peers in 1920, promising to respect and abide by the rules and spirit of the Olympics 'for the glory of sport and the honour of our teams'. Since 1972, an official has also taken an oath, promising complete impartiality in the true spirit of sportsmanship. And in 2010 the tradition of a coach from the Host Nation taking an oath was introduced. So now there are three.

La trêve olympique

Dans la Grèce antique, la trêve olympique durait traditionnellement jusqu'à trois mois, avant et pendant les Jeux, permettant aux cités-états en guerre de mettre de côté leurs conflits, de célébrer le vivre-ensemble et de vivre la paix inspirée par le sport.

La Fondation Internationale pour la Trêve Olympique a été créée en 1999 pour permettre le dialogue, encourager et inspirer l'humanité à imaginer la paix. Ses symboles sont une colombe de la paix, symbole de l'ambition du CIO de construire un monde meilleur et pacifié par le biais du sport, ainsi qu'une flamme représentant l'amitié chaleureuse et le vivre-ensemble mondial.

En 2011, le Royaume-Uni a présenté sa Résolution sur la Trêve olympique à l'Assemblée générale des Nations Unies. Celle-ci reprenait les principaux thèmes des Jeux de Londres 2012, notamment la promotion de communautés inclusives et apaisées, la régénération urbaine, la modification des mentalités en matière de handicap et l'inspiration des jeunes, et a reçu un soutien sans précédent des 193 États membres.

Le drapeau olympique

Le drapeau olympique a flotté pour la première fois lors des Jeux d'Anvers, en 1920. Les cinq anneaux entrelacés, imaginés par Pierre de Coubertin, fondateur des Jeux Olympiques modernes, représentent l'union des cinq continents habités de la planète.

L'hymne olympique

L'hymne olympique a été écrit en 1896 pour les premiers Jeux modernes par le compositeur Spirou Samara et le poète Kostis Palamas. Hymne officiel depuis 1958, il est joué à chaque cérémonie d'ouverture depuis 1960.

Les serments olympiques

En 1920, un athlète a pour la première fois prêté au nom de ses pairs serment de respecter et de suivre les règles et l'esprit des Jeux Olympiques « pour la gloire du sport et l'honneur de nos équipes ». Depuis 1972, un officiel prête également serment, jurant une impartialité totale, dans un véritable esprit sportif. Et une nouvelle tradition a été introduite en 2010 avec la prestation de serment d'un entraîneur de la nation organisatrice. Les serments sont donc maintenant au nombre de trois.

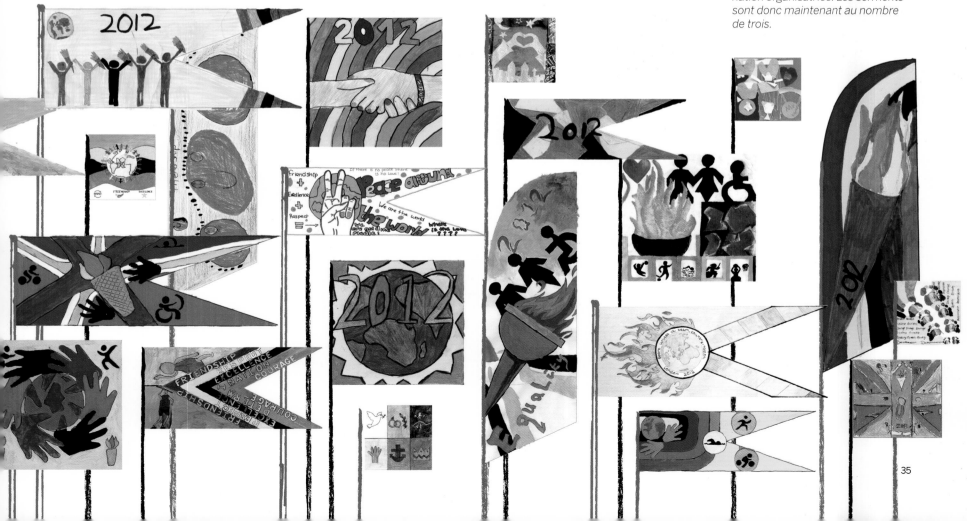

There is a Light That Never Goes Out

Une lueur qui ne s'éteint jamais

Principal Performers / *Artistes principaux*
Dame Evelyn Glennie, Elizabeth Roberts, Alex Trimble

Kindled from the rays of the sun at the Temple of Hera in Olympia, the Olympic Torch has spent 70 days travelling around the UK, carried by 8,000 inspirational Torchbearers chosen by their own communities for the light that they bring to the lives of others.

The journey ends this evening as the final Torchbearer lights the Cauldron, marking the official start of the London 2012 Olympic Games.

During the ancient Olympic Games in Greece, a fire was kept burning to symbolise and remind people of the Olympic Truce. The Torch is therefore a living, vulnerable reminder that the true ambition of the Olympics is not victory but peace.

The first Torchbearer was Prometheus, who stole fire from Mount Olympus and gave it as a gift to mankind.

La torche olympique a été allumée au temple d'Héra, à Olympie, grâce aux rayons du soleil. Elle a ensuite voyagé durant 70 jours à travers le Royaume-Uni, portée par 8000 relayeurs. Ces derniers ont été choisis en raison du rôle exemplaire qu'ils jouent au sein de leur collectivité.

Le voyage de la flamme s'achève lorsque le dernier porteur de la torche enflamme la vasque, marquant l'ouverture officielle des Jeux Olympiques de Londres 2012.

Durant les Jeux Olympiques de l'antiquité grecque, la flamme symbolisait la trêve olympique. La torche vient ainsi rappeler, par sa vulnérabilité, que l'objectif premier des Jeux n'est pas la victoire, mais la paix.

Le premier porteur de torche fut Prométhée, qui vola le feu sur le mont Olympe pour en faire don à l'humanité.

A 1,000-year-old riddle from the *Exeter Book*

A magical warrior walks this earth.
Listen to the wonder of his birth.
Silent husband stroke silent wife.
This one comes roaring into life.
In battle he is strong and wild.
But a maid may make him mild.
Feed him well and he will feed you.
Feed him too much and he will eat you.

Une énigme millénaire tirée du Livre d'Exeter

*Il est un guerrier aux pouvoirs magiques.
Voici l'incroyable façon dont il fut conçu.
Le mari et la femme s'effleurent en silence.
Lui s'éveille à la vie dans un rugissement.
Au combat, il est fort et indomptable.
Mais une jeune femme sait l'apprivoiser.
Nourrissez-le bien et il vous nourrira.
Nourrissez-le trop et il vous dévorera.*

A modern riddle by Frank Cottrell Boyce

Brightness falls from air.
Light comes out of the ground.
A single lens—two hundred lights dance round it.
Ten billion eyes look into it.
But not one eye sees me – hidden in its heart.
Until two hundred lights converge.
At the lens' focal point.
Kindling me to flame.
The light of all ten billion eyes.
One fire for every nation.
Brightness falls from air.
Light comes out of the ground.

Une énigme moderne, par Frank Cottrell Boyce

*La clarté descend du ciel.
La lumière monte du sol.
Un disque unique,
deux cents lumières dansant autour.
Dix milliards d'yeux le fixent.
Mais personne ne me voit, caché en son cœur.
Les deux cents lumières convergent.
Vers le centre de son disque.
Et déclenchent la flamme.
Allumant dix milliards d'yeux.
Un feu pour toutes les nations.
La clarté descend du ciel.
La lumière monte du sol.*

Answers: 1,000-year-old riddle: fire. Modern riddle: cauldron.

Réponses : Énigme millénaire : le feu. Énigme moderne : la vasque.

Our revels now are ended. These our actors,
As I foretold you, were all spirits and
Are melted into air, into thin air:
And, like the baseless fabric of this vision,
The cloud-capp'd towers, the gorgeous palaces,
The solemn temples, the great globe itself,
Yea, all which it inherit, shall dissolve
And, like this insubstantial pageant faded,
Leave not a rack behind. We are such stuff
As dreams are made on, and our little life
Is rounded with a sleep.

The Tempest, William Shakespeare

Mes divertissements sont maintenant finis. Tous ces acteurs,
Comme je vous l'ai dit, n'étaient que des esprits ;
Ils se sont dissous dans l'air en un souffle subtil ;
Et, tels que l'édifice sans base de cette vision,
Les tours qui se couronnent de nues, les palais magnifiques,
Les temples solennels, et aussi ce vaste globe lui-même
Et tout ce qu'il renferme, un jour disparaîtront,
Et, comme ce rêve léger qui s'évanouit,
Ne laisseront pas un débris de leur naufrage. Nous sommes faits
De la vaine substance dont se forment les songes ;
Et le cercle étroit de notre vie éphémère
Est arrondi par un sommeil.

La Tempête, *William Shakespeare*

Thomas Heatherwick's extraordinary 56m
tall sculpture, 'B of the Bang' was created
for the 2002 Commonwealth Games in
Manchester. It was inspired by Olympic gold
medallist Linford Christie's claim that he
started running not when he heard the bang
of the starting pistol but when he heard the
'B' of the bang.

L'extraordinaire sculpture de 56 mètres
de Thomas Heatherwick, B of the Bang, a
été créée pour les Jeux du Commonwealth
de 2002 à Manchester. Elle s'inspire de
la déclaration du médaillé d'or olympique
Linford Christie selon laquelle il commençait
à courir non pas à la détonation du pistolet,
mais lorsqu'il entendait le « B » du bang.

And in the end...

Et au final...

And in the end, the love you take
Is equal to the love you make

'The End', Lennon/McCartney

*Et au final, l'amour que tu reçois
Est égal à l'amour que tu donnes*

The End, *Lennon/McCartney*

Principal Performer / *Artiste principal*
Sir Paul McCartney

Who's Who?

Qui est qui ?

You'll see thousands of talented performers this evening who've been working with hundreds of creative people behind the scenes to devise and deliver the London 2012 Olympic Games Opening Ceremony.

Vous verrez ce soir des milliers d'artistes de talent qui, en coulisses, ont travaillé avec des centaines de créatifs pour concevoir et vous offrir la cérémonie d'ouverture des Jeux Olympiques de Londres 2012.

Principal Performers in alphabetical order
Artistes principaux par ordre alphabétique

Arctic Monkeys

Since releasing their number one debut single 'I Bet You Look Good on the Dancefloor' in 2005, Arctic Monkeys have released four consecutive number one albums, including their debut *Whatever People Say I Am, That's What I'm Not*. The Sheffield four-piece, Alex Turner, Matt Helders, Jamie Cook and Nick O'Malley, will soon start work on their next studio album.

Depuis leur premier single I Bet You Look Good on the Dancefloor, classé numéro un des ventes en 2005, les Arctic Monkeys ont sorti quatre albums, tous classés numéro un des ventes, dont leur premier opus Whatever People Say I Am, That's What I'm Not. Les quatre garçons de Sheffield, Alex Turner, Matt Helders, Jamie Cook et Nick O'Malley, commenceront bientôt à travailler sur leur prochain album studio.

Rowan Atkinson

Rowan is one of the best-known British comic talents of his generation. With his friend Richard Curtis, he created two memorable television characters, Mr Bean and Blackadder and has appeared in many successful West End stage productions and feature films.

Rowan est l'un des comiques britanniques les plus célèbres de sa génération. Avec son ami Richard Curtis, il a créé deux personnages mémorables de la télévision, Mr Bean et Blackadder, et on a pu le voir dans de nombreux longs métrages et productions théâtrales du West End, tous auréolés du même succès.

Sir Tim Berners-Lee

In 1989 Tim invented the World Wide Web while at CERN, the European Laboratory for Particle Physics. A graduate of Oxford University, he is a Professor at the Massachusetts Institute of Technology, Director of the World Wide Web Consortium and the Web Foundation. In 2004 he was knighted and in 2007 he was awarded the Order of Merit.

En 1989, Tim a inventé le World Wide Web, alors qu'il travaillait au CERN, le laboratoire européen pour la physique des particules. Diplômé de l'université d'Oxford, il est professeur au Massachusetts Institute of Technology et directeur du World Wide Web Consortium et de la Web Foundation. Anobli en 2004, il a été décoré de l'ordre du Mérite britannique en 2007.

Kenneth Branagh

Kenneth is best known for directing and starring in several film adaptations of Shakespeare's plays. He's also directed and acted in a number of other films and TV series, most recently *My Week with Marilyn*, *Thor*, *Wallander* and *Valkyrie*. He's received five Oscar nominations in five different categories.

Kenneth est avant tout connu en tant que metteur en scène et acteur de plusieurs adaptations cinématographiques de pièces de Shakespeare. Il a également exercé ses talents de réalisateur et d'acteur dans d'autres films et séries télévisées, notamment récemment My Week with Marilyn, Thor, Wallander et Walkyrie. Il a reçu cinq nominations aux Oscars dans cinq catégories différentes.

Principal Performers
Artistes principaux

Daniel Craig

Daniel is renowned as one of the finest actors of his generation on stage, screen and TV. He made his debut as James Bond in *Casino Royale*, followed by *Quantum of Solace* and the forthcoming *Skyfall*. Other recent credits include the film, *The Girl with the Dragon Tattoo*, and *A Steady Rain* on Broadway.

Daniel est connu pour être l'un des meilleurs acteurs de sa génération au théâtre, au cinéma et à la télévision. Il a pour la première fois joué le rôle de James Bond dans Casino Royale *avant de le reprendre dans* Quantum of Solace *et dans* Skyfall, *qui devrait bientôt sortir sur les écrans. Il s'est également illustré récemment sur le film* Millénium, les hommes qui n'aimaient pas les femmes *et sur la pièce* A Steady Rain *à* Broadway.

Dockhead Choir

The choir of 7-17-year-olds are drawn from Christian faith communities in Southwark, south London. They've all been singing in church from a very young age and include many brothers and sisters whose family roots are ethnically diverse.

Ce chœur d'enfants et d'adolescents âgés de 7 à 17 ans est issu de communautés chrétiennes de Southwark, dans le sud de Londres. Tous chantent à l'église depuis leur plus jeune âge et on trouve parmi eux de nombreuses fratries aux origines ethniques diverses.

Dame Evelyn Glennie

Dame Evelyn Glennie is the first person to successfully create and sustain a full-time career as a solo percussionist. Through overcoming the adversity of profound deafness she has become one of the world's most innovative musicians. As an international motivational speaker Evelyn draws on her experiences to captivate and enthral audiences.

Dame Evelyn Glennie est la première personne à avoir entamé et mené avec succès une carrière de percussionniste solo à plein temps. En surmontant l'obstacle de sa profonde surdité, elle est devenue l'un des musiciens les plus novateurs au monde. Conférencière motivationnelle intervenant au niveau international, Evelyn s'appuie sur ses expériences pour captiver et passionner ses auditoires.

At the heart of every life form there is rhythm. Movement, flow, change, renewal and repetition are all based on rhythm. It's only in rhythm that we can experience time. Without vibration, without oscillation, there is stasis, there is nothing. Stability and solidity are illusions. Everything oscillates and vibrates – from the bridge of steel and concrete to the energy shells around an atom. Even colours oscillate at different frequencies. We recognise and experience our world through rhythm. Everything vibrates, everything speaks. It is, in essence, a universe of sound.

Thomas Riedelsheimer, director of *Touch the Sound: A Sound Journey with Evelyn Glennie* (quote translated from German by Leslie Hills)

Au cœur de toute forme de vie, il y a le rythme. Mouvement, flux, changement, renouveau et répétition reposent tous sur le rythme. Il n'y a que dans le rythme que nous pouvons faire l'expérience du temps. Sans vibration, sans oscillation, il y a immobilité, il n'y a rien. La stabilité et la solidité sont des illusions. Du pont d'acier et de béton aux couches d'énergie qui entourent un atome, tout oscille et vibre. Même les couleurs oscillent à des fréquences diverses. Nous reconnaissons et vivons notre monde par le rythme. Tout vibre, tout parle. Notre univers est, fondamentalement, un univers de sons.

Thomas Riedelsheimer, réalisateur de Touch the Sound: A Sound Journey with Evelyn Glennie

The Kaos Signing Choir for Deaf & Hearing Children

The award-winning choir of 4-18-year-old deaf and hearing children incorporate singing and British Sign Language interpretation into their performances. They've performed for Princess Anne, won the North London Festival Choir Competition three times and featured on BBC TV and radio. Their global patron is Archbishop Desmond Tutu.

Récompensé par de nombreux prix, ce chœur composé d'enfants sourds et entendants de 4 à 18 ans pratique la chanson et l'interprétation en langue des signes britannique. Il s'est produit devant la Princesse Anne, a remporté trois fois le concours de chorales du North London Festival et est apparu dans des programmes de télévision et de radio de la BBC. Son parrain mondial est l'archevêque Desmond Tutu.

Sir Paul McCartney

Since writing his first song at the age of 14, Paul has dreamed and dared to be different. In the 60s he changed the world of music with The Beatles. Over the last 40 years he's continued to push the boundaries as a solo artist, with Wings, as part of The Fireman, as a classical composer and one of the world's greatest live performers.

Paul a écrit sa première chanson à l'âge de 14 ans et n'a depuis jamais cessé de rêver et d'oser être différent. Dans les années 60, il a bouleversé le monde de la musique avec les Beatles et a continué ces 40 dernières années à repousser les limites en tant qu'artiste solo, avec les Wings ou The Fireman, en tant que compositeur de musique classique et en tant qu'artiste parmi les plus proéminents de la musique en direct.

Mike Oldfield

Mike made his name with the groundbreaking 1973 musical suite, *Tubular Bells,* and his subsequent 24 albums all take a similar, singular, innovative path. A gifted composer, guitarist and multi-instrumentalist, he returns to the UK after years in semi-retirement, living, in his own words, a 'Robinson Crusoe-like' life in the Bahamas.

Mike s'est fait connaître en 1973 avec la révolutionnaire suite musicale Tubular Bells, et ses 24 albums suivants ont tous emprunté le même chemin singulier et novateur. Compositeur, guitariste et multi-instrumentiste de talent, il retrouve le Royaume-Uni après plusieurs années de semi-retraite aux Bahamas, où il mène dit-il la vie d'un Robinson Crusoë.

Dizzee Rascal

During a career spanning almost a decade, Dizzee has released four hit albums including *Boy In Da Corner* and the platinum *Tongue n' Cheek*, which produced five UK number one singles. Accolades and awards include the coveted Mercury Music Prize, an Ivor Novello Award and a BRIT Award.

Au fil de ses presque dix ans de carrière, Dizzee a sorti quatre albums auréolés de succès, dont Boy In Da Corner et Tongue n' Cheek, disque de platine dont cinq titres ont été numéro un des ventes au Royaume-Uni. Il a reçu de nombreux prix et distinctions, parmi lesquels le très convoité Mercury Music Prize, un Ivor Novello Award et un BRIT Award.

Principal Performers
Artistes principaux

Sir Simon Rattle

Chief Conductor and Artistic Director of Berliner Philharmoniker and former Music Director of City of Birmingham Symphony, Simon conducts leading ensembles and soloists worldwide. His long relationship with EMI has produced many distinguished recordings and his dedication to working with young people has been recognised with numerous international awards.

Chef d'orchestre et directeur artistique du Berliner Philharmoniker, Simon Rattle a été directeur musical du City of Birmingham Symphony et dirige ensembles et solistes de premier plan dans le monde entier. De sa longue relation avec EMI sont nés de nombreux enregistrements majeurs, et son dévouement à collaborer avec les jeunes lui a valu de nombreuses récompenses internationales.

Elizabeth Roberts

Born in Bethnal Green, Elizabeth is an accomplished performer in oratorio, opera and recital. She's appeared on two recordings with the BBC Symphony Orchestra and has performed throughout the UK, Europe and in Beijing. Operatic roles include Mimì (*La bohème*), Fiordiligi (*Così fan tutte*), Salome (*Hérodiade*) and Tosca (*Tosca*).

Elizabeth is joined by Junior Guildhall School of Music student Esme Smith, who co-wrote the soprano and choral score for 'Caliban's Dream'.

Native de Bethnal Green, Elizabeth est une chanteuse accomplie d'oratorios, d'opéra et en récital. Elle a participé à deux enregistrements avec l'Orchestre symphonique de la BBC et a chanté aux quatre coins du Royaume-Uni, en Europe et à Pékin. Ses rôles d'opéra comprennent Mimì (La Bohème), Fiordiligi (Così fan tutte), Salomé (Hérodiade) et Tosca (Tosca).

Elizabeth est accompagnée d'Esme Smith, étudiante à la Junior Guildhall School of Music et co-compositeur des partitions de soprano et du chœur de Caliban's Dream.

JK Rowling

JK Rowling is the author of the bestselling Harry Potter books. The series has sold more than 450 million copies worldwide, been distributed in over 200 countries and translated into 70-plus languages, as well as being turned into blockbuster films. She has an OBE for services to children's literature.

JK Rowling est l'auteur de la saga Harry Potter. Ces best-sellers se sont vendus à plus de 450 millions d'exemplaires dans le monde, sont distribués dans plus de 200 pays, ont été traduits dans plus de 70 langues et portés à l'écran dans de gros succès au box-office. Elle a été faite Officier de l'Empire britannique pour services rendus à la littérature de jeunesse.

Emeli Sandé

BRIT Awards Critics' Choice winner Emeli has written songs for some of the biggest names in pop. Revered by her peers and championed by artists like Alicia Keys and Coldplay's Chris Martin, she released her debut album *Our Version of Events* in 2012 which reached number one in the charts.

Prix de la critique aux BRIT Awards, Emeli a écrit des chansons pour quelques-uns des plus grands noms de la pop. Adulée par ses pairs et encensée par des artistes comme Alicia Keys et Chris Martin, de Coldplay, elle a sorti en 2012 son premier album, Our Version of Events, *qui s'est classé numéro un des ventes.*

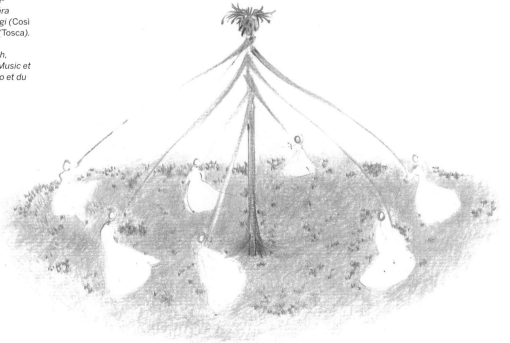

Alex Trimble

Alex is the lead singer of Northern Irish band Two Door Cinema Club. Their debut album, *Tourist History* was released in 2010 and has sold over one million copies. Their follow-up, *Beacon*, will be released in September 2012.

Alex est le chanteur du groupe nord-irlandais Two Door Cinema Club. Leur premier album Tourist History, sorti en 2010, s'est vendu à plus d'un million d'exemplaires. Leur deuxième opus, Beacon, sortira en septembre 2012.

Frank Turner

Frank is an award-winning folk/punk singer-songwriter whose fourth studio album, *England Keep My Bones*, reached number 12 in the UK charts last year. A rising star, earlier this year he played a sold-out headline show at Wembley Arena.

Frank est un auteur-compositeur-interprète folk punk primé dont le quatrième album studio England Keep My Bones a atteint la douzième place des ventes au Royaume-Uni l'an dernier. Étoile montante de la musique, il a fait salle comble à la Wembley Arena au début de cette année.

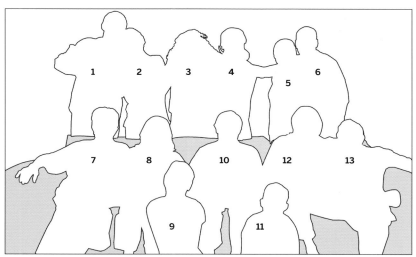

Thanks Tim family and friends are all volunteer performers (see p24)

La famille et les amis du volet Thanks Tim sont tous bénévoles (voir p. 24)

1 Stephen Concannon	**and...**	
2 Laura Eagland	Katie Appleby	
3 Jasmine Breinburg	Matthew Brinkworth	
4 Nathalie Miller	Henrique Costa	
5 Carly Enstone	Katie Farnsworth	
6 Sebastian Wilson	Stephanie Firth	
7 Louise Jefferson	Kane Foley	
8 Audrey Daley	Dinah Gray	
9 Alex Jarrett	Craig Jenner	
10 Brian Boston	Remmie Milner	
11 Maxwell Grappy	Jolyon Price	
12 Teresa Earle	Dhruv Rupapara	
13 Anthony Curran	Husna Torabally	
	Laura Winnan	

Performers
Artistes

Stadium Announcers
Layla Anna-Lee
Marc Edwards

Prologue / Green and Pleasant Land

Prologue Host
Curtis Walker

Frank Turner's Performers
Tarrant Anderson
Emily Barker
Christopher Capewell
Simon Cripps
Anna Jenkins
Benjamin Lloyd
James Lockey
Ben Marwood
Matthew Nasir
Nigal Powell
Gillian Sandell
Joanne Silverston
Francis Turner

Movement Assistants
Polly Bennett
Laura Cubitt
Paul Fillipiak
Robin Guiver
Joyce Henderson
Paul Kasey
Eric Mallett
Diane Mitchell
Anna Morrissey
Emily Mytton

Brunels
Nicholas Beveney
Rikki Chamberlain
Richard James-Neale
Adam Jones
Dermot Keaney
Alex McNally
Jermaine Oguh
Phil Snowden
François Testory
Tam Ward

Animal Handlers
Charles Atkinson
Lucy Atkinson
Daniel Brown
Mark Brown
Jill Clark
Nikki Cole
Joanne Coombes
Sophia Cordwell
Janette Duncan
Sally Dunsford
Katherine Eaglen
Ryan Evans
Gabby Farr
Roger Farr
Chris Few
Naomi Forrest
Olivia Forrest
Malvyn Groves
Jenny Harris
Michael Hartland
Claire Hawthorn
Lesley Hawthorn
Lisa Hawthorn
Lara Heath
Samantha Jones
Holly Levinge

Sharon Rafferty
Elizabeth Rutherford
Paul Stanley
Danny Stevens
Gavin Stevens
Nara Stevens
Shane Stevens
Steve Tubbs
Christopher Tucker
Katy Tucker
Leigh Tucker
Kay Weston

Pandemonium

Drum Consultants
Paul Clarvis
Mike Dolbear
John Randall
Ralph Salmins

Drum Captains
Barnaby Archer
Oliver Blake
Daniel Bradley
Rebecca Celebuski
Jason Chowdhury
Jonathan Colgan
Oliver Cox
Fabio de Oliveira
Robert Eckland
Daniel Ellis
Richard Elsworth
David Holmes
Oliver Lowe
Nicola Marangoli
James O'Carroll
Gerard Rundell
Ramon Sherrington
Corrina Silvester
Alex Smith
Owain Williams
Justin Woodward

Suffragettes
Rachel Bingham
Madeleine Bowyer
Kaye Brown
Lucy Casson
Janine Craig
Luisa D'Ambrosio
Louise Davidson
Alison Kirrage
Tracey Lushington
Meg McNaughton-Filipidis

Chimney Riders
Remy Archer
James Booth
Ben Brason
Graeme Clint
Chris Gage
Terry Lamb
Hasit Savani

Ring Riders
Eric Adame
Jono Fee
Adam Laughton
David Rimmer

Stilt Walkers
Gina d'Angelo
Desiree Kongerod
Adrian South
Mark Tate

Happy & Glorious

Stunt Performers
Gary Connery
Mark Sutton

Helicopter Pilots
Sam Edding
Marc Wolff

Flag Team Leader
Squadron Leader Lambert, Royal Air Force, RAF Brize Norton

Flag Raisers
Corporal Adam, Royal Air Force, RAF Leuchars
Able Seaman Drew, Royal Navy, HMS Excellent
Able Seaman Class 2 Fasuba, Royal Navy, HMS Drake
Sergeant Reains, Army, 1 Irish Guards

Flag Bearers
Gunner Bateman, Army, Kings Troop Royal Horse Artillery
Flight Lieutenant Cadman, Royal Air Force, RAF Cranwell
Marine Edwards, Royal Navy, Commando Logistic Regiment
Colour Sergeant Hiscock, Royal Navy, 10 Training Squadron RM Poole
Corporal of the Horse Puddifoot, Army, Household Calvary Mounted Regiment
Sergeant Raval, Royal Air Force, RAF Halton
Corporal Robins, Army, 20 Transport Squadron, RLC
Lieutenant Weller, Royal Navy, DES Abbeywood

Second to the right, and straight on till morning

Dance Captains/ Choreographic Assistants
Tim Hamilton
Carolene Hinds
Sam Lane
Junior Laniyan
Yami Lovfenberg
Richard Pitt
Russell Sargeant
Alan Vincent

Assistant Dance Captains/ Choreographic Assistants
Damien Anyasi
Julian Essex-Spurrier
Jreena Green
Warren Heyes
Emiko Ishi
Rebekkah Knight
Eilidh Ross

Dancers
Afi Agyeman
Ben Ajose-Cutting

Lucy Alderman
Abdul Ali
Michelle Andrews
Yaa Appiah-Badu
Clara Bajado
Isaac Vitamin Baptiste
Hanna Bardall
Sasha Biloshitsky
Martha Carangi Bishoff
Nader Kayzar Boulila
Lexi Bradburn
Angelica Brewster
Abigail Brodie
Renata Carvalho
Loveday Chamberlain
Darren Charles
Alexandra-Louise Cheshire
Konrad Ciechanowski
Lisa Clarke
Lee Crowley
Olivia Daniell
AJ Daniels
Brenan Davies
Shannen Devlin
Sara Dos Santos
Kage Douglas
Kieran Edmonds
Shangomola Edunjobi
Victoria Ekundayo
Rachel Ensor
Adrian Falconer
Lulu Fish
Kara Fogerty
Maureen Francis
Steph Furness
Poppy Garton
Jennifer Gauss
Tarryn Gee
Kit Glennie
Phil W Green
Hattie Lauren Grover
Dominika Grzelak
Chloe Hallett
Selina Hamilton
Anna Haresnape
Cathryn-Anne Harries
Dani Harris-Walters
Samantha Haynes
Samantha Hayes
Denny Haywood
Keith Henderson
Sarah Hitch
Anthony Jackson
Hannah Jackson
Julie Jade
Peter Johnson
Jahmai Jam Fu Jones
Naa-Dei Kwashie
Simon Lee
Kamila Lewandowska
Amanda Lewis
Issie Lloyd
Daniel Aaron Louard
Devon Mackenzie-Smith
Antoine Marc
Katie Marcham
Laura Kate Marlow
Lindsay McAllister
Stella McGowan
Ross McLaren
Lee Meadows
Azara Meghie
Ella Mesma
Hayley Michelle
Simone Mistry-Palmer
Tashan Muir
Wolfgang Mandela Mwanje

Chris Neumann
Ellesha Newton
Emma Nightingale
Abena Z Noel
Joanne Odro
Lauren Okadigbo
Isabel Kayzar Olley
Olufunmilola Fumy Opeyemi
Emma O'Regan
Mark Parton
Jole PJ Pasquale
Ashley Patricks
Lee Payne
Karis Pentecost
Bethan Peters
Marianne Phillips
Tania Pieri
Yohemy Prosper
Andrea Queens
Adam Rae
Avalon Rathgeb
Alexis KA Roberts
Julien Roussel
Amy Rowbottom
Jack Saunders
Justin Saunders
Julie Schmidt Andreason
Jody Schroeder
Nathaniel Scott
Aaron Entropy Shah
Benjamin Shogbulu
Francesca Short
Victoria Shulungu
Ashley David Simon
Candice Szczepanski
Sorsha Talbot-Hunt
Benjamin Taylor-Shepherd
Aleta Thompson
Nefeli Tsiouti
Katrina Vasilieva
Julie Vibert
Gavin Vincent
Keigan Westfield
Jezz-Lee Wood
Carly Woodridge
Katie Wymark
Adelle Young

Aerialist Captain
Matt Costain
Jono Fee
Robyn Miranda Simpson

Mary Poppins Aerialists
Katherine Arnold
Helen Ball
Anna Serena Bindra
Teresa Callan
Tamlyn Victoria Clark
Vanessa Cook
Pippa Coram
Laura Cork
Clare Elliott
Hege Eriksdatter Østefjells
Kimberley Eyles
Naomi Giffen
Sophie Page Hall
Maria Hippolyte
Allie Ho Chee
Marada Manussen
Victoria McManus
Tori Moone
Collette Morrow
Valerie Murzak
Michaela O'Connor
Nikki O'Hara
Claire O'Neill

Catrin Osborne
Amy Panter
Jennifer Paterson
Dela Seward
Zoey Tedstill
Philippa Vafadari
Natalie Verhaegen
Annette Walker

Nightmare Aerialists
Cornelius Atkinson
Matt Costain
Abagail Evans
Lucy Francis
Jack Horner
Kate Sanderson
Anthony Weiss

Trampoline Consultant
David-Roy Wood

Trampolinists
Nathan Adams
Anton Anderson
Libbie Brown
Cole Burrell
Tye Crawford
Roman Woody Elliott
Samantha Katkevica
Jessie Koon
Keziah Livingston
China Mattis
Logan Maxwell
Thomas Mitchelmore
Iona Moir
Parise Simpson
Francesca Sweet
Lewis Walsh

Elevating Bed Children
Leo Ayres
Yaris Lee-Lawrence
T'Khai Phillips
Fleur Sweet

Skaters
Amanda Valentine Constantinou
Leroy Ricardo Jones

Lead Puppeteers
Andrew Dawson
Tom Espiner
Sean Myatt
Rob Tygner

Puppeteers
Derek Arnold
Caroline Bowman
Ashleigh Cheadle
Fiona Clift
Iestyn Evans
Sean Garratt
David Grewcock
Brian Herring
Matthew Hutchinson
Rachel Leonard
Irena Stratieva
Ivan Thorley
Jon Whitten

frankie & june say... Thanks Tim

Dance Captains/
Choreographic Assistants
Bradley Charles
Danielle Rhimes Lecointe
Skytilz Mantey
Bruno Perrier
Nadia Sohowan

Assistant Dance Captains/
Choreographic Assistants
Jenni Bailey-Rae
Brendan Syxx Isaac
Charlene Mini Willets

Assistant Dance Captains
Gemma Hoddy
Nathaniel Sweetboy Impraim-Jones
Kofi Mingo
Theo Oloyade
Eloise Sheldon
Duwane Taylor
Mary Weah
Serena Williams

Dancers
Danella Abraham
Stephen Aspinall
Lindon Barr
Minica Beason
Conan Belletty
Karen Bengo
Ivan Blackstock
Filippo Calvagno
Simeon Campbell
Kieran Daley-Ward
Dominic Spin Daniel
Kerri De Aguiar
Kloe Dean
Israel Donowa
Odilia Egyiawan
Magnus Einang
Shannelle Fergus
Sam Field
Sam Fleet
Melissa Freire
Jemma Geanaus
Darron Gifty
Lucy Gilbert
Jeanette Gonzalez
Natasha Gooden
Jade Hackett
Clarissa Hagan
Carrie Hanson
Todd Holdsworth
Corinne Holt
Christina Ibironke
Rachel Kay
Mila Lazar
Kayla Lomas
Jaye Marshall
Miha Matevzic
Yolanda Newsome
Angela Nurse
Kelechi Nwanokwu
Andry Oporia
Holly Penny
Karim Perrineau
Jack Pointer-Mackenzie
Chantelle Prince
Kieron Providence
Michelle Queen
Serina Raymond
Nimmer Riaz

Tia Sackey
Alex Schoendorf
Michael Simon
Tomas Simon
Letitia Simpson
Stephan Sinclair
Tashan Sinclair-Doyle
Matt Sussman
Sian Taylor
Jodie Tye
Robyn Walker
Josh Wharmby
Dwain Talent White
Emily Williams
Aaron Witter
Zehra Zem

Starmen Aerialists
Eric Adame
Remy Archer
Alex Poulter
Ted Sikström

Power Skippers
James Booth
Ben Brason
Graeme Clint
Jono Fee
Chris Gage
Jack Helme
Terry Lamb
Dan Lannigan
Adam Laughton
Hannah Lawton
David Rimmer
Samantha Rockett
Hasit Savani
Steve Williams
Hadyn Wiseman

Zorb Performers
Conor Kenny
Rachael Letsche
Ahmahd Thomas
Kylie Walker

Abide With Me

Dancers
Jose Agudo
Kristina Alleyne
Sade Alleyne
Azzurra Ardovini
Helena Arenbergerova
Inma Asensio
Eva Assayas
Eulalia Ayguade Farro
Aymeric Bichon
Patsy Browne-Hope
Amy Butler
Magdaléna Caprdová
Melodie Cecchini
Rudi Cole
Vittoria De Ferrari Sapetto
Pauline De Laet
Laura De Vos
Yentl De Werdt
Kamala Devam
Vanessa Guevara
Thomasin Gülgeç
Kenny Wing Tao Ho
Reiss Jeram
Martijn Kappers
Matthias Kass
Nicholas Keegan
Sung Hoon Kim

KJ Lawson
Elias Lazaridis
Yen-Ching Lin
Katie Love
TJ Lowe
Colas Lucot
Katie Lusby
Maya Masse
Joachim Maudet
Cherish Menzo
Rhiannon Elena Morgan
Stephen Moynihan
Andrej Petrovic
Nikoleta Rafaelisová
Nicolas Ricchini
Chanel Selleslach
Gemma Elizabeth-Sarah Shrubb
Ryu Suzuki
Devaraj Thimmaiah
Teerachai Thobumrung
Melissa Ugolini
Lenka Vagnerová
Lisa Welham
Josh Wille

Bike a.m.

Keyboard Player
James Ford

Let the Games Begin

Flag Team Leader
Flag Raisers
Flag Bearers
(see Happy & Glorious)

There is a Light That Never Goes Out

Drum Consultant
Paul Clarvis

Drum Captains
(see Pandemonium)

And in the end...

Paul McCartney's Band
Rusty Anderson
Abe Laboriel Jr
Brian Ray
Paul Wickens

Danny Boyle
Artistic Director

Danny is a filmmaker whose work includes *Shallow Grave*, *Trainspotting*, *A Life Less Ordinary*, *The Beach*, *28 Days Later*, *Sunshine*, *127 Hours*, *Millions* and *Slumdog Millionaire*, which won eight Academy Awards. He has also directed work on stage at the Royal Court, Royal Shakespeare Company and, most recently, *Frankenstein* at the National Theatre. His first Olympic memory is Bob Beamon jumping out of the pit in Mexico 1968.

Danny est un metteur en scène qui a notamment réalisé les films Petits meurtres entre amis, Trainspotting, Une vie moins ordinaire, La Plage, 28 jours plus tard, Sunshine, 127 heures, Millions *et* Slumdog Millionaire, *récompensé pour ce dernier de huit oscars. Il a aussi exercé ses talents de metteur en scène sur les planches du Royal Court, de la Royal Shakespeare Company et, plus récemment, sur* Frankenstein, *au National Theatre. Son premier souvenir des Jeux olympiques : le saut hors cadre de Bob Beamon aux Jeux de Mexico, en 1968.*

Rick Smith for Underworld
Music Director

Underworld are Rick Smith and Karl Hyde – artists, composers, musicians and creative partners of 30 years standing. The duo first worked with Danny Boyle on *Trainspotting*, and most recently *Frankenstein* at the National Theatre. They are also two of the original founders of art and design collective, Tomato. Rick's favourite Olympic moment is Abebe Bikila running the marathon barefoot and winning gold, Rome 1960.

Derrière Underworld se cachent Rick Smith et Karl Hyde, artistes, compositeurs, musiciens et partenaires de création depuis 30 ans. Après une première collaboration avec Danny Boyle sur Trainspotting, *le duo a réitéré l'expérience avec* Frankenstein, *au National Theatre. Rick et Karl comptent parmi les fondateurs du collectif d'art et de design Tomato. Le moment olympique préféré de Rick : le marathon couru pieds nus par Abebe Bikila et sa médaille d'or aux Jeux de Rome, en 1960.*

Sascha Dhillon
Video Editor

Sascha has edited and assisted on a variety of film and television programmes over the past 15 years, including *The Big Breakfast*, *Mike Bassett: England Manager*, *Big Brother*, *Fame Academy*, *Five Children and It*, *The History Boys*, *Good* and *Mamma Mia!* His favourite Olympic moment is Daley Thompson whistling the National Anthem, Los Angeles 1984.

Sascha a été monteur et assistant sur plusieurs films et programmes télévisés ces quinze dernières années, notamment The Big Breakfast, Mike Bassett: England Manager, Big Brother, Fame Academy, Cinq enfants et moi, History Boys, Par-delà le bien et le mal *et* Mamma Mia! *Son moment olympique préféré : Daley Thompson sifflotant l'hymne national britannique aux Jeux de Los Angeles, en 1984.*

Mark Tildesley
Designer

Mark co-founded the Catch 22 Theatre Company, for whom he directed, designed and performed. He continued designing for the stage, including the Young Vic, Royal Opera House, and most recently *Frankenstein* at the National Theatre. Films with Danny Boyle include *28 Days Later* and *Sunshine*. Other films include *24 Hour Party People*, *The Constant Gardener* and *Happy-Go-Lucky*. His favourite Olympic moment is John Currie winning gold in figure skating, Innsbruck 1976.

Mark est cofondateur de la compagnie théâtrale Catch 22, pour laquelle il a été metteur en scène, concepteur de décors et acteur. Il a continué à exercer ses talents de décorateur au théâtre, notamment au Young Vic, à la Royal Opera House et plus récemment sur Frankenstein, *au National Theatre. Il a travaillé avec Danny Boyle sur plusieurs films, dont* 28 jours plus tard *et* Sunshine. *Au cinéma, ses autres collaborations comprennent* 24 Hour Party People, The Constant Gardener, *et* Be Happy. *Son moment olympique préféré : la médaille d'or de John Currie en patinage artistique aux Jeux d'Innsbruck, en 1976.*

Frank Cottrell Boyce
Writer

Frank is a children's writer and screenwriter. His Carnegie Medal winning book, *Millions*, was filmed by Danny Boyle. His most recent book is the first official sequel to Ian Fleming's *Chitty Chitty Bang Bang*. As a teenager, his emotional life was dominated by the rivalry between two great Olympians – Steve Ovett and Sebastian Coe.

Écrivain et scénariste pour enfants, Frank a remporté la Carnegie Medal avec son livre Millions, *porté à l'écran par Danny Boyle. Dans son ouvrage le plus récent, il livre une première suite officielle au roman* Chitty Chitty Bang Bang *d'Ian Fleming. Adolescent, il suivit la rivalité qui opposait alors deux monstres sacrés de l'Olympisme, Steve Ovett et Sebastian Coe.*

Adam Gascoyne
Visual Effects Supervisor

Adam is a co-founder of Union Visual Effects, London. His extensive career has covered all aspects of film production and post-production, including collaborations with Danny Boyle on *Slumdog Millionaire* and *127 Hours*. His favourite Olympic moment is Eric Moussambani swimming the 100m freestyle, Sydney 2000.

Adam a cofondé Union Visual Effects, situé à Londres. Au fil de sa riche carrière, il a couvert tous les aspects de la production et de la postproduction cinématographiques, travaillant notamment avec Danny Boyle sur Slumdog Millionaire *et* 127 heures. *Son moment olympique préféré : le 100 m nage libre d'Éric Moussambani aux Jeux de Sydney, en 2000.*

Suttirat Anne Larlarb
Designer

Suttirat Anne Larlarb has been part of Danny Boyle's creative team for seven years. She has been designing internationally for theatre and film since receiving her MFA at the Yale School of Drama in 1997. Credits include the films *Slumdog Millionaire* and *127 Hours*, and *Frankenstein* at the National Theatre. Her favourite Olympic moment is Mary Lou Retton winning gold for the USA in gymnastics, Los Angeles 1984.

Suttirat Anne Larlarb a intégré l'équipe créative de Danny Boyle il y a sept ans. Depuis l'obtention de son MFA à la Yale School of Drama en 1997, elle crée des décors et costumes de théâtre et de cinéma. Elle a notamment travaillé sur les films Slumdog Millionaire *et* 127 heures *ainsi que sur* Frankenstein, *au National Theatre. Son moment olympique préféré : la médaille d'or de l'Américaine Mary Lou Retton en gymnastique aux Jeux de Los Angeles, en 1984.*

Paulette Randall
Associate Director

Paulette is a freelance theatre director, television producer and writer. Credits include *Desmond's* (Channel 4), *The Real McCoy* (BBC2) and *Kerching!* (CBBC). She has directed five of August Wilson's plays, that celebrate the African American experience, at the Tricycle Theatre and is a former Artistic Director of Talawa Theatre Company. Her favourite Olympic moment is Tommie Smith and John Carlos' Black Power salute, Mexico City 1968.

Metteur en scène de théâtre, productrice de télévision et auteur indépendante, Paulette a notamment à son actif Desmond's, *sur Channel 4,* The Real McCoy, *sur BBC2, et* Kerching! (CBBC). *Elle a mis en scène cinq pièces d'August Wilson, célébrations de l'expérience afro-américaine, au Tricycle Theatre, et a été directrice artistique de la compagnie théâtrale Talawa. Son moment olympique préféré : le poing levé en hommage au Black Power de Tommie Smith et John Carlos aux Jeux de Mexico, en 1968.*

Tracey Seaward
Producer

Tracey most recently co-produced Steven Spielberg's Oscar nominated *War Horse*. She has a long standing collaboration with Stephen Frears producing, among other films, *The Queen* for which she received the BAFTA Award for Best Film and an Academy Award nomination. Other credits include Fernando Meirelles' *The Constant Gardener*, David Cronenberg's *Eastern Promises* and Danny Boyle's *Millions*. Her favourite Olympic moment is Allan Wells' wife Margot cheering her husband to gold in the 100m final, Moscow 1980.

C'est sur Cheval de guerre *de Steven Spielberg, nominé aux Oscars, que Tracey a le plus récemment exercé ses talents de coproductrice. Elle collabore depuis longtemps avec Stephen Frears et a notamment produit* The Queen, *(BAFTA Award du meilleur film) et a été nominée pour un Academy Award. Elle a aussi travaillé sur* The Constant Gardener *de Fernando Meirelles,* Les Promesses de l'ombre *de David Cronenberg et* Millions *de Danny Boyle. Son moment olympique préféré : les encouragements de Margot Wells à son mari Allan, qui décrocha l'or sur la finale du 100 m aux Jeux de Moscou, en 1980.*

Artistic Team
Équipe artistique

Toby Sedgwick
Movement Director

Toby was an actor for more than 30 years with extensive theatre credits. He appeared in Danny Boyle's film *28 Days Later* and was movement director on *Frankenstein* at the National Theatre. Choreography credits include *Nanny McPhee and the Big Bang*, *The 39 Steps* and *War Horse* for which he won an Olivier Award for Best Theatre Choreographer. His favourite Olympic moment is Richard Fosbury debuting the Fosbury Flop, Mexico City 1968.

Acteur depuis plus de 30 ans, Toby bénéficie d'une solide expérience théâtrale. On a pu le voir dans le film 28 jours plus tard, de Danny Boyle, et il a été directeur du mouvement sur la pièce Frankenstein, au National Theatre. En tant que chorégraphe, il a notamment travaillé sur Nanny McPhee et le big bang, The 39 Steps et Cheval de guerre, pour lequel il a remporté l'Olivier Award du meilleur chorégraphe de théâtre. Son moment olympique préféré : le premier saut en Fosbury de l'histoire, réalisé par Richard Fosbury aux Jeux de Mexico, en 1968.

Temujin Gill
Choreographer

Temujin is an Associate Artist at Greenwich Dance, ex-Jiving Lindy Hopper and founder of Temujin Dance. Credits include collaborations at the Young Vic, Half Moon Theatre and National Maritime Museum; presenting work at the Queen Elizabeth Hall, Sadler's Wells and the Lindy Hop extravaganza for Ray Davies' Meltdown Festival 2011; and working with Daniel Radcliffe. His favourite Olympic moment is Muhammad Ali winning the light heavyweight gold, Rome 1960.

Artiste associé de Greenwich Dance, ancien membre des Jiving Lindy Hoppers et fondateur de Temujin Dance, Temujin a collaboré avec le Young Vic, le Half Moon Theatre et le Musée national de la Marine. Ses œuvres ont été présentées au Queen Elizabeth Hall, au Sadler's Wells et au festival Meltdown de Ray Davies, en 2011. Il a également travaillé avec Daniel Radcliffe. Son moment olympique préféré : la médaille d'or de Mohamed Ali dans la catégorie poids mi-lourds aux Jeux de Rome, en 1960.

Sunanda Biswas
Co-Choreographer

Sunanda is one of the UK's foremost B-Girls and founder of Flowzaic, the UK's first all-female breaking crew. A founding member of Temujin Dance, she choreographed the BAFTA Award winning *Fishtank* and has worked with Mel B, Gabrielle and Take That. Other credits include Nike Dance Clash, Breaking Convention and B-Supreme Women in Hip-Hop Festival. Her favourite Olympic moment is the USA gymnastics team winning gold, Atlanta 1996.

Breakdanseuse émérite du Royaume-Uni et fondatrice de Flowzaic, première compagnie de breakdance féminine du pays, Sunanda est également un membre fondateur de Temujin Dance et a conçu les chorégraphies du film Fishtank, récompensé d'un BAFTA Award. Elle a travaillé avec Mel B, Gabrielle et Take That et s'est illustrée sur le Nike Dance Clash, Breaking Convention et le festival B-Supreme Women in Hip-Hop. Son moment olympique préféré : la médaille d'or de l'équipe américaine de gymnastique aux Jeux d'Atlanta, en 1996.

Akram Khan
Choreographer

Akram is a British-born choreographer celebrated internationally for the vitality he brings to cross-cultural, cross-disciplinary expression. His dance language, rooted in classical Kathak and modern dance training, continually evolves to communicate ideas that are intelligent, courageous and new. He performs his own solos and collaborative works with other artists, and presents ensemble works through Akram Khan Company. His favourite Olympic moment is the Greece 2004 Opening Ceremony.

Britannique de naissance, Akram est un chorégraphe qui s'est fait un renom international pour la vitalité qu'il insuffle à l'expression interculturelle et interdisciplinaire. Le langage porté par sa danse, enraciné dans une formation en danse kathak traditionnelle et en danse moderne, évolue continuellement pour communiquer des idées intelligentes, courageuses et novatrices. Il interprète lui-même ses solos et les chorégraphies qu'il crée avec d'autres artistes, et présente des œuvres d'ensemble avec l'Akram Khan Company. Son moment olympique préféré : la cérémonie d'ouverture des Jeux de 2004 en Grèce.

Kenrick H2O Sandy
Choreographer

Kenrick is a choreographer, performer, teacher and Co-Founder/Artistic Director of Olivier Awarded and Barbican Associate Artist Boy Blue Entertainment. Credits Include; *StreetDance 3D*, Tour De France 2007, BRIT Awards, National Movie Awards, BAFTA Awards, *Alesha's Street Dance Stars*, Peter Andre, Plan B, Victoria Beckham and The Saturdays. His favourite Olympic moment is Usain Bolt celebrating his record breaking win with the famous archer pose, Beijing 2008.

Kenrick est chorégraphe, danseur, professeur et cofondateur-directeur artistique de Boy Blue Entertainment, compagnie lauréate d'un Olivier Award et artiste associé du Barbican. Kenrick s'est notamment illustré sur StreetDance 3D, le Tour de France 2007, les BRIT Awards, les National Movie Awards, les BAFTA Awards, Alesha's Street Dance Stars ainsi qu'auprès de Peter Andre, de Plan B, de Victoria Beckham et des Saturdays. Son moment olympique préféré : la célèbre posture de l'archer adoptée par Usain Bolt pour célébrer son record du monde aux Jeux de Pékin, en 2008.

Thomas Heatherwick
Cauldron Designer

Thomas is one of Britain's most creative thinkers. His work includes the internationally renowned UK Pavilion at the Shanghai World Expo 2010, the Rolling Bridge in Paddington and London's new red double-decker bus. His studio's projects are characterised by a focus on innovative architectural solutions for cities and a dedication to craftsmanship and materials. His favourite Olympic moment is the archer Antonio Rebollo lighting the Olympic flame, Barcelona 1992.

Thomas est un des penseurs les plus créatifs de Grande-Bretagne. Il a notamment conçu le Pavillon du Royaume-Uni à l'Exposition universelle de Shanghaï 2010, reconnu internationalement, le Rolling Bridge de Paddington et le nouveau bus rouge à impériale londonien. Les projets réalisés par son studio se caractérisent par leur recherche de solutions architecturales innovantes pour les villes et un intérêt particulier pour le savoir-faire et les matières. Son moment olympique préféré : l'allumage de la flamme olympique par l'archer Antonio Rebollo aux Jeux de Barcelone, en 1992.

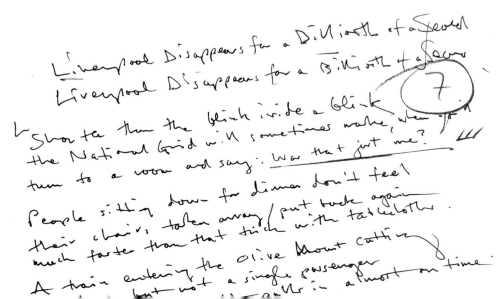

Liverpool Disappears for a Billionth of a Second, Paul Farley

Liverpool Disappears for a Billionth of a Second, Paul Farley

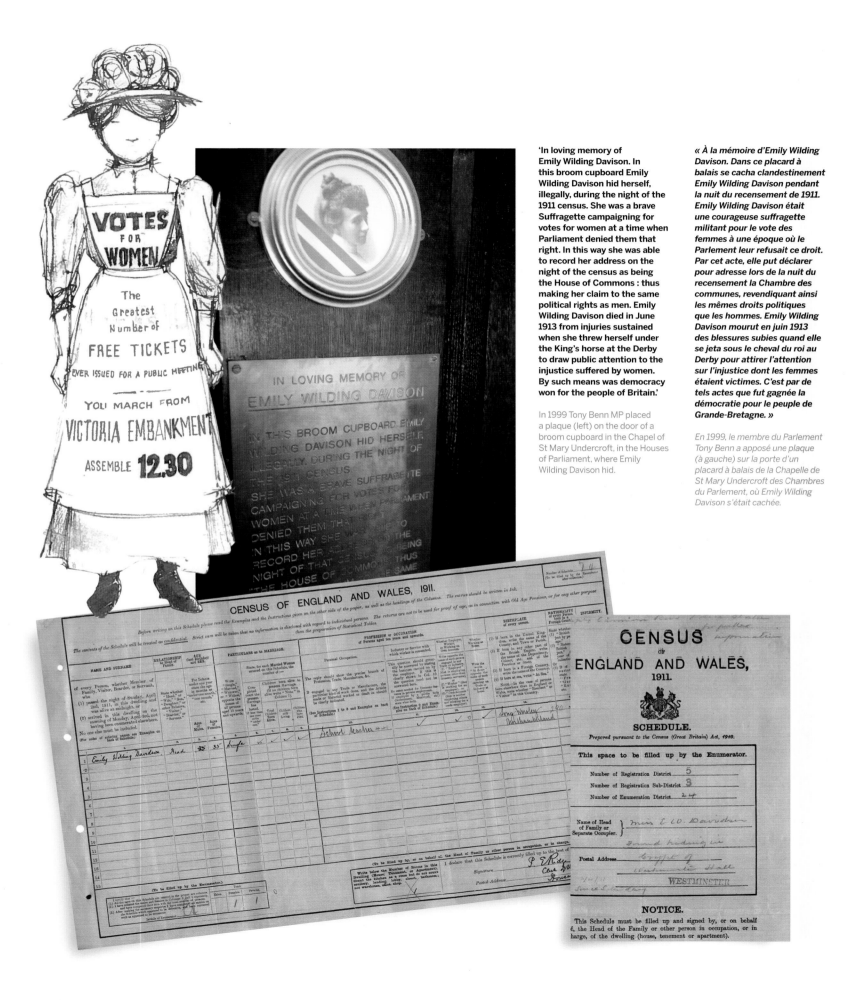

'In loving memory of Emily Wilding Davison. In this broom cupboard Emily Wilding Davison hid herself, illegally, during the night of the 1911 census. She was a brave Suffragette campaigning for votes for women at a time when Parliament denied them that right. In this way she was able to record her address on the night of the census as being the House of Commons : thus making her claim to the same political rights as men. Emily Wilding Davison died in June 1913 from injuries sustained when she threw herself under the King's horse at the Derby to draw public attention to the injustice suffered by women. By such means was democracy won for the people of Britain.'

In 1999 Tony Benn MP placed a plaque (left) on the door of a broom cupboard in the Chapel of St Mary Undercroft, in the Houses of Parliament, where Emily Wilding Davison hid.

« À la mémoire d'Emily Wilding Davison. Dans ce placard à balais se cacha clandestinement Emily Wilding Davison pendant la nuit du recensement de 1911. Emily Wilding Davison était une courageuse suffragette militant pour le vote des femmes à une époque où le Parlement leur refusait ce droit. Par cet acte, elle put déclarer pour adresse lors de la nuit du recensement la Chambre des communes, revendiquant ainsi les mêmes droits politiques que les hommes. Emily Wilding Davison mourut en juin 1913 des blessures subies quand elle se jeta sous le cheval du roi au Derby pour attirer l'attention sur l'injustice dont les femmes étaient victimes. C'est par de tels actes que fut gagnée la démocratie pour le peuple de Grande-Bretagne. »

En 1999, le membre du Parlement Tony Benn a apposé une plaque (à gauche) sur la porte d'un placard à balais de la Chapelle de St Mary Undercroft des Chambres du Parlement, où Emily Wilding Davison s'était cachée.

Executive Team
Équipe exécutive

Bill Morris
Director of Ceremonies,
Education & Live Sites

Bill joined London 2012 six years ago from the BBC where he started as a journalist, moved into radio and TV production and executive roles, before specialising in major events as Project Director Live Events. These included the BBC Music Live festival, the annual BBC Proms in the Park, the Olympic Torch Relay Concert in London's Mall, and the Queen's Concerts at Buckingham Palace (for which he was awarded the LVO in the Queen's Jubilee Honours List). He also coordinated broadcast live events across a number of BBC radio and television services, including Live 8 in 2005. Bill served on the Radio Academy's Council from the early 1990s, he was Chair 1998-2001, and was made a Fellow in 2001.

Avant de rejoindre Londres 2012 il y a six ans, Bill était à la BBC, où il a commencé comme journaliste puis a travaillé à la production radio et télévision et assumé des fonctions de direction. Il s'est ensuite spécialisé dans les grands événements, devenant directeur de projets sur les événements live comme le festival BBC Music Live, la manifestation annuelle BBC Proms in the Park, le concert du relais de la flamme olympique au London's Mall et les Queen's Concerts à Buckingham Palace (pour lesquels il a été fait Lieutenant de l'ordre royal de Victoria à l'occasion de la promotion du Jubilé de la Reine). Il a aussi coordonné plusieurs événements en direct diffusés sur les services de radio et de télévision de la BBC, dont la série de concerts Live 8, en 2005. Bill a intégré le conseil de la Radio Academy au début des années 90 et en a été président de 1998 à 2001. Il en est devenu membre associé (Fellow) en 2001.

Martin Green
Head of Ceremonies

Trained in writing and directing theatre, Martin spent five years as Head of Events for the Mayor of London where he was responsible for producing global events such as the London New Year's Eve fireworks, major music festivals and one-off events across the city. As Director of Events at the O2 he oversaw the reopening of this now hugely successful venue. He joined London 2012 in 2007 as Head of Ceremonies, where he has recruited and inspired a world class team to deliver the Torch Relays, Victory Ceremonies, Team Welcome Ceremonies, and Opening and Closing Ceremonies of the Olympic and Paralympic Games.

Formé à l'écriture et la mise en scène théâtrale, Martin a été pendant cinq ans responsable événementiel pour le maire de Londres, poste où il avait en charge la production d'événements globaux tels que les feux d'artifice du 31 décembre à Londres, les grands festivals musicaux et les événements ponctuels organisés au sein de la ville. En tant que directeur événementiel de l'O2, il a supervisé la réouverture de ce site qui rencontre aujourd'hui un immense succès. Il a rejoint Londres 2012 en 2007 en tant que responsable des cérémonies, poste où il a recruté et inspiré une équipe de tout premier plan pour organiser les relais de la flamme, les cérémonies de la victoire, les cérémonies de bienvenue aux équipes ainsi que les cérémonies d'ouverture et de clôture des Jeux Olympiques et Paralympiques.

Catherine Ugwu
Executive Producer, Production

Catherine is a creative director, executive producer and consultant and has been involved in some of the world's largest and most prestigious public events. She was Executive Producer for the Glasgow Handover Ceremony of the Delhi 2010 Commonwealth Games; Senior Producer for the strategic phase of the Opening, Closing and Victory Ceremonies of the 2010 Vancouver Winter Olympics; she produced the Opening Ceremony for the Asian Games in Doha, Qatar in 2006, the Closing Ceremony for the Commonwealth Games in Manchester in 2002 and a large-scale performance spectacle to mark the opening of the Millennium Dome, London in 2000.

Directrice de la création, productrice exécutive et consultante, Catherine a contribué à certains des événements publics les plus importants et les plus prestigieux au monde. Productrice exécutive pour la cérémonie de passage à Glasgow des Jeux du Commonwealth de 2010 à Delhi, elle a été productrice sénior pour la phase stratégique des cérémonies d'ouverture, de clôture et de la victoire des Jeux Olympiques d'hiver de 2010 à Vancouver. Elle a également produit la cérémonie d'ouverture des Jeux asiatiques de Doha, au Qatar, en 2006, ainsi que la cérémonie de clôture des Jeux du Commonwealth à Manchester en 2002 et un spectacle de grande envergure pour marquer l'ouverture du Dôme du millénaire, à Londres, en 2000.

Stephen Daldry
Executive Producer, Creative

Stephen started his career at Sheffield's Crucible Theatre and directed extensively in Britain's regional theatres. In London he was Artistic Director of the Gate and Royal Court theatres; he's directed at the National Theatre, the Public Theatre in New York and transferred many productions to the West End and Broadway. His production of *Billy Elliot: The Musical* is currently playing in London and on tour in the USA. It recently won more Tony Awards (10) than any other British show in Broadway history. He's also made four films: *Billy Elliot*; *The Hours*; *The Reader*; and *Extremely Loud & Incredibly Close*.

Stephen a commencé sa carrière au Crucible Theatre de Sheffield et a mis en scène de nombreuses pièces dans les théâtres régionaux britanniques. À Londres, il a été directeur artistique du Gate Theatre et du Royal Court Theatre. Il a également mis en scène des pièces au National Theatre et au Public Theatre de New York et a transposé de nombreuses productions dans le West End et à Broadway. Sa production Billy Elliot: The Musical *est actuellement à l'affiche à Londres et en tournée aux États-Unis. Elle a récemment remporté plus de Tony Awards (dix) que n'en a jamais reçu un autre spectacle britannique à Broadway. Stephen a également réalisé quatre films :* Billy Elliot, The Hours, The Reader *et* Extrêmement fort et incroyablement près.

Hamish Hamilton
Executive Producer, Broadcast/TV

Hamish, from Blackpool, is a Grammy nominated, multi-camera television and video director. He began his career as a trainee with BBC Scotland and as a TV director for the BBC Manchester Youth Programmes Unit. Pursuing his love of live music, he's directed the BRIT Awards, the MTV European Music Awards and the Victoria's Secret Fashion Shows for nine years. His credit appears on nearly 30 million live concert DVDs. His most recent work includes the Oscars, the MTV Video Music Awards and the Super Bowl halftime shows. He is also Creative Director of the television and event production company, Done and Dusted.

Originaire de Blackpool, Hamish est un réalisateur de télévision et de vidéos multicaméras nominé aux Grammy Awards. Après avoir débuté comme stagiaire à la BBC Écosse puis réalisateur TV pour l'Unité de programmes jeunesse de la BBC Manchester, son amour de la musique en direct l'a amené à réaliser les BRIT Awards, les MTV European Music Awards et les défilés de mode de la marque Victoria's Secret pendant neuf ans. Son nom apparaît au générique de près de 30 millions de DVD de concerts en direct. Ses réalisations les plus récentes concernent notamment les Oscars, les MTV Video Music Awards et les spectacles de la mi-temps au Super Bowl. Il est également directeur de la création de la société de production télévisée et événementielle Done and Dusted.

Mark Fisher
Executive Producer

Mark has been an adviser to London 2012 Ceremonies since 2007. A world-renowned designer and architect, his credits include *The Wall* for Pink Floyd in 1980 and Roger Waters in 2010; every Rolling Stones show since 1989 and every U2 concert since 1992; the Opening and Closing Ceremonies for the 2010 Commonwealth Games in Delhi, the 2010 Asian Games in Guangzhou and the 2008 Beijing Olympic Games. His theatre shows include *KÀ* and *Viva Elvis* for Cirque du Soleil in Las Vegas.

Conseiller auprès de London 2012 Ceremonies depuis 2007, Mark est un designer et architecte de renommée mondiale qui a notamment travaillé sur The Wall *pour Pink Floyd en 1980 et Roger Waters en 2010, tous les spectacles des Rolling Stones depuis 1989 et tous les concerts de U2 depuis 1992, les cérémonies d'ouverture et de clôture des Jeux du Commonwealth de 2010 à Delhi, des Jeux asiatiques de 2010 à Canton et des Jeux Olympiques de 2008 à Pékin. Au théâtre, il s'est notamment illustré sur les spectacles* KÀ *et* Viva Elvis *pour le Cirque du Soleil à Las Vegas.*

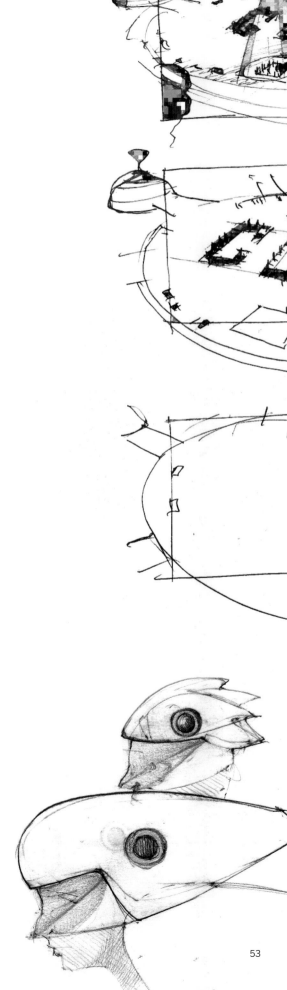

Production Team: Creative
Équipe de production créative

Aerial & Special Skills

Phil Hayes Aerial & Special Skills Consultant
Alex Poulter Aerial & Special Skills Associate

Audio Visual & Broadcast

Justine Catterall Head of Audio Visual
Adam Dadswell Presentation Manager
David Watson Digital Media Manager
Lizzie Pocock Audio Visual Department Coordinator
Charlotte Andrews Archive Coordinator
Emma Gaffney, Damien Pawle Assistant Video Editors

Steven Harris Video Documentation
Graham Carlow Photographer
Matt Askem Video Screens Director
Tracey Askem Video Screens
Production Assistant
Jane Jackson Broadcast Liaison Manager

Bike Choreography

Bob Haro
Bike Choreographer
Paul Hughes
Bike Project
Manager

Casting

Gillian Schofield Cast Manager, Professional
Sarah Chambers, Andrew Ramsbottom, Jane Salberg
Cast Coordinators, Professional
Penny Davies Cast Coordinator, Professional & Volunteers
Rhian Davies Assistant Cast Coordinator, Professional
Sarah Murray Casting Assistant, Professional
Solomon Wilkinson Casting Assistant, Volunteers
Nichola Bouchard, Katy Bryant Company Managers

Sara-Ellen Williams Cast Manager, Volunteers
Sara Berutto, Maz Bryden, Diane Leach, Trish McClenaghan, Laura Windows Senior Cast Coordinators, Volunteers
Barbara Lisicki Access Manager
Michael Foley, Glenda Genovesi, Vanessa Griffiths, Helen Lam, Haitham Ridha Cast Coordinators, Volunteers
Jenny Rogers Cast Coordinator, Schools
Cheryl Galbraith, Martin Malone, Lesley Raymer, Kieran Shekoni Assistant Cast Coordinators, Volunteers
Genevieve Baker, Hannah Caple, Joanna Griffith, Ellena Jones, Andrea Mangerie, Diana Prociv Casting Assistants, Volunteers

Costume, Hair & Make-Up

Tahra Zafar Head of Costume, Hair & Make-up
Lorraine Ebdon, Anna Lau Costume Supervisors
Matthew George Hair & Wigs Design Supervisor
Amber Sibley Make-up Design Supervisor
Katie Newitt Costume Department Coordinator
Lesley-Ann Halls Costume Department Volunteers Coordinator
Fiona Parker Assistant Costume Supervisor
Caroline Brett Senior Costume Buyer
Rebecca Mills, Samantha Langridge, Charlotte McGarrie Costume Buyers
Vanessa Bastyan Costume Workshop Fabrication Supervisor
Angie Pledge Costume Workshop Supervisor
Elaine Battye Costume Workshop Senior Costumier
Becky Johnson, Thea Keenan Costume Workshop Senior Fabricators
Cheryl Mason Costume Breakdown Supervisor
Nicola Beales, Helena Bennett, Robin McGrorty Costume Workshop Assistants
Maisie McCubbin Costume Workshop Junior
Olima Rolfe Creative Division Assistant
Jamie Mendonça Garment Stock Logistics & Driver

Lighting & Audio Design

Patrick Woodroffe
Lighting Designer

Over the last 30 years, Patrick has been responsible for the lighting of an extraordinary array of people and places including rock stars and opera singers, ballet dancers and ice skaters, kings, queens, presidents and desert sheiks, military camps and palaces, forests and waterfalls, racing cars, cruise liners and the World Cup.

Patrick a assuré ces 30 dernières années l'éclairage d'un extraordinaire éventail de personnalités et de lieux : stars du rock et chanteurs d'opéra, danseurs de ballet et patineurs, rois, reines, présidents et cheikhs du désert, camps militaires et palais, forêts et cascades, voitures de course, paquebots et Coupe du Monde.

Bobby Aitken
Audio Designer

Bobby is a world-renowned theatre sound designer. His work includes worldwide productions of *Ghost*, *Mamma Mia!*, *Dirty Dancing*, *We Will Rock You* and *Return to the Forbidden Planet*. Credits for large scale in-the-round opera include *Carmen*, *Madame Butterfly*, *Aïda*, *Cavalleria Rusticana* and *Pagliacci*, *Tosca* and *La Bohème*.

Concepteur sonore de renommée mondiale pour le théâtre, Bobby a collaboré aux productions mondiales de Ghost, Mamma Mia!, Dirty Dancing, We Will Rock You et Return to the Forbidden Planet. Il a également travaillé sur des opéras in-the-round de grande envergure comme Carmen, Madame Butterfly, Aïda, Cavalleria Rusticana, Pagliacci, Tosca et La Bohème.

Adam Bassett
Associate Lighting Designer
Scott Willsallen
Audio Systems Designer

Discover more about the Ceremony, including exclusive videos, at london2012.com/exploretheceremonies
Pour en savoir plus sur la cérémonie et découvrir des vidéos exclusives, rendez-vous sur london2012.com/exploretheceremonies

Production Team: Creative
Équipe de production créative

Design

Ala Lloyd Design Studio Manager
Emma Child Design Studio Coordinator
Basmah Arafeh, Rebecca Brower,
Hatty Morris Design Studio Assistants
James Collins Art Director
Anita Dhillon Graphic Designer
Brendan Houghton Storyboard Artist

Mass Movement

Steve Boyd Head of Mass Movement Choreography & Parade of Athletes

Steve has contributed to 11 consecutive Summer and Winter Olympic Games from Barcelona 1992 to London 2012. Other credits include Special Olympics, Commonwealth Games, Cricket World Cup, Asian Games and Super Bowl halftime shows. Prior to event production, Steve designed for several Condé Nast publications including *Vanity Fair* and *The New Yorker*.

De Barcelone 1992 à Londres 2012, Steve a participé à 11 Jeux Olympiques d'été et d'hiver consécutifs. Il a également collaboré aux Jeux olympiques spéciaux, aux Jeux du Commonwealth, à la Coupe du monde de cricket, aux Jeux asiatiques et aux spectacles de la mi-temps du Super Bowl. Avant la production événementielle, Steve a exercé ses talents de designer pour plusieurs publications du groupe Condé Nast, dont Vanity Fair *et* The New Yorker.

Gina Martinez Mass Movement Choreographer, Thanks Tim
Rocky Smith Mass Movement Choreographer, Second to the right
Nikki Woollaston Mass Movement Choreographer, Green and Pleasant Land
Nathan Wright Mass Movement Choreographer
Steve Boyd Mass Movement Choreographer, Pandemonium
Paul Neaum Manager, Parade of Athletes
Soha Frem, Bryn Walters Mass Cast Leaders
Ben Clare, Laura-Anne Gill, Vicki Igbokwe, Jeanefer Jean-Charles, Natasha Khamjani, Katie Pearson, Barbarana Pons, Wendy Steatham Mass Cast Coordinators
Edwina Allen, Taylor Anthony, Rachelle Conroy, Marianne Howard, Sean Mulligan, Brenda Jane Newhouse, Darragh O'Leary, Joseph Pitcher, Simone Sault, Carla Trim-Vamben, Claira Vaughan, Jayde Westaby Mass Cast Assistants

Music

Peter Cobbin, **Allan Jenkins,**
Kirsty Whalley
Associate Music Directors
Mike Gillespie Music Supervisor Underworld

Martin Koch Music Supervisor
Tom Jenkins Associate Music Supervisor
Clare Hazeldine Music Department Coordinator
Nick Gilpin Audio Supervisor
Mikey J Asante Music Editor for Kenrick Sandy

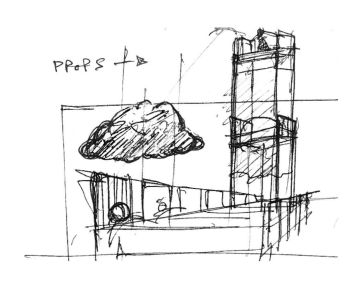

Producers

Claire Terri Associate Producer

Claire started her career as a professional dancer and choreographer before also moving into production. She was part of the teams creating the ceremonies for the 2004 Athens Olympic Games, 2006 Turin Winter Olympic Games, Rio 2007 Pan American Games, 2008 and 2009 Dubai World Cups, Delhi 2010 Commonwealth Games and Athens 2011 Special Olympics.

Claire a commencé sa carrière comme danseuse et chorégraphe professionnelle avant de se tourner aussi vers la production. Elle a fait partie des équipes conceptrices des cérémonies des Jeux Olympiques de 2004 à Athènes, des Jeux Olympiques d'hiver de 2006 à Turin, des Jeux panaméricains de 2007 à Rio, des Dubaï World Cup de 2008 et 2009, des Jeux du Commonwealth de 2010 à Delhi et des Jeux olympiques spéciaux de 2011 à Athènes.

Joan Schneider Production Manager, Opening Ceremony Films & Bike a.m.
Hallam Rice-Edwards Production Coordinator
Alex Barrett, Lex Donovan Production Assistants
Kaz Hill Headline Talent Manager
Sarah Casey Headline Talent Coordinator
Danielle Buckley Headline Talent Production Assistant

Publications

Fiona Richards Publications Manager
Jess Anstee Publications Coordinator

Stage Management

Sam Hunter Production Stage Manager
Guido Foa Deputy Production Stage Manager
Carola Altissimo, Liz Copp, Debbie Cronshaw, Hilary Davis, Ben Delfont, Anthony Field, Duane Harewood, Marianne Kuehner, Claire Loftus, Jordan Noble-Davies, Sam Pepper, Helen Smith, Ian Stephenson, Jorge Tapia, Peter Wakeman, Matt Watkins Senior Stage Managers
Holly Anderson, Miriam Bertaina, Abigail Dankwa, Lee Fowler, Miguel de la Fuente Graciani, Rhiannon Harper, Gareth Hulance, Bianca Jones, Dominique Pierre-Louis, Ryan Quelch, Gemma Thomas Stage Managers
Abigail Mills Associate Stage Manager
Julia Whittle Show Caller

Video Design & Visual Effects

Leo Warner Video Creative Director
Lysander Ashton Video Designer
Jonathon Lyle Associate Video Designer
Zsolt Balogh, Christian Debney, Lawrence Watson Video Animation Directors
Joseph Pierce Video Design Editor
Tim Caplan VFX Producer
Kaveh Montazer, Mervyn New VFX Artists
Noga Alon Stein VFX Coordinator

Internship Placements Lexi Boynton, Colm Dunhrosa, Jacqueline Field, Elizabeth Howe, Lexi Hyland, Anisha Patel, Janita Patel, Katie Radha Osterholzer, Claire Thorn, Daniel Vincze

Creative & Executive Administration

Tina Jaffray Senior Administrator, Creative
Jennifer Hutt Executive Assistant to the Head of Ceremonies and Executive Producer
Kate Hinchliffe Executive Assistant to the Producers
Nicky Cheung Personal Assistant to Director of Ceremonies, Education & Live Sites

Annie Corrigan Protocol Manager
Veronique Haddelsey Protocol Coordinator
Alison Wade Script Manager
Clare Ellis Administration Assistant

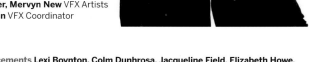

Production Team: Technical
Équipe de production technique

Technical Executive

Piers Shepperd
Technical Director

For 20 years, Piers has delivered technical production wizardry for mega events around the globe. Critically acclaimed projects in theatre and music include *We Will Rock You* and the Rolling Stones Licks World Tour. Other work includes the Athens 2004 Olympic Ceremonies, 2006 Doha Asian Games Ceremonies and 2010 Delhi Commonwealth Games Ceremonies.

Piers insuffle depuis 20 ans un peu de magie à la production technique des méga-événements de la planète. Encensés par la critique, les projets qu'il a réalisés dans les domaines du théâtre et de la musique comprennent We Will Rock You *et la tournée mondiale Licks des Rolling Stones. Il a également travaillé sur les cérémonies des Jeux Olympiques d'Athènes, en 2004, des Jeux asiatiques de Doha, en 2006, et des Jeux du Commonwealth de Delhi, en 2010.*

Andrew Morgan
Senior Administrator, Technical
Elena Dogani
Production Coordinator, Technical Contracts
Ross Nicholson
Production Assistant, Technical

Aerial & Special Projects

James Lee Technical Manager, Aerial & Special Projects
Glenn Bolton Senior Production Manager, Capital Works & Special Projects
Luke Mills Production Manager, Pyro, Flame & SFX
Edwin Samkin Deputy Production Manager, Pyro, Flame & SFX
Sammy Samkin Production Manager, Fireworks
Nick Porter Deputy Production Manager, Aerialist Training
Paul English Deputy Production Manager, Show Vehicles
Anna Cox Assistant manager, Special Projects
Emma Neilson Production Coordinator
Nick Levitt Production Manager, Torch Journey

Audio, Comms & Broadcast

Chris Ekers Senior Production Manager, Audio & Comms
James Breward Deputy Production Manager, Comms, CCTV & Mass Cast IEM
Alison Dale Deputy Production Manager, Principal Performer IEM & Wireless Mics
Trevor Beck Audio Playback
Richard Sharratt Audio FOH
Hannah Charlesworth
Deputy Production Manager, Backline
Steve Watson Audio Monitor Engineer
Steve Williams Audio Broadcast Systems Engineer
Andy Rose Audio Broadcast Sound Supervsior

Lighting, AV & Power

Nick Jones Technical Manager, Lighting, AV & Power
Andy Loveday Senior Production Manager, Lighting
Ben Pitts Production Manager, Lighting Set LX
Dan Sloane Production Manager, Video & LED Screens
Tim Routledge Senior Lighting Operator

Andrew Voller Lighting Operator
Pryderi Baskerville Lighting Operator
Lee Threlfall Set Lighting Production LX
Dave Bartlett Project Manager, Pixels
Mike Dawes Deputy Project Manager, Pixels

Staging & Scenic

Jeremy Lloyd Technical Design & Staging Manager
Nigel Mousley Senior Production Manager, Staging & Scenic
Steve Richards Senior Production Manager, FOP
Chris Clay, Dave Williams Production Managers, Staging & Scenic
Kieran McGivern Deputy Production Manager, Staging & Scenic
Scott Seaton Deputy Production Manager, FOP
Lianne Bruce Production Coordinator, Staging & Scenic
Johanna Eaden Production Assistant, Staging & Scenic
Tom White CAD Manager

Andrew Bailey, Ben O'Neill, Philip Wilding CAD Operators
Moose Curtis, Magnus Harding, Kevin Jones Staging Crew Chiefs
Peter English Head Carpenter
Phil Perry Staging Crew Chief, Rehearsal Venue
Ray Bogle Field of Play Crew Chief
Mike Grove Stage Manager, Main Stage
Rasti Bartek, Aran Chadwick, Glyn Trippick Consultant Engineers
Richard Bentley, John Prentice CAD Consultants

Technical Services

Scott Buchanan Technical Manager,
Technical Services & Special Projects
Annette Stock Production Manager, Schedule,
Crew & Contractors
Jess Noakes Production Coordinator, Technical Services
Dave Wilkie Production Manager, Plant & AP
Matthew Beardsley Production Coordinator, Crew & Logistics
Terry Hubble Production Staff Quartermaster
Laura Lloyd, Grant Peters, Kate Ramsey Production Staff Runners

Workshop & Props

Ted Irwin Technical Manager, Workshop & Props
Dan Shipton Production Manager, Props
Pam Nichol Deputy Production Manager, Props & Rehearsals
Eric Hickmott Production Manager, Workshop
Rhiannon Newman-Brown Production Coordinator, Workshop
Nick Bloom Deputy Production Manager, Carpentry
Jo Cole Deputy Production Manager Props, Crew & Volunteer Chief
Sherri Hazzard Deputy Workshop Manager, Props
Sally Christopher, Sean Flynn Production Coordinator, Props
Mark Moore Deputy Production Manager, Metal Fabrication

Will Sumpter Deputy Workshop Manager, Props
Steve Dart, John McGarrigle Props, LX
John Pratt Workshop Coordinator & Buyer
Dave Blacker Props Coordinator and Crew & Volunteer Chief
Tanya Bond Props Buyer
Stephen Jeffrey Crew & Volunteer Chief
Sarah Whiting Workshop Volunteer Coordinator
Krissy Lee Technical Assistant

Internship Placements Laura Rixson, Chris Tani

Production Team: Operations
Équipe de production opérationnelle

Operations Executive

Mik Auckland
Director of Operations and Health & Safety

A career as a stage manager and technical director in musical theatre led Mik to senior roles at the Sydney 2000 and Athens 2004 Olympic Games. In 2005 he joined Jack Morton Worldwide as Senior Technical Director. Mik subsequently worked on the Beijing 2008 Olympic Games and the 2010 FIFA World Cup as Consultant Technical and Operations Director.

Une carrière de régisseur et de directeur technique dans le théâtre musical a amené Mik à assumer des fonctions d'encadrement aux Jeux de 2000 à Sydney et de 2004 à Athènes. En 2005, il a rejoint Jack Morton Worldwide en tant que directeur technique senior. Mik a ensuite travaillé sur les Jeux Olympiques de 2008 à Pékin et sur la Coupe du monde de Football 2010 en tant que directeur technique et opérationnel consultant.

Adrian Bourke Senior Manager, Venues & Facilities
Joseph Frisina Senior Operations Manager
Donna McMahon Senior Manager, Logistics
Neil Russell Senior Manager, Health, Safety, Welfare & Medical
Hannah Dorey Senior Administrator
Nathan Farquharson Logistics Coordinator
Jacinta Gee Operations Coordinator
Luke Woodham Venues & Facilities Coordinator
Alice Larmer Logistics Production Assistant

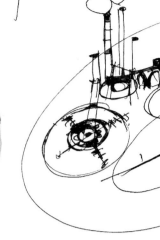

Health, Safety, Welfare & Medical
Show Operations & Scheduling

Conrad Schwarz Deputy Manager, Health & Safety
Sally-Ann Dod Health & Safety Advisor, Inductions & Contractor Liaison
Sarah Jones Medical Services Manager
Danielle Bromley, Steve Brown, Alan Law Health & Safety Consultants
Samantha Coles Coordinator, Health & Safety
Dean Jewel Show Operations & Schedule Manager
Paddy Bettington Show Operations & Schedule Assistant
Leah Harris, Sam Mount Schedule Production Assistants
Sally Downey Health & Safety Inductions Assistant

Logistics

Kirsty Thomson Operations Manager,
Catering, Cleaning & Waste
Julia Bowditch, Lynsey Jackson Coordinators, Catering,
Cleaning & Waste
**Rebecca Fletcher, Sandra Goetz, Gareth Lewis,
Ria Maycox, Alexander Thomas, Sarah Yates**
Production Assistants, Catering, Cleaning & Waste
Melissa McVeigh Operations Manager, Accreditation
Melanie East, Tyler Ffrench, Vincenzo Ianniello
Coordinators, Accreditation
Karen Cosgree, Emily Whitaker
Production Assistants, Accreditation
Laura Marakowits Operations Manager, Volunteers
Shelly Donaghy Coordinator, Volunteers
Grace Birkbeck, Laura Salvatore, Pete Thomson
Production Assistants, Volunteers
Valie Voutsa Operations Manager,
Accommodation & Travel
Marie Albrecht Assistant Manager,
Accommodation & Travel (Staff)
Leticia Gonzalez-Galvez Assistant Manager,
Accommodation & Travel (Principal Performers)
Eloise Crevier, Eirini Zoi
Production Assistants, Accommodation
Georgina Huxstep Operations Manager, Transport & Fleet
Sarah Hinchelwood Assistant Manager, Children's Transport
Matthew Howlett Assistant Manager, Fleet & Site Vehicles
Kate Blomfield, Asha Slade Coordinators, Transport
**Simon Galicki, Laura Gallen, Charlotte Howley,
Emma Lester, Emily Webber** Production Assistants, Transport
Debbie Paul Operations Manager, Principal Performer Logistics
Craig Lear Green Room Manager
Anna-Maria Kreuzer Coordinator, Principal Performer Logistics
Victoria Sandford, Kieran Smith, Ed Woodhouse
Production Assistants, Principal Performer Logistics

Venues & Facilities

Russel Bedford Operations Manager,
Workshop & Rehearsal Venues
Pete Williams Assistant Manager,
Rehearsal Venues
William Francis Coordinator, Workshop
& Rehearsal Venues
Sonya Gandras Coordinator, Rehearsal Venues
**Billy Cheeseman, Ralph Cullum,
Charlotte Jordan** Production Assistants, Venues
Robert Madeley Site Assistant, Rehearsal Venue
Lucinda Erskine-Crum Operations Manager,
Olympic Park
Al Parkinson Assistant Manager, Olympic Stadium
Toni Stockham Coordinator, Olympic Stadium
David Gregory Assistant Manager, Compound
Marcia Connell, Will Gunnett
Coordinators, Compound
Robert Schnaiberg Assistant Manager, MDS,
Storage & Freight
Sarah Adams, Olivia Pole-Evans
Site Assistants, MDS, Storage & Freight

Lottie Cresswell Assistant Manager, Common Domain
Chui-Yee Cheung Coordinator, Common Domain
Ryan Tate Coordinator, Venue
Lily Sutton Production Assistant, Venue
Holly Gregory Compound Assistant, Stadium
Trish Murphy Venue Manager, Eton Manor
Claire Ewings Assistant
Venue Manager, Eton Manor
Kayleigh Dean, Megan Wise
Venue Assistants, Eton Manor
Alina Murcott
Project Manager,
Water Polo Arena
Maddie Cupples
Assistant Manager,
Water Polo Arena
Emma-Jane Cotsell
Project Assistant,
Guard of Honour

Internship Placements Tanisha Malkki, Dimitry Ragozin

Production Team: Administration
Équipe de production administrative

Administration Executive

Sara Donaldson
Joint Chief Operating Officer

Sara has overseen the delivery of many high-profile events and campaigns, including the bid for London 2012. In 2000 she set up LIVE Communications and was awarded an OBE. She co-founded Unspun in 2008 with whom she led the strategic direction of England's bid for the 2018 FIFA World Cup and co-produced the Glasgow 2014 Commonwealth Games Handover in Delhi.

Sara a supervisé la mise en œuvre de nombreux événements et campagnes prestigieux dont la candidature de Londres aux Jeux de 2012. En 2010, elle a créé LIVE Communications et a été faite Officier de l'empire britannique. En 2008, elle a été l'une des cofondatrices d'Unspun, avec qui elle a assuré la direction stratégique de la candidature de l'Angleterre à l'organisation de la Coupe du Monde de la FIFA 2018 et coproduit le passage à Glasgow 2014 des Jeux du Commonwealth à Delhi.

Chris Laue
Joint Chief Operating Officer

A key team member from the beginning of London 2012 Ceremonies, Chris has served as Procurement and Contracts Director, Board Director, Producer and Interim Chief Operating Officer. Prior to moving to London, he was Creative Producer/Director for LiveCity Vancouver, the city's live sites for the 2010 Olympic and Paralympic Winter Games.

Membre clé de l'équipe de London 2012 Ceremonies depuis le début, Chris a exercé les fonctions de directeur des achats et des contrats, de membre du conseil d'administration, de producteur et de directeur des opérations par intérim. Avant de s'intaller à Londres, il était producteur créatif et directeur pour LiveCity Vancouver, qui regroupe les sites accueillant les manifestations en direct des Jeux Olympiques et Paralympiques d'hiver de 2010.

Dion Carter
Finance & Commercial Director

Dion had 18 years post-qualified experience in industry before joining London 2012 Ceremonies. He's been responsible for the development of finance and procurement teams and is the architect of the financial systems, policies, procedures and financial governance.

Dion avait derrière lui 18 ans d'expérience dans le secteur quand il a rejoint London 2012 Ceremonies. Il a pris en charge le développement des équipes Finances et Achats et a mis au point les systèmes, politiques et procédures financiers ainsi que la gouvernance financière.

Finance

Andrew Slater Financial Controller
Veronica Bailey Management Accountant
Kathleen Anderson Production Accountant
Mladen Ivezic, Farishta Yousuf
Senior Purchase Ledger Administrators
Hayden Porritt Purchase Ledger

Human Resources

Chidimma Chukwu Finance, Payroll & HR Clerk
Rebecca Janiszewska Human Resources Manager
Geraldine Daly, Derek Taylor, Cherise Scotland Human Rescources Coordinators
Selina Donald Executive Assistant to Chief Operating Officer

Internship Placement Christianne Gandossi

Information Technology

Campbell McKilligan
Head of IT & Comms
Dilraj Sachdev Database Manager
Allan Whatmough Application Developer
Gyula Keresztely-Krall
Systems Administrator

Grant Cassin Mac Specialist
**Abdullah Al-Mamoon, Regis Joffre,
Rica Mackay, Irfan Mohammed,
Khizzar Younis** Desktop Engineers
Marita Samuel IT Department Coordinator
Mick Turvey Service Desk Manager

Legal

Will Hutchinson Head of Legal (Culture,
Ceremonies, Education & Live Sites)
Chris Loweth Senior Ceremonies Lawyer
Shirin Foroutan Senior Ceremonies
Legal Advisor

Procurement & Contracts

Simon Aspland
Head of Procurement & Contracts
**Natalie Foster, Robert Graham,
Ilyas Rahman, Stephanie Tillman,**

Marlon Trotman Procurement & Contracts
Administrators
Monique Pennycooke, Rachel Williams
Procurement & Contracts Coordinators

Ceremonies, Education & Live Sites

Caroline Ainley Financial Control Accountant
Anna Blackman Programme Manager
Mark Smith Finance Manager
Kristina Richmond Procurement Manager

London 2012 Ceremonies Ltd

Scott Givens
Managing Director

Scott is an Olympic Ceremonies and mega-event
producer with more than 300 spectaculars to his
credit. Leading the team at creative production firm
FiveCurrents, he has worked on 11 Olympic Games,
and was awarded the prestigious Olympic Order. His
productions have also received numerous Emmy
Awards, Telly Awards and Sports Business Awards.

*Scott est un producteur de cérémonies olympiques
et de méga-événéments avec plus de 300 shows
spectaculaires à son actif. Chef de file de la société
de production créative FiveCurrents, il a travaillé
sur 11 éditions des Jeux Olympiques et a reçu le
prestigieux Ordre Olympique. Ses productions ont
également remporté de nombreux Emmy Awards,
Telly Awards et Sports Business Awards.*

Board of Directors
Scott Givens (Chair)
Sara Donaldson
Martin Green
Chris Laue
Bill Morris
Catherine Ugwu
Frank McCormack (non-executive)
Alan Robertson (non-executive)

London 2012 Ceremonies
Committee

Bill Morris (Chair)
Charles Allen
Doug Arnott
Jackie Brock-Doyle
Seb Coe
Paul Deighton
Martin Green
Will Hutchinson
Catherine Ugwu
Neil Wood

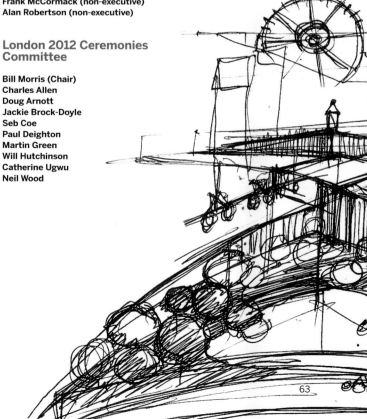

Production Credits
Générique de production

Special Thanks

AgustaWestland
BMW
British Fashion Council
Crystal CG
Dr. Martens
GoPro
Massey Ferguson
Samsung
Site-Eye Time Laps Films
Swarovski
Trekinetic
Tumblr

Acknowledgements

3 Mills Studios
Arri Lighting
Arri Media
Blind Summit
Corporation of London
EON Productions
Fife Council
Flying Pictures Ltd
Great Ormond Street Hospital
Greater London Authority
Island Records
The London Eye
NHS
Palace Scenery
The Red Arrows
RSPCA
Sir Robert McAlpine Ltd
Transport For London
Vans
Westminster City Council
Yamaha
Helle Absalonsen
Omer Ali
Tom Balkwill
Nick Barnes
Neil Blair
Barbara Broccoli
Mark Down
Richard Curtis
Richard Folkes
Kye Forte
Al Gurdon
Su-Man Hsu
Hugh Hudson
Sir Nicholas Hytner
Geoff Jukes
Lois Keidan
Joe Lawlor
Chris Livett
Jamie Longstreet
Daniel Marks
Father Alan McLean
Lucy Moffat
Christine Molloy
Paul O'Reilly
Pankhurst Family
Geoff Posner
Lord David Puttnam of Queensgate
Steve Rushbrooke
Mark Rylance
Sir Nicholas Serota
Amanda Softly
Patrick Stalder
Andy Stephens
Jane Thompson
Stephanie Tillman

Audience Pixel Content

Created by Crystal CG
Fillipo Bianchi
Will Case
Shi Cheng
Ed Cookson
Liberty Dakin
Kate Dawkins
Cath Elliott
Neil Evan
Henry Flitton
Andrew Gooch
Jude Greenaway
Jing Huang
Liu Jian
Zhang Jianzhi
Chai Ke Fu
Zhu Keming
Lou Leaver
Al Liddell
Mark Lindner
Giles Maunsell
Andrew McKinna
Pete Mellor
Chris Ratcliffe
Nicol Scott
Jamie Shiels
Martin Stacey
Zsuzsanna Voros
Joe Winston
Cheng Xinrong
Shi Yan
Liu Yi
Zhang Zhihong

Audio Visual

59 Productions
Giessika Strataki
M.I.E.Ltd
Sim Canetty-Clarke
Mark Grimmer
Akhila Krishnan
Tobias Lloyd
Tom Moss
Max Tipple

Casting

1st Choice Animals
Architen Landrell Associates
AYH
Big Dance
Byrne Bros
Careys
Clipfine
Core Group
Crosby's
Design Team
E&S Heating & Ventilation
East London Gymnastics Club
Ellmers
Equity
GBG
Hart Doors
Hed
Honeywell
Imtech Meica
Keller
Keltbray
Kitsite
Lloret
London 2012 Festival
London 2012 Nations and Regions Group
MPG
Populous
Prater
Protec

S Lucas
Seele
Senator
South Essex Gymnastics Club
T Clarke
Watson Steel
Wendover Veterinary Centre
Willerby Landscapes
WRR
Miles Allen
Phil Aller
Alexander Anderson
Steve Artus
Mark Atkins
Timothy Ayres
Jon Barnett
Joel Bennett
Adam Bessell
Davinder Bhatia
Julian Blackler
Jurek Blaszczak
Ruth Bradford
Tony Bradford
Adam Bradshaw
Clive Brennan
Leo Brennan
Ellis Bright
John Brooks
Ben Broomfield
Jake Brown
Tracy Brown
Martin Burden
Amos Burke
Sarah Burns
Mario Carelse
Gary Carter
Vanessa Celosse
Johann Chan
Alex Coleborn
Martyn Cooper
Paulo Cotrim
Alex Crawford
Collarbone Ron Crawley
Lucy Cuppleditch
Aram Delgado
Robert Desmond
Bruce Dixon
Joel Down
Jess Duffy
Danny Dwyer
Clive East
Ryan Elcock
Jake Ellis
Joe Embrey
Jaygun Evans
Chris Fishburn
Alaina Fletcher
Jason Forde
Robbie Francis
Ian Franklin
Lloyd Gale-Ward
Jamie Girven
Colin Goodman
Steve Gower
Steve Green
Dayle Guy
Ryan Hall
Simon Hall
Scott Hamlin
Sebastian Denver Hejna
James Heyes
James Hitchcox
Tom Holmes
Richard Hoult
Michael Hoy
Sarah Hughes
Tamas Jano

Paul Jeffries
Ronnie Johnson
Martin Gareth Jones
Oliver Jones
Ben Joyce
Tom Justice
Kate Kartal
Ho Ke
Dina Koulama
Elaine Lancaster
Isaac Lesser
Ian Lloyd
John MacDonald
Joe Maher
Chris Mahoney
Lily Makurah
Bob Manchester
Ben Manuel
Jack Marchant
Luke Marchant
Caroline Maxted
Steve Maxted
Peter McDermott
Alan McKenzie
Paul Mckeown
John McMillan
Paul Meacher
Jeff Meerdink
Tom Milham
Ric Moore
Tian Moses
Ross Nelson
Justin Neville-Rolfe
Terry O'Connell
James O'Neill
Norbert Onodi
Jeremy GW O'Sullivan
PJ O'Sullivan
Tom Palmer
Vince Parkes
Vladimir Parshikov
Anthony Pearson
Keelan Phillips
Sean Pointing
Jason Pooley
Matt Priest
Billy Purcell
Martin Purvis
Kit Rackham
Ada Raczynska
Morag Reavley
Yasemin Richards
Natalia Rodionova
Nathan Rowe
Daniel Rudd
James V2 Samuel
Zack Shaw
Sandra Simon
Louie Smith
Adrian Spender
John Spicer
Stan
Tika Stefano
Craig Stevens
Paul Stewart
Alan Swain
Jon Taylor
Craig Teague
Stephen Thurgood
Neil Tunnicliffe
Kelvin Waterman
Claira Watson Parr
Andrew Waud
Mark Webb
Stefan Weidmann
Lola Karolina Welch
Mark Welch

Stephanie Wheatley
James White
Michelle Wilkinson
Gareth Wilson
Joshua Wyles

Chaperones
Marsia Charman
Mary Chilton
Meredith Coombes
Ann Cranmer
Natalie Emuss
Pauline Glanville
Sonal Jeram
Dineshkumar Jeram
Melanie Sargeant
Daniel Twine
Deborah Wright

Costume
Allan Williams Textile Printers
Angels the Costumiers
Beadles Skates
BFS Buttons
Birute Fashions
Citrus Rain
Cosprop Ltd
Eden Studios
Empee Silks
Fashion Enter
FFGM
Hanley Band Uniforms
Laceys
Nicola Kileen Textiles
PAG Leisurewear
Phil Reynolds Costumes
Schultz + Wiremu
STI Line Ltd
Taylan Designs Ltd
TRAID
Trimway Ltd
Western Supplies
Whaleys
Zone Creations
Debbie Boyd
Sue Crawshaw
David David
Emma Hardy
Yasemin Kascioqlu
Sasha Keir
Angela Kelly and all her team
Nasir Mazhar
Margarida Santos
Neal Scanlan
Christopher Shannon
Will Skeet
Jane Smith
Michael Van der Ham
Mervyn Wallace
Marion Weise
Chris Winter

Costume, Hair and Make-up Specialist Crew
Nikki Belding
Jennifer Barnard
Elizabet Berrgren
Sylvaine Champeau
Katy Cherry
Charlie Cooper
Andrea Cracknell
Sarah Deans
Ian Denson
Emma Fairfield
Liam Farrelly
Leon Fernholdt
Pam Foster

Mandy Gold
Karen Gurney
Kit Hall
Gustav Hoegen
Gemma Hoff
Lauren Isles
Lizzie Judd
Marialena Kapotopoulou
Adam Keenan
Alexandra Kharibian
Shelley King
Sukie Kirk
Spencer Kitchen
Charlotte Lander
Josh Lee
Melanie Lenihan
Morna Macpherson
Cat McLoughlin
Kimberley Murray
Kirsteen Naismith
Emily Newbold
Jo Nielsen
Tanya Noor
Jess O'Shea
Rosie Octon
Jon Revell
Mary Richardson
Milo Sabariz
Amy Sachon
Joe Scott
Emma Sheffield
Charlotte Simpson
Elaine Solomon
Helen Spink
Mariella Spoto
Kerry Spring
Guy Stevens
Jane Stoner
David Stringer
Janine Summerhayes
Wendy Topping
Sékou Traoré
Jo Tuplin
Gemma Vincent
Aurelie Vogt
Laura Watkins
Nicola Webley
Julia Wilson
Laura Wisinger
Jenna Wyatt

Design
4D modelshop
London Graphic Centre
Space Syntax
Transport for London
Gerry Bunzl
Bec Chippendale
Charlie Cobb
Nick Evans
Gina Fields
Will Fricker
Tom Godfrey
George Guest
Karolina Kendall-Bush
Bronislawa Pratt
Jacqueline Pyle
Lorraine Richer
Dennis Schnegg
Martin Sutherland

Finance
Albert Goodman LLP
IT Associates Ltd

Human Resources
Beder-Harrison & Co

Information Technology
Adobe
Electranet
Jigsaw 24
Lesar
Netapp
Symantec

Legal & Clearances
Department for Education
Nion Hazell
Kate Penlington
Michael Simkins LLP
Barbara Zamoyska

Music
Abbey Road Studios
Air Studios
Angel Studios
Dakota Music Ltd
High Contrast
PRS for Music
PPL
Universal Music Group
Kris Burton
Malcolm Corbett
Gareth Fry
Eleanor Gussman
Jon Harris
Tim Hurrell
Amy Majumdar
Pete Malkin
Anis Marks
Kathryn McDowell CBE
Darren Price
Danielle Short
Marc Stevens
Ruth Sullivan
Rich Walsh

Operations
Arriva
British Waterways
Bunzl
Cabot Car Hire Ltd
Civil Aviation Authority
Clarendon Serviced
Apartments - London
Corinthia Hotel
Ford Dagenham
George Rogers Catering
Go Ahead
Grosvenor Facilities Services
Limited
Gravis Capital Partners LLP
(GSP)
Holiday Inn Express London
Hyatt Regency London - The
Churchill
IDS Develop Ltd
Joint Local Authority Building
Control
Joint Local Authority
Regulatory Services
Leasedrive Rental
Management
London Borough of Barking and
Dagenham Council
London Development Agency
National Air Traffic Services
Port of London Authority
Sam's Cars
Sands Catering
Sanofi
Sheraton Park Tower
Showpax Ltd
Tesco Bromley By Bow

Thames Water
Thrifty Car & Van Rental
Town Hall Hotel & Apartments
Travel by Appointment Ltd
Wing Commander Dawn
Lindsey

Procurement
Bravo Solutions

**Stage Management
Specialist Crew**
Eleanor Butcher
Grace Cameron
Stuart Campbell
Shaun Corcoran
Henrietta Curtis
Anthony Earles
Chloe French
Gemma Friel
George Hims
Scarlett Hooper
Osnat Koblenz
Tom Leggat
Dan Miller
Connor Mitchell
Zanna Orage
Georgia Paget
Christopher Mark Smith
Phillipa Sutcliffe
Sarah Sweet
PK Thummukgool

Task Force 27
Including representation from:
Government Olympic Executive
Greater London Authority
London 2012 Ceremonies Ltd
London Organising Committee
of the Olympic & Paralympic
Games Ltd
London Rail
London Underground
Metropolitan Police Service
Network Rail
Transport for London
Westminster City Council /
London Councils

Technical
Adam Bassett Lighting Design
Aggreko UK
Ainscough Crane Hire
Airworks BV
Artem
Atelier One
Aztec Modelmakers Ltd
Brilliant Stages
Bruce Banks Sails
Buro Happold
Creative Technology
Cumbria Clock Company
Delta Sound Inc (UK)
Factory Settings
FCT Flames
Filmscapes
Flying FX Ltd
Four One Four
Gallowglass
Hamble River Harbour Masters
Howard Eaton Lighting
Ifor Williams Trailers
Kimbolton Fireworks
Land Development Services
Le Mark Group
Lee Warren
Livett's Launches

Neg Earth
Pfeifer
Power Logistics Services
PRG UK
Pyrojunkies
Quantum Special Effects
Riedel Communications GmbH
& Co
River Hamble Harbour Masters
Serious Stages
Service Graphics
Sheetfabs
Show Canada
Showforce Services
Souvenir Scenic Studios
Stage One Creative Services
Stageco Belgium NV
Steel Monkey Engineering
Tait Technologies
The Technical Department
Total Fabrications
Transam Trucking
UK Loco
Unique Creations
Unusual Rigging Ltd
Wardlaw t/as Showstars
Whitechapel Bell Foundry
WIcreations
Alison Prior
Carl Robertshaw
Adam Taylor

Technical Specialist Crew
Guy Aldridge
Chris Aram
Gibson Arpino
Hamish Bamford
Mike Becket
Malcolm Birkett
Mike Bownds
Francesca Boyle
Belinda Clisham
Gary Connery
Terry Cook
David Patrick Emerson
Dan Evans
Jonathan Finch
Andy Fugle
Dario Fusco
Jason Gilbert
Ian Glassbrook
Chelsey Goord
Andrew Graves
Alex Hatton
William Hayman
Martin Hinkins
Patrick Hollingsworth
Brendan Houghton
Linford Hudson
Hannah Knox
Ingrid Mackay
Cattrina Mott
Nick Mumford
Sienna Murdoch
Rebecca Nelson
Jem Nicholson
Stephanie Pasiewicz
Chris Patton
Pip Ratcliffe
Jo Savill
Simon Sayer
Michael Scott
Elliot Sinclair
Anna Stamper
Erica Stokes
Pauline Stone
Mark Sutton

Jamie Taylor
Chris Tidmarsh
Tim Timmington
Elizabeth Vass
Joe Vassallo
Frances Waddington
Zoe Walker
Rachel Walsh
Oliver Welsh
Sharn Whitehead
Andrew Wilkinson
Jack Willis
Marc Wolff
Robert Woodley
Richard Young

Broadcast & Film

Broadcast
BBC
CTV Outside Broadcast
Bill Morris, Technical Producer
Emily Cobb, Outside Broadcast
Production Manager
Done & Dusted
Melanie Fletcher, Producer
Barrie Dodd, Camera
Supervisor
Olympic Broadcasting Services

**Isles of Wonder /
Happy & Glorious**
Produced by the BBC
Lisa Osborne
Adam Gascoyne
Liz Allman
Tamana Bleasdale
Caterina Boselli
Nicolas Brown
Zoe Brown
James Buxton
Julie Clark
Mark Clayton
Alex Gladstone
Jodie Gray
Joanna Gueritz
David Gunkle
John Marzano
Adrian McCarthy
Michael McDonough
Mervyn New
Sam Renton
Benjamin Richards
Gemma Ryan
Deborah Saban
Will Samuelson
Astrid Sieben
David Smith
Richard Todd
Andrew Wood

Four Nations
BBC Northern Ireland
BBC Scotland
BBC Wales
Historic Scotland
National Trust
Leonie Bell
David Brown
Roisin Browne
Francesca Canty
Derek Livesey
James Lucas
Chris Myers
Ian Russell
Cian Smyth
Kate Southwell

Gwyn Williams
Rhian Williams

**Chariots of Fire /
Thanks Tim**
Simon Baker
David Brown
Luke Coulter
Jamie Edgell
Hugh Gourlay
Jo Harrop
Richard Hewitt
Ed Kellow
Lizzie Kelly
Daniel Landin
Olivia Lloyd
Nathan Mann
Jason Martin
Adrian McCarthy
Orla O'Connor
Sylvia Parker
Amelia Price
Larry Prinz
Oliver Roberts
Ewan Robertson
Gemma Ryan
Deborah Saban
Gordon Segrove
Colin Strachan
Dorothy Sullivan
Gary Weekes
Tim White

Torch Journey
RKCR/Y&R
Studio aka
Jon Bray
Ben Davis
Alex Gladstone
David Gunkle
Yvonne Ryan
Kenny Underwood
Daisy Wallace

Music Credits
Générique musique

Sailor's Boots
Performed by Frank Turner, appearing courtesy of Xtra Mile Recordings / Polydor Records
Written by Turner
Universal Music Publishing Ltd

Wessex Boy
Performed by Frank Turner, appearing courtesy of Xtra Mile Recordings / Polydor Records
Written by Turner/Powell
Universal Music Publishing Ltd / Nigel Powell

I Still Believe
Performed by Frank Turner, appearing courtesy of Xtra Mile Recordings / Polydor Records
Written by Turner
Universal Music Publishing Ltd

Surf Solar
F.Buttons
Written by Power/Hung
Copyright control / ATP Recordings

Eton Boating Song
Eton College School Concert Choir and Orchestra
Written by Drummond/Cory/Wodehouse

Theme to *The South Bank Show*
Written by Paganini
Arranged by Lloyd Webber

God Save the Queen
Sex Pistols
Written by Lydon/Matlock/Jones/Cook
Rotten Music Ltd / Warner/Chappell Music Publishing Ltd / Universal Music Publishing Ltd
Under license from Universal Music Operations Ltd

Theme to *EastEnders*
Written by May/Osborne
Originally performed by Simon May
SonyATV / BBC

Under The House
P.I.L.
Written by Lydon/Atkins/Levene

London Calling
The Clash
Written by Strummer/Jones/Simonon/Headon
Universal Music Publishing Ltd
Sony Music Entertainment UK Ltd

Pomp and Circumstance Op.39: March, No 1 in D
London Symphony Orchestra
Written by Elgar

Smile
Lily Allen
Written by Allen/Babalola/Lewis/Dodd/Mittoo

Licensed courtesy of EMI Records Ltd
Universal Music Publishing Ltd / Sparta Florida Music Group Ltd / Music Sales Ltd

Map of the Problematique
Muse
Written by Bellamy
Loosechord Ltd
All rights administered by Warner/Chappell Music Publishing Ltd

Jerusalem
Performed by the Dockhead Choir
Choir Coordinator: Mag Shepherd
Written by Christie/Blake/Parry
Universal Music Publishing Ltd / Sony/ATV Music Publishing

Londonderry Air (Danny Boy)
Performed by the Belfast Philharmonic Phil Kids Choir and JAM Junior Academy Of Music
Music traditional / Lyrics by Weatherly

Flower of Scotland
Performed by The Big Project
Arranged by Kim Edgar
Written by Williamson

Bread of Heaven
Performed by Only Kids Aloud, Only Vale Kids Aloud and the WNO Singing Club
Arranged by Tim Rhys-Evans
Written by Hughes

Nimrod
Performed by LSO On Track, an orchestra comprising of young musicians from 10 east London boroughs and LSO members
Conducted by François-Xavier Roth
Assistant Conductor: Matthew Gibson
Arranged by Gareth Glyn
Written by Elgar

And I Will Kiss
Underworld, featuring a performance by Dame Evelyn Glennie
Drums: Paul Clarvis, Mike Dolbear, John Randall, Frank Ricotti, Ralph Salmins, Corrina Silvester and Ian Thomas
The 1000 Pandemonium Drummers, including Barnaby Archer, Oliver Blake, Daniel Bradley, Rebecca Celebuski, Jason Chowdhury, Jonathan Colgan, Oliver Cox, Fabio de Oliveira, Robert Eckland, Daniel Ellis, Richard Elsworth, David Holmes, Oliver Lowe, Nicola Marangoni, James O'Carroll, Gerard Rundell, Ramon Sherrington, Alex Smith, Owain Williams and Justin Woodward

Dame Evelyn Glennie Drum Score arranged by Paul Clarvis and Rick Smith
Orchestra: LSO On Track (see 'Nimrod')
Conducted by François-Xavier Roth
Assistant Conductor: Matthew Gibson
LSO On Track Orchestrated by Geoffrey Alexander
Brass Band: The Grimethorpe Colliery Band
Brass Band Orchestrated and Conducted by Sandy Smith
Steel Band: Nostalgia
Singers: Paul Ayres, Will Balkwill, Zoe Brown, Ronan Busfield, Pete Challis, Mark Connell, Emily Dickens, Kevin Doody, Elizabeth Drury, Ewan Gillies, James Hall, Johnny Herford, Katy Hill, Jimmy Holliday, Eloise Irving, Gareth John, Oliver Jones, Christopher Lowrey, Drew Mason, Philippa Murray, Sean Needham, Robyn Allegra Parton, Catherine Pope, Alison Rose, Domhnall Talbot, Reuben Thomas, Matt Thorpe and Amy Wood
Solo Violin: Sonia Slany
Written by Smith/Hyde
Mute Song / BMG Chrysalis

Arrival of the Queen of Sheba
Orchestra: London Symphony Orchestra
Conducted by Geoffrey Alexander
Written by Handel

Music for the Royal Fireworks: IV. La Rejouissance
Orchestra: London Symphony Orchestra
Conducted by Geoffrey Alexander
Written by Handel

The Dam Busters' March
Orchestra: London Symphony Orchestra
Conducted by Geoffrey Alexander
Written by Coates
Chappell Music Ltd

James Bond Theme (from *Dr. No*)
The John Barry Orchestra
Written by Norman
EMI Music Publishing Ltd

Sundowner
Blanck Mass
Written by Power
P&C 2011 Blanck Mass / Rock Action Records

Sundowner
Orchestra: London Symphony Orchestra
Arranged by Rick Smith
Orchestrated by Geoffrey Alexander
Written by Power

P&C 2011 Blanck Mass / Rock Action Records

God Save the Queen (National Anthem)
Performed by The Kaos Signing Choir for Deaf and Hearing Children
Signductor: Ali Wood

Tubular Bells
Performed by Mike Oldfield
Alistair Mulloy, Luke Oldfield, Ash Soan
Musical Director: Robin Smith
Written by Oldfield
Stage Three Music Ltd

In Dulci Jubilo
Performed by Mike Oldfield
Recorder: Andy Findon
Musical Director: Robin Smith
Written by Bach
Arranged by Oldfield
Stage Three Music Ltd

Chariots of Fire
Performed by the London Symphony Orchestra
Conducted by Sir Simon Rattle, appearing courtesy of EMI Classics
Pianist: Iain Farrington
Arranged by Howard Goodall
Orchestrated by David Butterworth
Singers: Will Balkwill, Zoe Brown, Ronan Busfield, Emily Dickens, Elizabeth Drury, James Hall, Johnny Herford, Katy Hill, Jimmy Holliday, Eloise Irving, Gareth John, Oliver Jones, Christopher Lowrey, Philippa Murray, Robyn Allegra Parton, Catherine Pope, Alison Rose, Domhnall Talbot, Reuben Thomas and Amy Wood
Written by Papathanassiou
EMI Music Publishing Ltd

Girls in Grey
Charles Williams and His Concert Orchestra
Written by Williams
Chappell Recorded Music Library Limited

Theme to *The Archers* ('Barwick Green')
Written by Wood
Cavendish Music Library

Black and White Rag
Winifred Atwell
Courtesy of Decca Music Group Ltd
Written by Botsford
EMI Music Publishing Ltd
Under license from Universal Music Operations Ltd

Push the Button
Sugababes
Written by Austin/Buchanan/Buena/Range
Courtesy of Universal-Island Record Ltd

Under license from Universal Music Operations Ltd

Enola Gay
Orchestral Manoeuvres In The Dark
Written by McCluskey
EMI Music Publishing Ltd

Food Glorious Food
Written by Bart
From the original soundtrack recording of Oliver appearing courtesy of Sony Music Entertainment Inc
Lakeview Music Publishing Co Ltd
Arranged by Green
Recorded by Sony

When I Was a Youngster
Rizzle Kicks
Written by Alexander-Sule/Stephens/Street/Dring/Edwards/Ray
Panache Music Limited/Fairwood Music (UK) Limited/Chrysalis Music ltd/Stage Three Music Publishing Ltd
Courtesy of Universal-Island Records Ltd
Under license from Universal Music Operations Ltd

Going Underground
The Jam
Written by Weller
Universal Music Publishing Ltd
Courtesy of Polydor UK Ltd
Under license from Universal Music Operations Ltd

Wonderful Tonight
Eric Clapton
Written by Clapton

My Generation
The Who
Written by Townshend
Courtesy of Polydor UK Ltd
Under license from Universal Music Operations Ltd
Fabulous Music Ltd

(I Can't Get No) Satisfaction
The Rolling Stones
Written by Jagger/Richards
ABKO Music Inc
Courtesy of ABKCO Music & Records Inc

My Boy Lollipop
Millie Small
Written by Levy/Roberts
EMI Music Publishing Inc
Courtesy of Polydor UK Ltd
Under license from Universal Music Operations Ltd

All Day and All of the Night
The Kinks
Written & arranged by Davies
Courtesy of Sanctuary Records Group Ltd
Under license from Universal Music Operations Ltd
Edward Kassner Music Co Ltd

She Loves You
The Beatles
Written by Lennon/McCartney
Licensed courtesy of EMI Records Ltd
Sony/ATV Music Publishing

Tiger Feet
Mud
Written by Chinn/Chapman
Licensed courtesy of EMI Records Ltd
Universal Music Publishing Ltd

Trampled Under Foot
Led Zeppelin
Written by Page/Plant/Jones/Bonham
Licensed courtesy of Warner Music UK Ltd
Flames Of Albion Music Inc, All rights administered by Warner/Chappell North America Ltd

A Message to You, Rudy
The Specials
Written by Thompson
Licensed courtesy of EMI Records Ltd
Carlin Music Corp

Starman
David Bowie
Written by Bowie
Licensed courtesy of RZO Music
Published by Tintoretto Music/RZO Music Ltd / EMI Music Publishing Ltd / BMG/Chrysalis Music Ltd

Bohemian Rhapsody
Queen
Written by Mercury
EMI Music Publishing Ltd
Under license from Universal Music Operations Ltd

Pretty Vacant
Sex Pistols
Written by Cook/Matlock/Jones/Rotten
All rights on behalf of itself and Rotten Music Ltd administered by Warner/Chappell Music Publishing Ltd & Universal Music Publishing Ltd
Courtesy of Universal Music Catalogue
Under license from Universal Music Operations Ltd

Blue Monday
New Order
Written by Morris/Hook/Sumner/Gilbert
Be Music publishing. All rights administered by WB Music Corp
Licensed courtesy of Warner Music UK Ltd

Relax
Frankie Goes To Hollywood
Written by Gill/Johnson/O'Toole
Perfect Songs Ltd

Courtesy of Union Square Music Ltd under license from ZTT Records Ltd
Arranged by Trevor Horn
Recorded by ZTT Records Ltd

Back to Life (However Do You Want Me)
Soul II Soul (featuring Caron Wheeler)
Written by Wheeler/Law/Romeo/Hooper
EMI Music Publishing Ltd / Sony/ATV Music Publishing / WB Music Corp
All rights on behalf of WB Music Corp
Administered by Warner/Chappell North America Ltd

He's Gonna Step On You Again
Happy Mondays
Written by Demetriou/Kongos
Tapestry Music Ltd
Licensed courtesy of Warner Music UK Ltd

Sweet Dreams (Are Made of This)
Eurythmics
Written by Lennox/Stewart
Universal Music Publishing Ltd
Appearing courtesy of Sony Music Entertainment UK Ltd
Recorded by Sony

Bitter Sweet Symphony
The Verve
Music by Jagger/Richards
Lyrics by Ashcroft
Licensed courtesy of Virgin Records Ltd
ABKO Music Inc

Firestarter
The Prodigy
Written by Dudley/Horn/Jeczalik/Langan/Flint/Howlett/ Deal/Morley
Appearing courtesy of Beggars Group Media Ltd
Contains samples of 'SOS' Performed by The Breeders Courtesy of 4AD / Elektra
'Close to the Edit' Performed by Art Of Noise Courtesy of ZTT Records Ltd
EMI Music Publishing Ltd/ Perfect Songs/Universal Music Publishing Ltd

Born Slippy NUXX
Underworld
Written by Smith/Hyde
Appearing courtesy of Cooking Vinyl
Mute Song Ltd/Chrysalis Music Inc./Sherlock Holmes Music Ltd
Recorded by Rick Smith, Karl Hyde & Darren Emerson t/a Underworld, under exclusive license to Cooking Vinyl Ltd

I'm Forever Blowing Bubbles
Written by Vincent/Brockman/Kellette/Kendis

Carlin Music Ltd / EMI Music Publishing Ltd

Song 2
Blur
Written by Albarn/Coxon/Rowntree/James
EMI Music Publishing Ltd

Bonkers
Performed by Dizzee Rascal, appearing courtesy of Dirtee Stank / Universal Island Records
Written by Mills/Van Helden
Notting Hill Music Ltd / Bug Music Ltd
Arranged by Armand Van Helden
Recorded by Dirtee Stank Records

Nimma Nimma
AR Rahman
Written by Rahman
Universal Music Publishing Ltd

Valerie
Mark Ronson featuring Amy Winehouse
Written by Payne/McCabe/Harding/Chowdhury/Pritchard
Appearing courtesy of Sony Music Entertainment UK Ltd
Recorded by Sony

Uprising
Muse
Written by Bellamy
Loosechord Ltd
All rights administered by Warner/Chappell Music Publishing Ltd

Random Antics
Mikey J feat. Kano
Written by Asante/Robinson
Kano appears courtesy of Bigger Picture Music
Michael 'Mikey J' Astante appears courtesy of Mikeyjdotnet
Blue Mountain Music / Copyright Control

Pass Out
Tinie Tempah
Written by Okugwu/McKenzie

Heaven
Emeli Sandé
Written by Sandé/Spencer/Khan/Chegwin/Craze
Licensed courtesy of Virgin Records Ltd
EMI Music Publishing Ltd / Sony/ATV Music Publishing

Abide With Me
Performed by Emeli Sandé, appearing courtesy of Virgin Records Limited
Music by Monk
Lyrics by Lyte

Welcome
Produced by Lincoln Barrett,

John Harris and Rick Smith
Mixed by Simon Gogerly
The complete list of music heard in this section will be credited online at: london2012.com/exploretheceremonies

I Bet That You Look Good on the Dancefloor
Performed by Arctic Monkeys, appearing courtesy of the Domino Recording Company
Written by Turner
EMI Music Publishing Ltd
Recorded by The Domino Recording Co Ltd

Come Together
Performed by Arctic Monkeys, appearing courtesy of the Domino Recording Company
Written by Lennon/McCartney
Sony/ATV Music Publishing

Fanfare of the Common Welshman
Orchestra: London Symphony Orchestra
Written by Jenkins
Copyright Control

Olympic Anthem
Orchestra: London Symphony Orchestra
Arranged by Kirsty Whalley and Guy Barker
LSO Orchestrated and Conducted by Geoffrey Alexander
Brass Band: The Grimethorpe Colliery Band
Brass Band Orchestrated and Conducted by Sandy Smith
Written by Samaras/Palamas

Caliban's Dream
Underworld, featuring performances by the Dockhead Choir, Dame Evelyn Glennie, Only Men Aloud, Elizabeth Roberts, Esme Smith and Alex Trimble, Alex Trimble is appearing courtesy of Kitsune SARL and Glassnote Entertainment Group LLC
Orchestra: London Symphony Orchestra
LSO orchestrated and conducted by Geoffrey Alexander
Soprano Lead and Choral Score Written and arranged by Rick and Esme Smith
Singers: Will Balkwill, Zoe Brown, Ronan Busfield, Emily Dickens, Elizabeth Drury, James Hall, Johnny Herford, Katy Hill, Jimmy Holliday, Eloise Irving, Gareth John, Oliver Jones, Christopher Lowrey, Philippa Murray, Robyn Allegra Parton, Catherine Pope, Alison Rose, Domhnall Talbot, Reuben Thomas and Amy Wood
Drums: Paul Clarvis, Barnaby Archer, Oliver Blake, Daniel Bradley, Rebecca Celebuski,

Jason Chowdhury, Jonathan Colgan, Oliver Cox, Fabio de Oliveira, Mike Dolbear, Robert Eckland, Daniel Ellis, Richard Elsworth, David Holmes, Oliver Lowe, Nicola Marangoni, James O'Carroll, Gerard Rundell, Ramon Sherrington, Corrina Silvester, Alex Smith, Owain Williams and Justin Woodward
Drum score arranged by Rick Smith and Paul Clarvis
Written by Smith/Hyde
Mute Song / BMG Chrysalis

Eclipse
Pink Floyd
Written by Waters
Roger Waters Music Overseas Ltd (NS)
All rights administered by Warner/Chappell Artemis Music Ltd

The End
Performed by Sir Paul McCartney, appearing courtesy of MPL Communications Limited
Written by Lennon/McCartney
Sony/ATV Music Publishing

Hey Jude
Performed by Sir Paul McCartney, appearing courtesy of MPL Communications Limited
Written by Lennon/McCartney
Sony/ATV Music Publishing

Clearance Credits
Autorisations

Film

Bedknobs and Broomsticks courtesy of Disney Enterprises Inc
Billy Elliot courtesy of Universal Studios Licensing LLC
Breakfast at Tiffany's courtesy of Paramount Pictures
Brief Encounter courtesy of ITV Studios
Footage from *Casablanca* licensed by Warner Bros Entertainment Inc
Chariots of Fire clips courtesy of Twentieth Century Fox and Warner Bros Entertainment Inc all rights reserved
City Lights by Charles Chaplin © 1931 Roy Export S.A.S. all rights reserved, renewed copyright a 1958 Roy Export S.A.S. all rights reserved, music composed by Charles Chaplin except 'La Violetera' by and copyright ã José Padilla
Don't Look Now courtesy of STUDIOCANAL Films Ltd and Paramount Pictures
Dr No courtesy of Danjaq LLC and United Artists Corporation © 1962 Danjaq LLC and United Artists
East Is East courtesy of Film4/Screenocean
Four Weddings and a Funeral © 1994 Orion Pictures Corporation, courtesy of Metro-Goldwyn-Mayer Studios Inc, all rights reserved
Footage from *The Full Monty* courtesy of Twentieth Century Fox, all rights reserved
The Graduate courtesy of STUDIOCANAL Films Ltd
Gregory's Girl © 1981 National Film Trustee Company Ltd, courtesy of Metro-Goldwyn-Mayer Studios Inc, all rights reserved
Kes © 1970 Woodfall America Inc, courtesy of Metro-Goldwyn-Mayer Studios Inc, all rights reserved
Lady and the Tramp courtesy of Disney Enterprises Inc
The Man Who Fell to Earth courtesy of STUDIOCANAL Films Ltd
A Matter of Life and Death courtesy of ITV Studios
My Beautiful Launderette courtesy of Film4/Screenocean
Footage from *North By Northwest* licensed by Warner Bros Entertainment Inc
Oliver! courtesy of Columbia Pictures
Oliver Twist courtesy of ITV Studios
Footage from *Planet of the Apes* (1968) courtesy of Twentieth Century Fox, all rights reserved
Footage from *William Shakespeare's Romeo + Juliet* courtesy of Twentieth Century Fox, all rights reserved
Shrek © 2001 DreamWorks Animation LLC, used with permission of DreamWorks Animation LLC
Footage from *Singing in the Rain* licensed by Warner Bros Entertainment Inc
Footage from *Slumdog Millionaire* © 2008 Celador Films Ltd and Channel 4 Television Corporation, courtesy of Twentieth Century Fox, all rights reserved
The Snowman © Snowman Enterprises Ltd 1982, 2012
Footage from *Titanic* (1997) courtesy of Twentieth Century Fox and Paramount Pictures Corporation, all rights reserved
Toy Story courtesy of Disney/Pixar
Trainspotting courtesy of Film4/Screenocean
Twilight courtesy of Summit Entertainment, LLC
Wall-E courtesy of Disney/Pixar
Wallace & Gromit - The Wrong Trousers © Aardman Animations / Wallace & Gromit Ltd 1993
Wayne's World courtesy of Paramount Pictures
The Wickerman courtesy of STUDIOCANAL Films Ltd
Excerpt from the film *Withnail and I* courtesy of HandMade Limited and © 2012 HandMade Limited, all rights reserved

Television

BBC & BBC Worldwide
The Cosby Show clips courtesy of Carsey-Werner, LLC
Britain's Got Talent Clips courtesy of FremantleMedia/ Simco Ltd
Cuéntame Cómo Pasó courtesy of Grupo Ganga Producciones
Desmond's courtesy of Humphrey Barclay Productions/Channel 4/Screenocean ITV Studios
Brookside courtesy of Mersey TV and Lime Pictures/Channel 4/Screenocean
Footage from *Modern Family* courtesy of Twentieth Century Fox and Paramount Pictures Corporation, all rights reserved

Archive Footage

Courtesy of:
AP Archive / British Movietone
British Pathé
Framepool
Getty
Olympic Television Archive Bureau

General

The Beatles themed imagery and images from *Yellow Submarine* (1968) used by kind permission of Apple Corps Ltd and Subafilms Ltd
James Bond™ character used by kind permission of Danjaq, LLC and United Artists Corporation
Worldview-2 satellite image of London acquired on 28 March 2012 © DigitalGlobe inc / provided by European Space Imaging GmbH
Chariots of Fire scene used with kind permission of Enigma Productions
The Cure at Troy © Seamus Heaney and reprinted by permission of Faber and Faber Ltd
Swimming poster (2011) by Howard Hodgkin
Historical Olympic posters © 1948-2012 International Olympic Committee (IOC)
'MCMXIV' from *The Complete Poems* © Estate of Philip Larkin and reprinted by permission of Faber and Faber Ltd
Captain Hook character used by kind permission of Great Ormond Street Hospital Children's Charity
Text extract from *Peter Pan* by JM Barrie, alterations to original text agreed by kind permission of Great Ormond Street Hospital Children's Charity
Cyclorama inspired by David Hockney – 'Summer Sky' 2008, photograph of an inkjet-printed computer drawing on paper © David Hockney, photo credit Richard Schmidt
Cruella de Vil character used by kind permission of Laurence Fitch Ltd/Film Rights Ltd and The Walt Disney Company
Shipping forecast extracts used courtesy of Met Office, Maritime and Coastguard Agency and the BBC
Childcatcher Character used by kind permission of Metro-Goldwyn-Mayer Studios Inc and Danjaq LLC
The Pig from the album *Animals*, licensed by Pink Floyd Music Ltd and Pink Floyd (1987) Ltd
The Prism from the album *The Dark Side of the Moon*, licensed by Pink Floyd Music Ltd and Pink Floyd (1987) Ltd
Mary Poppins character used by kind permission of the estate of PL Travers
Winston Churchill (1973) Statue located in Parliament Square, sculpted by Ivor Roberts-Jones used by permission of the trustees of the Roberts-Jones Trust
Lord Voldemort character used by kind permission of JK Rowling, Warner Bros Entertainment Inc, and Bloomsbury Publishing Plc
Ratty, Mole & Toad illustrations © The Estate of EH Shepard, reproduced with permission of Curtis Brown Group Ltd
Image licensed under Shutterstock.com
Pages from *The Daily Sketch* (Thursday 5th June, 1913), reproduced with permission by Solo Syndication
Smiley design licensed by The Smiley Company
London Underground maps, roundel, and New Johnston typeface used by kind permission of Transport for London
LOndOn 2012 poster (2011) by Rachel Whiteread

Programme

AP/Press Association
Simon Annand
Chad Baker
'Bike' by Syd Barrett © Westminster Music Ltd
John Churchman/Getty Images
Gregory G Dimijian/Science Photo Library
Photo of Don Foster MP courtesy of Dods
'Prayer' is taken from *Mean Time* by Carol Ann Duffy published by Anvil Press Poetry in 1993
Albert Einstein quote © The Hebrew University of Jerusalem
Mat Hennek
Getty Images
Antony Gormley, 'Field for the British Isles', 1993 (detail) Terracotta Variable size: approx. 40,000 elements, each 8-26 cm tall
Charlie Gray
Bike Arch © 2007 Mark Grieve and Ilana Spector, photo by Frank Roberto
'B of the Bang' image (And in the end...) courtesy of Heatherwick Studio
Cover design by Heatherwick Studio
'Summer Sky' 2008 inkjet printed computer drawing on paper 34 1/4 x 45 1/2" edition of 25 © David Hockney, photo credit Richard Schmidt
iStock
'I'm Forever Blowing Bubbles' written by James Kendis, James Brockman, John Kellette and Nat Vincent, used by kind permission of Carlin Music Corp on behalf of Redwood Music Ltd, EMI Publishing Ltd and Warner/Chappell Music Inc
MJ Kim
Michal Krakowiak/Getty Images
'MCMXIV' from *The Complete Poems* © Estate of Philip Larkin
'The End' words & music by Lennon/McCartney, published by Sony/ATV Music Publishing
© *Small Island* by Andrea Levy first published in Great Britain in 2004 by Headline
MPL Communications Ltd
Parliamentary copyright images are reproduced with the permission of Parliament
Philipp Rathmer
Tony Scarpetta
Peter Searle
Wild Swimmer by Jo Shapcott, commissioned by the Olympic Delivery Authority and Winning Words to be permanently installed in the Olympic Park
Shutterstock
Clive Streeter/Getty Images
Photo of Tessa Jowell by John Swannell
John Swannell/Royal Household/Camera Press
Hortense et Queenie, © La Table Ronde, 2006
Ellen Carys Tullett
Universal Images Group Editorial/Getty Images
Wall to Wall
Extract from HG Wells *The Wheels of Chance* used by permission of Literary Executors of the Estate of HG Wells
Erik Weiss
Stefan Wermuth/Reuters/Action Images
Daniel Craig photograph © Greg Williams
Rachel Whiteread, *House*, 1993, © Rachel Whiteread, photographed by Sue Omerod
'Flower of Scotland' written by Williamson, published by Corries Music Ltd
The London Breed by Benjamin Zephaniah, © Benjamin Zephaniah, is reproduced by permission of United Agents on behalf of Benjamin Zephaniah

If you'd like this programme in another language or format please email info@enquiries.london2012.com or phone 44 (0)845 267 2012 quoting LOC2012/CER/1386.

Published under licence from London 2012 by Haymarket Network, Teddington Studios, Broom Road, Teddington, Middlesex TW11 9BE. Tel 44 (0)20 8267 5000. Reprinting in whole or in part is forbidden except with prior permission of the publisher. Due care is taken to ensure that the content of this programme is accurate, but the publisher and printer cannot accept liability for errors, omissions or alterations. Additionally, Ceremonies Producers acknowledge the contribution of anyone involved in the Ceremony whose name does not appear in the programme due to publication deadlines. Any alterations or additions to the credits will be available online at london2012.com/exploretheceremonies.

Printed at an environmentally aware ISO14001 printer on FSC certified paper.

Si vous souhaitez obtenir ce programme dans une autre langue ou sous un autre format, veuillez envoyer un e-mail à l'adresse info@enquiries. london2012.com ou appelez le 44 (0)845 267 2012 en indiquant LOC2012/CER/1386.

Publié sous licence de Londres 2012 par Haymarket Network, Teddington Studios, Broom Road, Teddington, Middlesex TW11 9BE. Tél. : 44 (0)20 8267 5000. Reproduction totale ou partielle interdite sans autorisation préalable de l'éditeur. Malgré les efforts pour garantir l'exactitude du contenu de ce programme, l'éditeur et l'imprimeur ne peuvent être tenus responsables des erreurs, omissions ou altérations qui pourraient y figurer. Les producteurs reconnaissent en outre la contribution de tout participant à la cérémonie dont le nom n'apparaîtrait pas dans le présent programme en raison des délais de publication. Toutes les modifications ou les ajouts aux crédits seront consultables en ligne sur london2012.com/ exploretheceremonies.

Imprimé sur papier certifié FSC chez un imprimeur certifié ISO14001 sensibilisé aux questions environnementales.

FSC
www.fsc.org
MIX
Paper from responsible sources
FSC® C013417

The BBC and the Olympics
La BBC et les Jeux Olympiques

The London 2012 Olympic Games are by far the largest set-piece broadcasting event in the BBC's history. But our Olympic links go back more than 100 years, before the BBC even existed. Our White City complex in West London stands on the site of the finishing line for the 1908 Marathon – the very first Marathon of the modern Games.

These are the 15th Summer Olympic Games broadcast by the BBC. It's a sequence that began with the 1948 Games in London, when the BBC pioneered the televising of the Olympics with pictures viewed in homes for the first time, and one that has run unbroken since the 1960 Games in Rome.

But 2012 is on a different scale from anything we've seen before. For the first time, in partnership with the host broadcaster OBS, we will cover every venue live around the clock – more than 2,500 hours of sport crammed into little more than a fortnight. BBC One and BBC Three will be supplemented by an additional 24 television channels for the duration of the Games. The same content, and much more, will be available on both web and mobile.

But for us, London 2012 means much more than sport. As you sit here tonight, you're watching the culmination coverage of a Torch Relay that's covered the length and breadth of our land. The BBC has followed it every inch of the way, shining a light on the amazing stories of the Torchbearers and their communities. We've even seen the Torch make its way through Albert Square, the home of our beloved *EastEnders* drama, passing iconic on-screen landmarks such as the The Queen Vic pub.

We have also enthusiastically supported the London 2012 Festival with its music, arts and entertainment; and the BBC has made two of the films you'll see tonight within the Opening Ceremony. We're proud to have worked with LOCOG to deliver the best of British creativity to the world.

The London 2012 Olympic Games are the biggest sporting event in the UK in our lifetimes. We will offer services to our audiences that mean they'll never miss a moment – as well as the opportunity to join together to celebrate this unique summer.

Mark Thompson, BBC Director General

Les Jeux Olympiques de Londres 2012 sont de loin le plus grand événement organisé diffusé par la BBC depuis sa création. Mais nos liens avec les Jeux Olympiques remontent en réalité à plus d'un siècle, avant même la naissance de la BBC. Notre complexe de White City, dans l'ouest de Londres, se trouve sur le site de la ligne d'arrivée du marathon de 1908, le tout premier marathon des Jeux modernes.

Ces Jeux sont les 15ᵉ Jeux Olympiques d'été diffusés par la BBC, les 15ᵉ d'une séquence inaugurée avec les Jeux de 1948 à Londres, où la BBC se fit pionnier des Jeux Olympiques télévisés en diffusant pour la première fois leurs images dans les foyers. Une séquence qui, depuis les Jeux de 1960 à Rome, n'a connu aucune interruption.

Mais 2012 est sur une tout autre échelle que tout ce que nous avons vu jusqu'à présent. Pour la première fois, en partenariat avec OBS, diffuseur hôte, nous couvrirons chaque site en direct, 24 heures sur 24, soit plus de 2 500 heures de sport condensées dans un peu plus de deux semaines. Vingt-quatre chaînes de télévision supplémentaires viendront compléter BBC One et BBC Three pendant toute la durée des Jeux. Le même contenu, et bien plus encore, sera disponible à la fois sur Internet et sur mobile.

Mais pour nous, Londres 2012 signifie bien plus que du sport. Du siège où vous êtes assis ce soir, vous assistez au point d'orgue d'un relais de la flamme qui a parcouru de long en large notre pays. La BBC en a suivi chaque centimètre, mettant en lumière les histoires extraordinaires des porteurs de la flamme et de leurs communautés. Nous avons même vu la flamme traverser Albert Square, théâtre du feuilleton EastEnders que nous aimons tant, passant devant des icônes du petit écran comme le pub The Queen Vic.

Nous avons également soutenu avec enthousiasme le Festival de Londres 2012 avec sa musique, ses arts et ses divertissements, et la BBC a réalisé deux des films que vous verrez ce soir pendant la cérémonie d'ouverture. Nous sommes fiers d'avoir travaillé avec le LOCOG (Comité d'organisation des Jeux Olympiques et Paralympiques de Londres) pour offrir au monde le meilleur de la créativité britannique.

Les Jeux Olympiques de Londres 2012 sont le plus grand événement sportif que nous avons vu et verrons au Royaume-Uni de notre vivant. Nous offrirons à nos publics des services qui leur permettront de ne jamais manquer aucun moment, ainsi que l'occasion de nous rassembler tous ensemble pour célébrer cet été unique.

Mark Thompson, directeur général de la BBC

Volunteers
Bénévoles

Prologue Lucy Abrahams, Angela Adler, Doreen Agyei, Marian Agyeman, Vivienne Ahmad, Minhaj Ahmed, Eren Ali, Hannah Allen, David Alli-Balogun, Syed Al-Nahiyan Ishtar, Praveen Amarasinghe, Komal Amin, Clare Anderson, Faye Andrews, Vicky Annand, Bevlyn Anyaoku-Clough, Adria Aranda-Balibrea, Niellah Arboine-Todd, Dioni Arvanitaki, Lorna Asante, Sophie Ashdown, Tania Austin Herdman, Sola Awoberu, Tessa Baartmans, Amanda Bailey, Julia Bailey, Lucy Baker, Tatiana Baratto, Sonja Barber, Cassandra Bardot, Ursula Barzey, Michael Beard, Katharina Beck, Kate Beeching, Gabi Beer, Geoff Bell, Kate Bennett, Gloria Bernard, Anne-Marie Bevan, Sana Bhadelia, Varun Bhanot, Alexander Bishenden Moon, Rosa Bishenden Moon, Lynn Blackman, Kat Blake-Pink, Katherine Blightman, Wendy Blow, Elisa Bodden, Lydia Bolwell, Emma Bond, Laura Bonifacii, Nicole Boran, Sylvie Bornat, Jessica Bosworth, Rhiannon Brace, Penny Breia, Hannah Broad, Karen Brock, Elizabeth Brooks, Larissa Brown, Camilla Brueton, Julie Bryant, Kirsty Bullen, Katy Burke, Richard Burke, Mulgrew Cameron, Annie Campbell, June Campbell, Charles Campbell-Peek, Amy Carrick, Nicola Carsons, Albert Carter-Phillips, Finn Casey, Emma Chalk, Danielle Chamberlain, Chor Hon Chan, Ann Charles, Qi Chen, Natalie Chivers, Nazish Choudhury, Severino Chuquivala-Jos, Ernests Cirulis, Lauren Coates Lewis, Bianca Cole, Annie Coleman, Anne Corbett, Penny Costa, Anne Costello, Sarah Cowan, Lois Crane, Claire Cranmer, Cristiane Crauford, Jumar Cristobal, Melisande Croft, Oliver Crooke, Gillian Dacey, Eleni Danika, Leaphia Darko, Carol Davis, Miranda Dawkins, Rhiannon Daye, Cara de Reuck, Barbara De Rios, Maryam Delavar, Zu Ning Ding, Yaxin Ding, Alexander Dmochowski, Amada Dorta Cerpa, Jane Dotzek, Rachel Drew, Thorsten Dreyer, Adrian Dutch, Kara Earl, Insiah Edgecombe, Helen Edwards, Georgia Emm, Marialaura Ena, Jason Eustice, Lilinaz Evans, Charlotte Eves, Christina Farley, Victoria Farmer, Matteo Fernandes, Madeleine Field, Liz Findlay, Ann Foley, Cabe Franklin, Arnold Frazer, Feonia French, Emma Fuller, Sonja Garsvo, Aaron Gauntlett, Fiona Gaze-Fitzgibbon, Raphael Geldsetzer, Annie Gleeson, Judith Glossop, Graciete Gomes De Pina Costa, Serena Gonsalves-Fersch, Claudia Gonzalez Burguete, Juliet Goulding, Rhian Greaves, Aprille Green, Steve Griffin, Bethany Grogan, Robert Grogan, Keith Grout, Eleanor Gussman, Jan Halloran, Lynsey Hamilton, Madeline Hammond, Kate Hands, Beatrice Harbour, Penelope Harris, Tayfun Hassan Onder, Carole Hayward, Peter Hayward, Felicity Hearn, Naomi Heathcote, Rosemary Henderson, Emily Herrett, Amy Hession, Grace Hewitt, Jan Hickman, Anna Hirst, Clare Hodgkin, Cynthia Holness, Veronica Hooles, Ellen Hooper-Doku, Jonathan Hoxby, Michelle Hsieh, Ethan Huang, Kellie Hughes, Nicola Hunter, Susan Innes, Judith Irwin, Eleanor Ivens, Wioletta Jablonska, Ian Jacobsberg, Aissatu Jalloh, Sue James, Amy Jankiewicz, Yvette Jarvis, Judy Jenkin, Eleanor Jenkins, Xiya Jia, Jo Johnson, Hebe Johnson, Luke Johnson, Cat Jones, Dylan Jones, Susan Jones, Jill Jordan, Lydia Julien, Christopher Karwacinski, Molly Kavanagh, Finnbar Keating, Teresa Kennedy, Beth Kershaw, Aida Khalil Gomez, Montserrat Kidwell, Suzanne King, Alex Kolton, Ursula Kopp, Silvia La Greca Bertacchi, Laura Lagana, Jenny Laidlaw, Kirsten Laird, Treveni Lall, James Larter, Sami Latif, Heidi Latronico-Ferris, Elaine Lau, Ana Lavekau, Hilary Lawrence, Van Le, Julia Lee, Inova Lee, Camilla Leonelli, Sok Leong, Dez Lewis, Sisi Li, Joseph Linton, Manila Lippi, Illia Lisak, Sofia Lisak, Jingjing Liu, Nicola Lloyd, Tracy Lodge, Fabia Lonnquist, Mia Lowry, Julie Lung, Ellis Lusted, Katherine Lynch, Rachel Lyons, Amy Majumdar, Sacha Mandel, King Mason, Ashby Mayes, Michael Mcauliffe, Geraldine Mcewan, Angela Mcintosh, Marie Mclernon, Thomas Mclucas, Kate Mcswiney O'Rourke, Hema Mehta, Dom Melaragni, Charlene Michael, Lina Michael-Imobioh, Madeleine Mills, Sally Mills, Pam Milsom, Chris Minton, Margaret Mitchell, Hannah Mizon, Jasvir Singh Modaher, Natalie Mooney, William Morley, Annette Morley, Mary Morrell, Natasha Morrison-Osbourne, Anusha Muhundan, Lesley Mulley, Menelik Mulugeta Claffey, Nicky Mutale, Muhammed Neeliyath, Demelza Nelson, Sam Thi Nguyen-Neugarten, Benjamin Norris, David Nunn, Jacob O'Ceallaigh, Chinedu Ofoegbu, Rofiat Ogundapo, Joyce Ogunfeyimi, Ines-Amael Olenga Disashi, Sofia Oloyede, Joey O'Neill, Stan Onyejekwe, Julie Oram, Karen Orwell, Afua Osei-Asibey, Natalie Osei-Owusu, Sabrina Oufella, Joseph Owen, Amy Page, Jyoti Patel, Sharron Patrick, Debra Payne, Jennifer Payne, Sarah Payne, Stephen Payne, Laura Pethers, Andrea Phillips, Pickard Price Pickard Price, Rebecca Pinder, Michel Pinte, Pearl Prashar, Rachel Pratt, Hannah Pyper, Wesley Quadros, Me! Raghwani, Heenal Raichura, Shanmugapriya Raju, Suzanne Read, Shayne Reason, Fiona Reid, Cheryl Richardson, Angela Riches, Ezra Rimell, Elizabeth Rook, Maria Rosiak, June Rowlands, Vicky Royall, Mayra Ruiz, Davina Russell, Shereen Russell, Lois Russell-Moyle, Zahida Saddiq, Christina Sage, Victoria Salcevich, Nathalie Salic, Jasvin Sanghera, Buledy Sangwa, Alexander Sarriegui, Denise Savill, Natalie Schofield, Peter Scott, Lorayne Seaholme, Lily Seddon-Cox, Rutu Shah, Sonia Shah, Laura Sheldon, Caterina Shepherd, Fiorenza Shepherd, Ingrid Shiel, Alex Sierra Rodriguez, Maria Sierra-Negrete, Joao Roberto Silva Barros, Mandy Simpson, Nisha Sivalingam, Anna Slater, Graham Smith, Lauren Smithers, Luella Solomon, Mim Spettigue, Philly Spurr, Leili Sreberny-Mohammadi, Justas Stanislovas, Julie Stanning, Tracy Stedman, Elizabeth Stevenson, Azul Strong, Paula Suciu, Janet Ann Sullivan, Penelope Summers, Lucy Sutton, Daniel Swani, Carole Swift, Paul Tame, Nhyim Tandooran-Sentain, Hellen Thatcher, Anjila Thomas, Carmenleta Thomas, Helen Thomas, James Thomas, Donna Africa Thompson, Amanda Thorne, Elias Tomarkin, Angela Tomkinson, Victoria Tucker, Karen Tweddle, Silviya Valkova, Jose Antonio Vazquez Mata, Natalia Velaz Ripa, Jayro Viapree, Aaran Vijayakumaran, Caroline Viple, Charlotte Vowden, Andy Wakeford, Samantha Walker, Sarah Walker, Rebecca Wallace, Aileen Walsh, Nancy Wang, Matthew Ward, Rachel Wedderburn, Polly Wells, Lucy Whyte, Bernadine Williams, Lorraine Williams, Clare Wills, Kirsty Witherden, Chris Wolff, Chi-Chung Wong, Gulfem Wormald, Hollie Wynne, Nelia Yakupova, Jun Yang, Carlotta Yannopoulou, Sarah Yarrall, Pei Ye, Rosalind Zeffertt, Cen Zhang, James Zhang-Ly, Min Zhou, Julie Zhu **Green and Pleasant Land** Leance Abi, Maliek Abrahams-Maynard, Yaqub Abukar, Phoebe Adams, Opeyemi Adeyiga, Samuel Adu, Sundeep Aeri, Fatima Ahmed, Hibak Ahmed, Romeo Ajala, Elizabeth Akeju, Victoria Alade, John Alderman, Jolanta Alexandre, Khadijah Alhamdan, Safia Ali, Zahrah Ali, Jaya Rela Alifandi, Sonia Allen, Deshi Alleyne-Fung, Alex Alma, Ricardo Amaya, Kajan Anand, June Andersen, Valerie Anderson, Sylvia Andonopoulos, Stephen Angell, Bronwen Anthony-Downs, Alba De Luna Arce De Kelbaba, Paul Arkilander, Oruccan Arslan, David Ashley, Nicola Ashley, Zachary Aspery, Firdaous Attioui, Kieran Auguste, Christina Babatunde, Sanjit Badhan, Simone Bahr, Alex Bailey, Lisa Bailey, Sue Bailey, Zoe Baird, Blessing Bakare, Victoria Bakare, Bronwen Baker, Holly Baldwin, Ralph Ballard, Jane Barber, Katy Barker, Ashshan Barnaby, Zuriel Barnes-Maselino, Fadumina Barre, Helena Barrowclough, Neil Barton, Simon Bass, Alex Bates, Deepak Batta, Gebru Bayeh, Joshua Beckford, Samuel Beckford, Corinthia Bell, Gemma Benjamin, Mia Benjamin, Christine Benn, Julie Bennett, Lauren Bethune, Eva Bianchi Burgos, Hannah Billington, Catherine Blackwell, Natalia Blake, Natalie Blenford, Hayley Boateng, Nia Boateng, Tyra Boateng, Lailia Boaten-Rolfe, Marc Boettcher, Mateusz Boniewicz, Mariam Boota, Lucia Borrero, Moira Borrero, Sonia Borrero, Joost Bosdijk, Brian Boston, Rachael Bowker, Martin Braham, Catherine Bray, Catherine Breen, Hayley Brightman, Jamie Broadbent, Christian Bromley, Holly Brou, Lizzie Brown, Kate Brown, Brianca Browne, Omari-J'Nay Brown-Smith, Chris Buck, Jane Bugg, Ken Bullen, Ellie-Marie Bunn, Victoria Burton, Des Busteed, Gemma Butterworth, Abraham Byleveldt, Joseph Byrne, Tom Cadley, Calum Callaghan, Max Campbell, Millie Campbell, Nigel Campbell, Shian Campbell, Margaret Canty-Shepherd, Alicia Caprice, Rosalyn Caprice, Christine Carter, Matthew Carter, Lucy Casal, Linda Cearns, Kawthar Chakrouni, Shimari Chang, Muhammad Choudhury, Ann Clark, Sianna Clark, Matt Clawson, Jodie Clerck, Jason Cole, Isabella Collins, Elizabeth Colman, Stephen Concannon, Rachel Connolly, Charles Conrath, Nicola Constantinou, Suliann Conteh-Njawah, Tom Conway, Lynne Copperthwaite, Barry Costas, Helen Coupe, Deja Creary, Tony Crease, Alicia Crockford-Jeffries, Marco Cruse, Mark Cumberworth, Demelza Cundy, Paola Cuneo, Anthony Curran, Kaitlin Cutress, Przemyslaw Czuj, Matthew Dale, Audrey Daley, James Dartnall, Darren David, Jacqueline Davidson, Owen Davies, Alasdair Daw, Anita Dawit, Dina Dawit, Fiona Dawit, Shammai Dawit, Jhon De Souza Leao, Olivia -Rose Deer, Ruth Deer, Lauren Derry, Isabella Dixon, Ella Dokk-Olsen, Serena Dolan, Zakairiya Donaldson, Tamara Donn, Hugo Doswald, Elijah Doueu, Stephen Drew, Moira Duhig, Lindy Dumas, Rachel Dunkley, Jenny Dunne, John Dunne, Michelle Durant, Laura Eagland, Teresa Earle, Onella Edde, Sophie Ede, Nils Edelman, Anne Elise Efejuku, Annette Efejuku, Marie Antoinette Efejuku, Lucy Elwell, Ann Emmons, Alex Enciso Ripoll, Helen Enebeli, Billy Eskelson, Grace Evans, Rory Evans, Oluwabukola Eweoya, Audrey Eyre, Lindsay Fallows, Akin Fashola, Yu Feng, Susan Jane Ferguson, Michael Fernandez, Michael Flannery, Julian Ford, Tyane Forde, Selina Frazer, Antonio Furione, Matthew Gardner, Regat Gebreu, Sabrina George, Sue Germon, Robert Ghazi, Deborah Gibbon, Matthew Gibson, Steven Gibson, Sabina Giri, Vesela Gladicheva, Tim Goldman, Matt Goldsmith, Thomas Goodman, Kamaal Gordon, Kamari Gordon, Colin Granger, Siobhan Grealy, Melanie Greenstock, Maya Greenwell, Patrik Grega, Lisa Gwinnell, John Hague, Henry Hall, Sharon Halliday, Frances Hamilton, Rhys Hamilton, Kate Hammond, Jennifer Handovsky, Megan Handovsky-Boyd, Kailan Hanson, Daniel Harland, Nicolette Harley, Cameron Harmon, Anita Harper, Patrick Harrild, Michael Harris, Kelly Harrison, David Harvey, Kerry Harwood, Jasmine Hassan, Camille Hastings-Prosser, Sebastian Hau-Walker, Paige Hazel, Sian Henderson, Virginia Henry, Andres Hermosa, Harry Hill, Emma Hills, Isaiah Hills, Maddy Hilton, Helena Hird, Gary Hoang, Dianne Hoctor, Vince Hoctor, Jamie Hodge, Patricia Hodgins, Neil Holloway, Anthony Holme, Craig Hopkinson, Charlotte Horobin, Gareth Horton, Antonio Hrinko, Simon Hubbert, Danny Hughes, Zakir Hussain, Chikwe Ibeakanma, Cleopatra Idemudia, Hayder-Marie Igbonachi-Obioma, Khadeejah Imran, Alice Ingham, Lewis Inglis, Kay Instrell, Irmak Islek, Hugo Iturralde Caballero, Evelina Jakaite, Christine Janssen, Pavithra Jayakumar, Louise Jefferson, Beverley Jenkins, Mark Jenner, Steven Johnston, Bethany Johnstone, Hilary Jones, Linda Jones, Kelly Joyce, Paul Jubb, Malachi Junaid, Katia Kaczynski, Aminata Kamara, Harriet Kamu, Sharad Kanwar, Sedef Karayel, Maame-De Karikari Brobbey, Adwoa Karikari-Brobbey, Eryk Karys, Louise Kearney, Dorothea Keeper, Humphrey Keeper, Ayman Kemal, David Kenneth-Elue, Selma Khelifi, Thea King, Richard King, Aryna Kokoryna, Andrea Kovacs, Samantha Kowalczyk, Shanice Kowfie, Gramos Krasniqi, Rahime Krasniqi, India Kumar, Anita Kusi, Maxine Kwok-Adams, Ken Lalobo, Winnie Lam, Zubeida Lambat, Ryan Langley, Marcos Lastra Castro, Laiba Latif, Yahya Latif, Ayshah Lawrence, Anjola Lawson, Boluwatife Lawson, Una Le Meur, Ryan Lee, Danielia Lee, Jean-Jacques Lescure, Franciszka Lesniak, Olaf Lesniak, Alexander Limb, Katharine Limb, Rachel Limb, Sarah Limb, Hanna Lindley-Jones, Jonathan Lipton, Elizabeth Lleshi, Susan Long, Jennifer Lord, Lindsey Lovatt, Graham Lovell, Jonathan Lovett, Robyn Luckham, Sophie Luker, Emily Luong, Colin Mabey, Vincent Macias, Nicholas Mackay, Clare Mackmin, Jasia Macmeikan, Katherine Makulska, Dorcas Malemba, Rami Malik Chowdhury, Marcie Mallea, William Maloney, Simone Mameli, Emmanuel Mandangi, Sinead Mandlik, Brian Manning, Elayne Manton, Hannah March, Madeleine Marshall, Lucy Marti, Atiya Martins, Duke Maselino, John Maskell, Paul Massey, Tyrik Matthews, Zara Matthews, Chikara Mbakwe, Rosanna Mcdonald, Belinda McFarlane, Estie Mclaurin, Maxine Mcminn, Constance Meade, Cristian Medeiros, Richard Merrick, David John Miller, Paul Milner, Joshua Mintori, Jasu Mistry, Debjani Mitra, Jasdeep Mlait, Conti Moll, Moganie Moodley, Russell Moon, Christine Moore, Angela Morgan, Caterina Moropoulou, Samuel Morson, Elena Mortelliti, Sam Moutet, Kabir Mughal, Lesley Murphy, Zara Mutabazi, Ed Naish, Surinder Nandra, Tasha Nelson, Sheridan Nelson, Tarundeep Neta, Guneet Neta, Catherine Neufeld, Hazel Neville, Tom Newman, Sofina Nichollis, Leigh Norgrove, Alun North, Jevan Nuby, Pamela Nuttall, Stephen Oatley, Ciara O'Brien, Fintan O'Connor, Kate O'Connor, Shanaya Ojeda, Christian Okadigbo, Olurotimi Oke, Lorenzo Okpewo, Ebenezer Okyere-Mireku, Libby O'Leary, Emmanuel Omogbai, Rachel Omogbai, Osas Omorodion-Umaru, Deborah Omoruanzoje, Safiyya Onanuga, Ilze Ose, Adebukonla Osinusi, Noel Otley, Fureel Otubu, Faith Oyegun, Stanley Padmore, Archie Page, Emily Palmer, Kathryn Papworth-Smith, David Parker, Melissa Parmar, Tracy Parr, Ann Parsons, Lesley Parsons, Marion Pastellas, Maariyah Patel, Rubina Patel, Alan Paterson, Alan Patient, Kasper Pauley, Siobhan Paull, Aoife Pearson, Maria Pedraza, Yun Yun Pei, Linyu Peng, Lara Perkins, Mark Peters, Jayne Phillips, Clare Pike, Sajeevaney Pillai, Jeanette Pinho, Kenni Poulsen, Nyima Pratten, Helen Preston, Charlotte Priestley, Dalia Puertas Jimenez, Charlotte Pye, Laurent Quenelle, Sarah Quinn, Christine Radu, Fawziyah Rafique, Mahdhi Rahman, Zia Ralston, Jenny Rampling, Steve Ranford, Jen Rankin, Ali Rashid, Alex Read, Olivia Reardon, Alison Redford, Alex Reece, Paris Reefer, Selvin Reid, Sarvjit Renoo, James Rhodes, Allan Richards, Liz Ridgewell, Marc Ridley, Oscar Ridout, Julia Ridout, Mya Robert, Adam Robertson, Paul Robinson, Chris Rogers, Phil Rosenberg, Matt Ross, Christine Ru Pert-Em-Hru, Gerald Ruddock, Jennifer Ruffell, Kareena Rummun Soobaraydoo, Kieran Rushton, Terence Russ, Jo Ryan, Tim Ryan, Serhad Sahin, Nick Sait, Bolaji Salokun, Jolene Sampson, Joseph Sanders, Tony Sanders, Lee Sargent, Annapoorany Sathiyamoorthy, Jimmy Savvas, Chris Scott, Vanessa Scott, Heather Scratcher, Lesley Anne Scutter, Chloe Selby, Alpha Sesay, Anna Sewell, Atifah Shah, Idris Shaikh, Zeenat Shaikh, Joseph Shambrook, Maisie Sheehy, Esther Shepherd, Magdeline Shepherd, Ruth Shepherd, Oliwia Siemion, Andrew Sigley, Gabriel Silveira, Chrissy Simmonds, Miriam Simmons, Alexis Simpson, Gerald Simpson, Natalie Simpson, Martin Skipper, Bartosz Skonieczny, Annetta Slade, Kungwa Small, Natalie Smellie, Alfie Smiley, David Smith, Elaine Smith, Jaheem Smith, Sarah Smith, Ann Snell, Lesley Snelson, Rick Snow, Bernie Solly, Leah Spence, Simon Springall, Chris Stacey, Daniel Stacey, Glenda Stamp, Oksana Stasyuk, Mark Stephenson, John Stewart, Coby Stickland, Demi Stickland, Claire Stone, Graham Storey, James Storm, Craig Strachan, Sam Stutterheim, Charlotte Sutton, Miriam Swainsbury, Hannah Sweeney, Yvonne Swift, Josephine Swindell, Thomas Swindell, Bellmani Takueni, Sophie Tamlyn, Mackenzie Tang, Stephen Tang, Nikki Taylor, Susan Terenzio, Ewoenam Tetteh, Johanna Tewolde, Maria Tewolde, Mary Thomas, Samuel Thomas, Thugipa Thurendiran, Kate Thurlow, Kerry Tokley, Susannah Traill, Georgia Tredgett, Amanda Truelove, Chris Truscott, Anne-Marie Tucker, Robert Turner, Kayla Tyson, Maria Uddin, Ashiana Umarji, Ibrahim Umer, Jennifer Usman Vargas, Lara Varga, Non Vaughan-O'Hagan, Sandra Vince, Andrew Vourdas, Jennifer Wade, Patrick Wagstaff, Patricia Wakefield, Tim Wakeling, Chelsea Walker, Michelle Walker, Heather Wallington, George Walsh, Grace Walsh, Patrick Walton, Cecilia Ward, Hana Ward, Andrew Warren, Flavia Watts, Lara Wear, Charlie Webb, George Webb, Joseph Webb, Sam Webster, Marina White, James Whittington-Phillips, Ruan Whyler, Shannon-Louise Whyte, Diana Williams, Florence Williamson, John Wilson, June Wilson, David Worswick, Rachel Wray, Emma Wyton, Linda Patricia Wyton, Tommy Wyton Wyton, Aki Yamamoto, Udara Yapa, Carlos Yebra López, Canev Yorganci, Rosemary York, Mert Zeytun **Pandemonium** Derek Abbey, Ian Abbott, Laura Abbott, Zenab Abdirahman, Zak Abdullah, Lynsey Abernethy, Joyce Abosi, Massimo Acquisto, Glen Acton, Acuña Acuña Quintana, Daniel Adaja, Dominic Adaja, Jane Adams, Mosun Adebayo, Victor Adedayo-Ogunruku, Cornelius Adenekan, Tolu Adepegba, James Adutt, Otibho Agbareh, Abiodun Agbeleye, Solomon Aggninie, Andrea Agrell, Angela Agyei, Des Agyekumhene, Patrick Ahern, Shamsuddin Ahmed, Marcus Aitman, Abdu Akemel, Adeola Akitoye, Rimi Aktar, Imad Al Dakkak, Rafiqul Alam, Javier Albarracin Perea, Alister Albert, Charles Albert, Rachel Alcock, Kelly Al-Dakkak, Charlotte Aldhouse, Julie Aldred, Holly Alexander, Karen Algacs, Peter Algacs, Mehmet Ali, Mohammed Ali, Seb Alias, Sudheer Alladi, Claire Alleguen, Brian Allen, Jim Allen, Jonny Allen, Michael Allen, Steven Allen, Barney Alley, Laura Alleyne, Tom Allin, Amonn Al-Mahrouq, Ed Alton, Nazare Alves, Dilesh Amlani, Zahra Amlani, Beverley Amoah, Ryan Amstad, Sabrina Anderson, Sean Anderson, David Anderton, Rene Andrew, Thomas Andrews, Matthew Anello, Karl Anns, Angelina Ansah, Marius Antanavicius, Gerard Antony, Sally Antwi, Veronica Apolinario, Lucy Appleton, Dejaar Arabshahi Fard, Baven Arasaretnam, Ricardo Araujo, Kathleen Arbuckle, Alan Archer, Gabrielle Archer, Emma Arden, Stefan Arestis, Kate Argent, June Arinze, Toni Armiger, Keith Armour, Alex Armstrong, Ben Armstrong, David Armstrong, Amanda Arnold, David Arnold, Hamilton Arroyo Ospina, Samuele Aru, Michael Arulanantham, Ravi Arya, Khelisyah Ashamu, Ewan Ashburn, Ian Ashby, Thomas Ashcroft - Nowicki, Andrew Ashford, Peter Ashley, Stella Asonye, Susan Aspinall, Gina Atherton, Steve Atkins-Steel, Greta Attridge, Gill Attrill, Usharani Augstine, Omar Augustus-Brown, Amit Aujla, Ashley Austen, Fabio Avarello, Lawrence Ayeni, Alastair Ayliffe, Shervin Azarian, Subash Bacheta, Jimmy Badal, William Badham, Alex Badrick, Abenaa Baffoe, Kirsty Baffour, Muhammed Bah, Joe Bai, Richard Bailey, Anthony Bailey, Alasdair Bain, Stephen Baines, Tejvir Bains, John Bainton, Alex Baker, Alexandra Baker, Cheryl Baker, Emily Baker, John Baker, Richard Baker, Maathini Balachandran, Vicki Baldwin, Laura Bale, David Balfour, Liz Ball, Steve Ball, Charlotte Ballard, Haiko Ballieux, Bernie Bane, Morli Bangura, Susan Banks, Andrew Bannister, Judy Bannister, Kevin Bannister, Amrit Barard, Karen Baratram, Marvin Barbe, Yvanna Barbe, Martyn Barber, Geoff Bargas, Jennie Barham, Tuahid Barik, Lynn Barker, Clive Barley, Jason Barlow, Matthew Barnes, Rachael Barnes, Peter Barnett, Virginia Baron, Tim Baros, Denise Barr, James Barr, Susan Barr, Lisa Barrett, Kathryn Barriskill, John Barron, Kieran Bartlett, Jo Barton, Sally Barton, Arafat Bashir, Corinne Bass, Edward Bateman, Arthur Bates, Helen Bates, Greg Battarbee, David Batten, Hepburn Battersby, Roy Batty, Erik Baurdoux, Audrey Baxter, Ole Baxter, Neil Bayley, Tristan Baylis, Matthew Bazeley, Anthony Bealing, Mark Bealing, Nick Beat, Kat Beaty, Mark Beautement, Sven Becker, Alexander Beckett, Garrath Beckwith, Phil Bedwell, Volker Behrends, Hiruy Belaye, Timothy Belcher, Martin Bell, Rashidat Bello, David Belnick, Volodymyr Bendikov, Conrad Benjamin, Gillian Bennet, Charlotte Bennett, Clive Bennett, Daryl Bennett, James Bennett, Simon Bennett, David Benny, Hilary Benson, Tim Benson, James Benwell, Niv Ben-Yehuda, Lucy Beresford-Knox, George Beretas, Carolyn Berkeley, Birte Berlemann, Matt Bernard, Sally Berridge, Adam Berry, Daniel Bessong, Melissa Bethune, Katrina Betteridge, Valeria Bettini, Mark Bevan, John Beveney, Tim Beveridge, Harpreet Bhal, Jasmeet Bhambra, Bhav Bhawsar, Bhundia Bhundia, Jamie Biddle, Adam Biggs, Dave Biggs, Gary Biggs, Sammy Bikoulis, Annie Billing, Kate Binchy, Jean Bincliffe, Caroline Bircham, James Bird, Katie Birmingham, Kathryn Birrell, Dav Bisessar, Emily Bishop, Konrad Bishop, Rodney Bishop, Steve Bishop, Liz Blackburn, Alan Blackmore, Ian Blackshire, Katie Blake, Nathaniel Blake, Padraig Blake, Angela Blakemore, Paul Blakemore, Rob Blakemore, Emma Blamey, Tibor Blok, Adam Joseph Bloomfield, Chris Bloomfield, Thomas Bloomfield, Darren Boakye-Adjei, Peter Boakye-Wreh, Margaret Boden, Paro Bodini, Bertrand Bodson, Jemma Bogan, Nadine Bogan, Jon Bola, Sylvie Bolioli, Clive Bolton, Sumanth Bommarthi, Helen Bond, Cynthia Bonds, Kaysea Bonds, Elena Bonfiglio Esper, Sophie Bonnefoi, Jodie Borer, Murray Borthwick, Thomas Borwick, Jo Bott, Jenn Botterill, Andrew Bottomley, Adrian Bouillin, Natasha Boult, James Bourton, Barbora Bousova, David Bower, Fredrica Bowkett, Sean Bowles, Nicholas Bowman, Ian Boyd, Sean Boyle, Vicky Boyle, Rich Bradish, Shaun Brannigan, Becky Brass, Martin Braund, Philip Brecht, Philip Bremang, Laura Brennan, Simon Brett, Steve Brett, Rachel Brewer, Cathrine Bright, James Bright, Tristan Bright, David Brighton, Jayson Brinkler, Nigel Brinklow, Steve Broad, Phyllis Broadbent, Joe Brookman, Laura Brooks, Jonathan Brooks, Beccy Brown, Ben Brown, Cathy Brown, David Brown, Delroy Brown, Jen Brown, Karen Brown, Kat Brown, Lennox Brown, Louise Brown, Robert Brown, Sarah Brown, Scott Brown, Stuart Brown, Susan Brown, Bernita Brumant, Elvena Brumant, Evangelica Brumant, Sylvester Brumant, Keith Brunger, Keith Bryan, Deborah Bryant, Ben Buckby Jones, Kathy Buley, Stephen Bulfield, Julia Bull, Clare Bullen, Jenny Bunclark, Caroline Bunker, Sally Bunker, Catherine Bunten, Deborah Burke, Paul Burne, Penny Burrows, Sophie Burrows, Michael-Deon Burton, Olivier Buschino, Andrew Butler, Grant Butler, Sarah Butler, Tom Butler, Stephen Byrd, Bruce Cade, Michael Cafferkey, Xinzheng Cai, Stefan Caiafa, Asa Cairns, Allan Callaby, Alex Callaghan, Jonathan Calvert, Candy Calvert-Ansari, Adrian Calvo Valderrama, Daniel Cameron, Kadian Cameron, Melanie Cameron, Samuel Cameron, David Cammock, Hollie Campbell, Sean Campbell-Hynes, Scott Campling, Vikki Canniford, Ben Canning, William Cantwell, Orlando Capitanio, Robert Capper, Benedict Carandang, Ben Carpenter, Carol Carr, Melanie Carr, Eliene Santana Carreiro Carreiro, John Carstairs, Jason Carter, Anne-Marie Carter, Adam Cartwright, Diogo Carvalho, Maureen Carvana, Anucska Case, Michael Casey, Sony Castillon, Joanna Cavan, Louise Cave, Omer Cavusoglu, Scott Cawley, Valeria Cazas, Anxo Cereijo Roibas, Richard Chadwick, Dia Chakravarty, Ruth Chalke, Liz Chamberlain, Rebecca Chamberlain, Richard Chamberlain, Chris Chambers, Philip Chambers, Mark Champion, Sylvia Chan, Harsharan Chana, Kenneth Chapman, Noor Charania, Andrew Charles, Darius Chatfield, John Chatfield, Kakia Chatsiou, Leo Chauhan, Vinesh Chauhan, Tarun Chavda, Raj Rani Chawla, Will Chegwidden, S Chelvan, Donald Chen, Kahtoong Cheong, Robert Cherry, Suet Yee Cheung, Chinenye Chigbu, Raymond Chihata, John Child, Nick Childs, Peter Childs, Brandon Chin, Marianne Chipperfield, Chiutsu Chiutsu, Arfuman Choudhury, Shaz Choudhury, Beverly Christie, Daniel Chu, Sandy Chui, Trevor Church, Rosa Cisneros, Matt Clack, Anne Clark, Charles Clark, Elaine Clark, Hugh Clark, Ian Clark, James Clark, Nick Clark, Hayden Clarke, Phil Clarke, Ricardo Clarke, Simon Clarke, Wesley Clarke, Katie Cleanthous, Christine Cleaver, Trevor Clitheroe, Marion Close, James Clossick, David Coatesworth, Rachael Coggins, Joseph Cohen, Heather Coke, Christina Coker, Foluke Cole, Jonathan Cole, Neil Coleman, Eddie Coleman, Ashley Coleridge, Nicola Coles, Chris Collier, Lynn Collier, Mark Collins, Gail Collins, Kieran Collyer, Michael Colman, Carla Colquhoun, Mark Philip Compton, Paul Conlan, Eki Connolly, Patrick Connolly, Amy Connor, Scott Connor, Amelia Cook, Stephen Cook, Declan Cooke, Simon Cooksey, Matthew Cooksey, Lisa Coomey, Jamie Cooper, Natalie Cooper, Matthew Copeland, Julia Copeland, Paul Copeland, Andrew Copley, Mathew Copping, James Copple, Raymond Corder, Simon Cork, Thomas Cornell, Peter Cornford, Roy Correa, Simona Costanzo, Chris Costello, Jim Costello, Josie Coster, Marie-Caroline Cotel, Susan Cotton, Lesley Covington, Alistair Cowan, Anthony Cowan, Christopher Cowan, Iain Cowell, Janine Cowie, Annette Cox, Daniel Cox, Ian Cox, Colin Coxall, Philippa Cradock, Ross Craib, Gareth Crane, Steven Crane, Alec Creed, Nick Creed, Andres Crespo, Nicholas Creswell, Terrie Creswell, Blair Crichton, David Crick, Darren Crisp, Suzanne Cross, Gillian Crow, Keith Crowe, Shannon Crowe, Sharon Crowe, Simon Crowhurst, Shaun Crowther, Pez Cuckow, Danielle Cudjoe Vincent, Christopher Cudmore, Martin Cullen, Andrew Culpan, Brian Cumming, Nadia Currie, Sarah Cusack, Victoria Custerson, John Cuthbert, Rodney Da Silva, Vander Da Silva, Vena Dacent, Neerav Dahya, Vince Dalaimo, Peter Dale, Kwabena Dallaway, Michelle Dalmacio, Adam Dalton, Barbara Dandy, Christopher Daniel, Chris Daniels, Tunde Danmole, Susmita Das, Adam Davey, Peya Davidovic, John Davidson, Lorna Davidson, Chloe Davies, Jill Davies, Mark Davies, Meryt Davies, Michael Davies, Peter Davies, Phill Davies, Toby Davies, Wendy Davies, Christine Davis, David Davis, Havva Davis, Jan Davis, John Davis, Thomas Davis, George Davison, Kathy Davison, Paul Davison Davison, William Davison, Sally Daw, Adam Dawes, Hayley Dawson, Phil Dawson, Jacqueline Day, Alexandre Yemaoua Dayo, Raquel De Almeida, Leonardo De Almeida Pancione, Scott De Blasio, Silvia Maria De De Mello, Carlos De Oliveira Gomes, Kim De Ram, Pedro De Sousa, Rene De Sousa, Carla De Sousa Coutinho, Charles Dean, Helen Dear, Samuella Dedji, Alesha De-Freitas, Matthew Deighton, David Dellaire, Patrick Dempsey, Emma Dengate, Rob Dennett, Christopher Derbyshire, Julius T Dete, Annick Devillard-Pickavance, Ruth Dewdney, Emma Dewhurst, Kevin Hugh Deyna-Jones, Mani Dhani, Mohan Dhar, Jag Dhesi, Nuno Dias, Jairo Diaz, Rimini Dick-Carr, Guy Dickens, Roger Dickson, Gillian Dinan, Chan Divani, Ben Dixon, Marina Dixon, Nigel Dixon, Sam Dixon, Amanda Dodd, Michael Dodd, Dennis Dolina, Jessykar Donald, Oliver Donaldson, Peter Donn, Carl Donoghue, Catherine Dook, Maria Dos Santos Veiga, Imran Dosani, Emily Douglas, Sue Douglass, Colm Downes, Frederick Dows, Beverley Drain, John Dray, Phill Drew, Dmitry Drozdov,

Kathleen Drum, Chris D'Souza, Miriam Dubois, Peter Dudas, Mark Dudley, Gwyneth Duhy, Fiona Duncan, Holly Dunlop, Ross Dunning, Dave Duxbury, Stephen East, Daniela Eavis, Vicki Eddens, Iain Edmondson, Talya Edmondson, Michelle Edney, Rebecca Edwards, Tom Eeles, Jonathan Efoloko, Elizabeth Eley, Henry Eliot, Penny Elkins, Nicola Elliott, Thomas Elliott, Adrian Ellis, Chris Ellis, Philip Ellis, Sophie Ellis, Jennifer Emerson, Russell Endean, Nicole English, Shane Enright, Ryan Epps, Anna Eriksson, Patrick Erni, Giles Ernsting, Taiwo Eshinlokun, Rahim Esmail, Rachel Espeute, Louise Etheridge, Marc Etherington, Russell Eubanks, Adrian Evans, Cheryl Evans, David Evans, James Evans, Jim Evans, Mark Evans, Rachel Evans, Richard Evans, Lauren Eve, Simon Evison, Elke Fabian, Zuza Fabiszak, Remi Fadare, Felipe Fagundes, Marcos Fagundes, Richard Fairs, Yuan Fang, Michelle Farber, Julia Farestvedt, Matt Fargie, Ana Clara Faria Do Amaral, Margaret Farmiloe, Susan Farnsworth, Alison Farrell, Rebecca Farrow, Del Fay, Ann Feloy, Carol Felton, Carol Felts, Gary Fentiman, David Fenton, Harris Fenton, Colin Fergusson, Peter Ferguson, Denis Fernando, Fernando Ferreira Dos Santos, Jack Ferro, Rebekah Fielding-Haynes, David Figg, Caroline Firman, Caroline Fisher, Sarah Fisher, Simon Fisher, Gill Fitnum, Alistair Fitzpatrick, Liam Fitzpatrick, Martin Fitzgerald, Preston Fitzgerald, Jazz Flaherty, Jim Fletcher, Nicolas Fleury, Peter Flew, William Flinn, Adriana del Carmen Florez Lopez, Jan Flower, Katherine Fodor, Ian Foley, Paul Foley, Timothy Foley, Matthew Folson, Richi Fontaine, Oliver Foot, Scott Forbes, Aundray Forde, Judith Forde, Michelle Forde, Andrew Forey, Paolo Fornasiero, Elliot Forward, Bray Foster, Colin Foster, Cru Fox, Hugh Fox, Steve Fox, Sue Foyle, Gregory Frame, Phil Francis, Roy Francis, Otis Leroy Francis, Craig Francis, Miriam Franz, Giuseppe Fraschini, Emma Frayne, David Freeborn, Bill Freeman, Shaun Freeman, Claire French, James French, Jonathan French, Sergio Freschi, Michael Frewin, Scott Friesen, Graham Frosdick, Christopher Frost, Robert Frost, Matt Frye, Dancemastergozi Fulani, Sean Fullerton, Polly Fung, Lorraine Furneaux, Justin Fynes, Henry Fynn, Anvar Gabidullin, Christian Gabriel, Jemima Gaddam, Matt Gage, Charlie Galarza, Emma Gale, Chris Galloway, Cordula Galster, Ej Gamboa, David Gamez, Dimisha Gami, Christian Gangeri, Poushali Ganguli, Duncan Ganley, Bin Gao, Qinquan Gao, Manuel García Sanchez, Kathryn Garden, Karen Gardiner, Charlotte Garey, Simon Garlinge, Christian Gastaldello, Sonia Gaus Agusti, Lucia Gavalova, Claude Gayle, Andrea Gazzola, James Gbadamosi, Jennifer Geary, Amanda-Jane Geddes, Andrew Geddes, Lara Gee, Thomas Gell, Tina Gellie, Cally Gentle, Jackie Gentle, Simon Gentry, Lorraine George, Velko Georgievski, Theodosis Georgiou, Lisa Gervais, David Gethin, Lee Gibbons, Joyce Gibbs, Julian Gibbs, Bramwell Gibson, Nick Gibson, Jagjit Gidda, Kieran Giffen, Howard Gilbert, Chris Gilchrist, Justin Giles, Chris Giles, Adrian Gill, Robert Gill, Sukhdev Gill, Sean Gillen, David Gillson, Gilly Gilmour, Luke Girvan, Shaz Gitay, Danny Gleeson, Denesh Gnanalingam, Darren Goad, Bryan Goddard, Tim Goddard, Aidan Godwin, Michelle Goel, Sandeep Gohil, Suzanne Goldberg, Janine Goldblatt, Doreen Golding, Max Goldman, Chris Gomersall, John Gomez, Nestor Raul Gomez Usme, Joseph Gonzales, Alina Gonzalez, Leo Gonzalez, Maria Goodall, Dan Goodhind, Peter Goodrick-Clarke, Renee Goodwin, Dennis Gordon, Justin Gordon, Peter Gordon, Malcolm Gorrie, Stewart Goshawk, Lydia Gosnell Dougan, Himanish Goswami, Amanda Gotham, Philip Goudal, Keef Gould, Marilyn Gould, Neil Goulder, Raju Govindasamy Muthuswamy, John Graddon, Matthew Graham, Bruce Graham, Eric Grainger, Piero Grandinetti, John Grant, Andy Gray, Julius Gray, Lizi Gray, Felix Greaves, Matthew Green, Robert Green, Sadeysa Greenaway-Bailey, Vistra Greenaway-Harvey, Elisabeth Greenbank, Roberta Greenhalgh, Daniel Greenhow, Alison Gregory, James Gribble, Kim Griffiths, Lynda Griffiths, Laura Grist, Antti Gronlund, Victoria Groves, Alan Guest, Xiaofei Gui, Louisa Gummer, Amanda Gunn, Yan Guo, Anil Gupta, Rajeev Gupta, Alaettin Gurarslan, Kiran Guraya, Abigail Gurr, Keiji Gurung, Mike Guy, Guzman Guzman Gonzalez, Jo Gweshe, Elsa Gwilliam, Keif Gwinn, James Gwynne, Carol Gysin, Peter Hackmann, Aceil Haddad, Kie Haddow, Loretta Hadjikoumi, Emina Hadzifejzovic, Nick Hafezi, John Hail, Helen Haile, George Hajiantonis, Matthew Hale, Stef Hale, Rebecca Hales, Alison Hall, Joey Hall, Phill Hall, Thomas Hall, Will Hall, Muj Hameed, Beverley Hamilton, Craig Hamilton, David Hamilton, David Hampson-Ghani, Edward Han, Ian Hancock, Diana Hancox, Steven Handley, Christopher Hanratty, Carol Hanson, Flo Hanson, Ryu Harada, Jonathan Harbourne, Daniel Harding, Tamsin Harding, Phil Hardisty, Joshua Hargense, James Hargreaves, Anjali Hariharan, Dorinia Harley, Kenneth Harlick, Jordan Harold, Melanie Harper, Roachelle Harper, Edward Harris, Jack Harris, James Harris, Judith Harris, Richard Harris, Rob Harris, Bridget Harrison, Nancy Harrison, Richard Harrison, Stephen Harrison, Kim Hart, Gideon Hart, Lucy Hartley, Ben Hartley, Robert Hartop, Jamie Harvey, Kate Harvey, Paul Harvey, Syed Raza Hasan, Stephen Haskins, Douglas Hassal, Arthur Haste, Oluseghun Haughton, Tom Haughton, Paul Hawes, Virginia Hawke, Peter Hawker, Catherine Hawkes, Matthew Hawksworth, Andrew Hawtin, Marge Hay, Kevin Haycock, Richard Hayes, Ben Hayter, Lesley Hayward, Dominic Hayward-Peel, Sijin He, Janet Head, Tim Hearn, Nicola Heather, Jo Hedges, Peter Hegan, Alex Henderson, Liam Henderson, Shirley Henry, Anne Henwood, Brad Hepburn, David Hepburn, Ferenc Hepp, Gavin Heppelthwaite, Ruth Herbert, Fabian Hermosa Alarcon, Henry Herrera, Tobias Herrmann, Cristina Heselden, Andrew Hesselden, Jason Hewitt, Jonathan Hewett, Stephen Hewitt, Max Heywood, Kathleen Hicks, Mandella Higgins, Karl Hildebrandt, Dave Hill, Nicola Hill, Tim Hill, Louise Hilliard, Catherine Hillis, Steve Himbury, Kirsty Hinchliff, Wayne Hincks, Felicity Hindle, Doug Hing, Rich Hinwood, Graham Hirst, Alex Hirst, Naomi Hiscock, Martin Hissey, David Hitchen, Louisa Hitchen, Stephanie Hitchins, Sarah Hixson, Andrew Hodges, Janet Hodgson, Nicola Hogg, Nick Hogwood, Wilfred Hohenkirk, Janet Holden, Emma Holden, Laura Hollands, Marica Holliday, Chris Hollis, Zoe Holloway, Alex Holmes, Andy Holmes, Catrina Holmes, Matthew Holmes, Michael Holmes, Jeffrey Holt, Lewis Holt-Brown, Jenny Honeybill, Bhupinder Hoonjan, Barry Hooper, Clifford Hopes, Ildi Horvath, Julie Horwood, Helen Hosking, Manzor Hossain, Peter Hotchkiss, Christine Houghton, Chris Houston, Edward Howard, Howell Howell, Max Hoy, Chris Hoye, Sylvia Hoye, Michal Hrncir, Matt Hryciw, Boyi Huang, Jane Huang, Zixiang Huang, Raymond Huggins, Dorothy Hughes, Katrina Hughes, Keith Hughes, Richard Hughes, Jill Huguet, Meleta Huie - Drummond, Charlie Huins, Anthony Hull, Nathan Humphreys, Nigel Humphriss, Robert Hunt, Tim Hunt, Robin Hunte, Drew-Levi Huntsman, Paul Hurford, Chris Hurst, Darren Hurst, Josue Hurtado, Riz Husain, Adal Hussain, Adnan Hussain, Akthar Hussain, Mudaser Hussain, Shaon Hussain, Wasif Hussain, Joshua Hustwick, Moses Hutchinson-Pascal, Jason Huynh, Hadi Ibrahim, Amanda Idowu, Mohammed Idriss, Tina Ilsley, Haider Ilyas, Mary Impey, Jerry Inniss, Vicky Instone, Cyrus Iravani, Stephen Irvine, Matthew Irving, Robert Irving, Helen Isaacs, Alberto Isidro, Nurul Islam, Munira Ismail, Sajith Ismail, Helen Ives, Ben Izard, Chris Jack, Annette Jackson, Karen Jackson, Cristiane Jacobs, Ilan Jadoul, Manish Jagatiya, Milena Jakupovic, Caryl James, Aubrey James, Michael James, Paul James, Roger James, Stephen James-Yeoman, Dzestina Janarauskaite, Stuart Janes, Liam Jarnecki, Zuri Jarrett-Boswell, Gary Jarvis, Sunny Jaspal, Isobel Jayawardane, Loriston Jeakngs, Mark Jeary, Martin Jee, Suzie Jeeves, Monica Jelley, Lewis Jenkins, Pam Jezard, Megha Jhaveri, Jingyuan Jiang, Mohamed Jiva, Genevieve Job, Kulvinder Johal, John John, Angela John-Baptiste, Andrew Johnson, Colin Johnson, Edwin Johnson, Kerrisa Johnson, Larry Johnson, Nathan Johnson, Vanessa Johnson, Mark Johnson-Brown, Adrian Johnston, Andrew Johnston, Carole Jolly, Patrick Jolly, Alexander Jones, Allan Jones, Caris Jones, Charles Jones, Gwendoline Jones, Helena Jones, Jenn Jones, Martin Jones, Matthew Jones, Natalie Jones, Nicholas Jones, Rebecca Jones, Steve Jones, Sue Jones, Suzanna Jones, Beverley Jordan, Christine Josef-Santos, Harold Joseph, Hazel Joseph, Joel Joseph, Judith Joseph, Roshini Joseph, Sandra Joseph, Anil Joshi, Madhuri Joshi, Mukesh Joshi, Nikita Joshi, Helen Jousselin, Cameron Judd, Graham Judge, James Jukes, Grzegorz Junka, Vinay Kabra, Mohau Kachula, Eugenia Kaka, Monika Kalde, Tejinder Kalsi, Lilly Kambo, Maulik Kamdar, Laxmi Kanbi, Daryl Kane, Joshua Kanu, Alice Kaphan, Janikunai Karolina, Carla Kaspar, Sema Kaur, Brian Kavanagh, Grainne Kavanagh, Shelagh Kavanagh, Grant Kay, David Kearney, Romany Kebar, John Keech, Daniel Keen, Alicia Keeping, Joe Keerthiratna, Philip Kelly, Neil Kelsey, Peter Keltie, Alastair Kember, Howard Kemp, Benyam Kenbata, Josie Kennedy, Lindsay Kennedy, Georgina Kennington, Jenny Kent, Katherine Kent, Stephen Kent, Kelly Kenubia, Peter Kenyon, Matt Keogh, Kanji Kerai, Amerz Kerwick, Alex Kessie, Claudia Keston, Catherine Ketsimur, Sam Key, Simon Key, Pareena Khairdin, Cyril Khamai, Jahanzeb Khan, Muhammed Khan, Tariq Khan, Kamal Khaveripour, Kibue-Ngare Kibue, Hilary Kidman, John Kim, Yerrie Kim, Anthony King, Blair King, Kirsten King, Steve King, Warren King, Paul Kingham, Nicola Kingman, Cassie Kingston, Jackie Kinnear, Hellen Kirby, Angela Kiss, Tim Kiss Freitas, Charlotte Kitteridge, Andrea Kitzberger, Carol Kleinschmidt, Elizabeth Kliman, Ryan Kliszat, Chris Knight, Lesley Knight, Eve Knights, Melanie Knoedler, Deborah Knox-Hewson, Zoltan Komlosi, Demetri Komodromos, Liane Kordan, Tyrese Koroma, Amita Kotecha, Arun Kottekudy, Helen Kowald, Luisa Krampoutsa, Lukas Krohn-Grimberghe, Nils Krumrey, Hannah Kubias, Romans Kulikovs, Vinay Kumar, Siva Kumaravel, Alexandre Kündig, Alexander Kustow, Patricia Labro, Olu Ladeinde, Peter Laemmle, Jonathan Lahraoui, Shaun Laird, Kulvinder Lal, Amitabh Lall, Irfan Lamba, Miles Lampitt, Nicholas Lane, Cathryn Langdon, Sarah Langslow, Danny Langston, Jayne Larnie, Richard Larsen, Erika Laszlo, Krishan Lathigra, Alan Lau, Hong-Tin Lau, Natalie Laudat, Ade Lawless, Krishna Lawrence, Maria Lawrence, Nigel Lawrence, Jan Lawry, Laura Lawson, Samantha Lawson, Joseph Lawton, Gary Laybourne, Matty Laycock, Dea Le Bargy, Emmanuelle Le Drian, Kieran Leahy, Welber Leao, Gary Joseph Learmonth, Victoria Lebor, Yann Leclercq, Sunee Lee, Andrew Lee, Christopher Lee, Le Kai Lee, Brian Leggett, Andrew Lennard, Nicholas Lennon, Oliver Leonard, James Leppard, Lee Lester, Jessica Leung, Itay Levin, Angela Lewis, Desmond Lewis, Leonie Lewis, Lewis Lewis, Mark Lewis, Michael Lewis, Naomi Lewis, Travers Lewis, Yang Li, Ying Li, Shuang Li, Yunlu Li, Huai-Chih Liang, Bo Li-Bean, Jakub Lichota, Cary Lied, Elsa Lignos, Wendy Lim, Yihsien Lin, Ming Lin, John Lines, Stanley Malcolm Lippeatt, James Lister, Kevin Liu, Jianning Liu, Ben Liu, Campbell Livingston, Andrew Livingstone, Alison Lloyd, Gary Lloyd, Bradley Lloyd-Prest, Simon Loach, David Lobley, Anthony Lobo, Chris Locke, Andrew Lockett, Keith Lockwood, David Lockwood, Mark Londesborough, Marie Lonergan, Stephen Long, Dave Longman, Michael Longridge, Rafael Lopez-Bravo, Vicky Lord, Katie Louch, Derek Love, Jeffery Lovejoy, Sarah Lowes, Dominic Lown, David Lozano, Zhiyuan Lu, Xialan Lu, Brett Lucas, Adam Lucas, Angela Lucas, James Lucas, Robert Lucas, Terry Luddington, David Lumby, Michael Wai Ko Lung, Priscilla Lungu, David Lyon, Lynne Lytton, Zibi Maciag, Elizabeth Macintyre, Peter Mack, Matthew Macmorland, Alan Macpherson, Hugh Macpherson, Reddy Madadi, Vaishnavee Madden, Chris Madell, Peter Magee, Sophie Maggs, Vasili Magnis, Deborah Magri-Overend, Shaun Maguire, Gary Mahoney, Jock Maitland, Stefan Majczak, Kevin Makepeace, Paras Malde, Sepehr Malekahmadi, Duncan Mallison, Malloy Malloy, Sally Manderson, Stephen Mangiurea, Geoff Manley, Chloe Mann, Andrew Manning, Annabel Mansell, Kevin Maple, Luke Mappley, Lilian Maranciuc, Darren Marash, Rebecca Marcano, Hannah Marcazzo, Michele Marchionni, Roman Marie, Cassandra Marillier, Max Marino, Andrew Mark, Dominic Markes, Sarah Marks, Emily Marrison, Carlos Marroquin De La Cruz, Alex Marsh, Simon Marsh, John Marshall, Steve Marshall, Tracey Marshall, Elaine Martel, Leonard Martin, Lynda Martin, Wendy Martin, Louis Martinelli, Sara Martins Martins Pereira Duarte, Milena Marucci, Darren Mason, Nadeem Masood, Heather Mathew, Michaela Mathieu-Marius, Oliver Matjasz, Alistair Matson, Mutsumi Matsuba, Ellie Matthews, Helen Matthews, Melissa Matthews, Nicky Matthews, Peter Matthews, Philip Matton, Sally Maxwell, Christopher May, Rachel Mayes, Henry Mayhead, Darren Mccabe, Sarah Mccaffrey, Judeth Mccall, Acquaye McCalman, Lionel McCalman, Robert Mccamon, John Mccann, Matthew Mccourt, Michael Mccoy, Charmaine Mccracken, Paul Mccrudden, Raymond Mccullagh, John Mccusker, Ewan Mcdonald, Oprah Mcdonald, Edward Mcdonald-Toone, Easton Mcewan, Timothy Mcgeever, Rowlands Mchale, Rachael Mcilroy, Tim Mcinerny, Ian Mcinnes, Martin Mckechnie, Sue Mckenzie, Conor Mckeown, Mark Mckinnon, Hugh Mclaren, Katherine Mclean, James Mcloughlin, Daniel Mcloughlin, Sean Mcmanus, Emma Mcpeake, Warren Mcwilliams, Lucy Meachen, Robert Mead, Jillian Meadows, Gemma Mears, Roopal Mehta, Christopher Melia, Giuseppe Membrino, Shauna Mennis, Seema Menon, Emmanuel Mensah, Leandro Mariano Mera Otero, Rachel Merrett, Caroline Merritt, Nick Metcalf, Yan-Ping Mew, Jane Michele, Kate Middleton, Keith Middleton, Katherine Midgley, Paul Milford, Wendy Millar, Graham Miller, Alex Millington, Carl Mills, Juliana Mills, Stephanie Mills, Rob Millwood, Adrian Milner, Ben Milway, Raj Mistry, Jonathan Mitchell, Kev Mitchell, Kurt James Mitchell, Liz Mitchell, Neil Mitchell, Paul Mitchell, Bradley Mock, Ranjit Modhawadia, Ahmed Mohideen, Jonny Molloy, Dominic Moloney, Andrew Mondia, George Monisse, Annabelle Monks, Clyde Monserrate, Waleed Montasser, Hannah Montrose, Jack Moody, Steve Moody, Simon Mooney, Katharine Moore, David Moore, Kevin Moore, Anthony Moran, Daniel Moravanszky, Alexandre Moreau, Alexandra Morgan, Liz Morgan, Alex Morgan, Kathy Morley, Katie Morris, Ruth Morris, Tim Morrish, Alan Morrison, Anya Morrison, Ian Morrison, Mac Morrison, Kristofre Morton, Juliusz Mosek, Rachel Moses, Sarah Moss, Celia Moutell, Thandie Moyo, Ann Moyse, Marcus Mozley, Lawal Muhammad, Dennis Muir, Laura Muir, Martin Mulgrew, Joe Mulkerrin, Thomas Mullaney, Stephen Mulley, Babita Mundra, Jim Munro, Jean Wangari Muoria-Sal, Sid Murad, Francesca Muro, Mary Muro, Claire Murphy, Jacqueline Murphy, Linda Murphy, Murphy Murphy, Sam Murphy, Joe Murray, Philippa Murray, Daniel Musikant, Clare Myers, Janet Naghten, Zoltan Nagy, Samra Naim, Rosemin Najmudin, Angela Nascimento, Nisha Natalia, Aseem Natekar, Manjula Natkunan, Dave Nattriss, Eileen Naughton, Andrew Naylor, Russell Neal, Tom Needham, Susan Nelson, Sonia Nelson-Williams, Tim Neumann, Stephen Neville, Tim Newbould, Annabel Newell, Alastair Newens, Andy Newman, Ross Newsome, Veronica Newson, Ellis Ngui, Margaret Ngui, Beth Nguyen, Katie Nicholas, Richard Nicholson, Sue Nicholson, Lauren Nickless, Gerhardus Niemand, Mauro Niewolski, John Nixon, Phil Nixon, Tristan Noakes, Marianna Nodale, Atsuhiro Noguchi, Craig Nolan, Abdud Nordien, Allison Noreiga-Clarke, Carolyn Norgate, William Norris, Inderjeet Notta, Elia Ntaousani, Deirdre Nugent, Jaime Nunez-Lopez, Stephen Nunn, Aileen Nurse, Victor Nutakor, Will Oakey, John O'Brien, Sarah O'Brien, Brendan O'Connor, John Odell, Stuart O'Dell, Aderemi Odeniran, Olly Offord, Phil O'Flaherty, Eoin O'Flynn, Steve O'Gallagher, Bernadene Ogle, Neil O'Grady, Paul O'Hara, Peter O'Hare, Mudimo Okondo, Oritsetimeyin Okoro, Patricia Olabre, Tomasz Olejniczak, Hugo Oliveira, Charlene Oliver, Jarrad Oliver, Peggy Oliver, Ayotunde Olutimehin, Saira O'Mallie, David O'Neale, Sarah Ong, Onkar Onkar, Nigel Oram, Lizzy Orcutt, Louisa Orr, Graham Orriss, William Orrock, Juan Ortiz Fernandez, Takeshi Osada, Rex Osafo-Asare, Lionel Osborne-Wakely, Jonathan Oser, Kieron O'Shea, Siobhan O'Shea, Inka Oshodi, Fiona Owen, John Owen, Nicky Owen, Robert Owen, Thomas Owen, Ayo Oyewusi, Cemile Ozkan, Marcin Pachura, Martin Padilla Borrero, Pedro Pages, Marjorie Palfrey, Monica Palmer, Scott Palmer, Trevor Palmer, Helen Pankhurst, Laura Pankhurst, Verinder Pardesi, Lisa Parfitt, Pauline Park, Claire Parker, Edward Parker, Sally Parker, Deb Parsons, Matt Parsons, Edward Parsons, Parthi Parthipan, Jonathan Partridge, Clinton Pascoe, Neringa Paskeviciute, Bharat Patel, Bhaskar Patel, Nimisha Patel, Prabha Patel, Yatin Patel, Susan Paterson, Padmraj Patil, James Paton, Sharon Paul-Taylor, Adrian Pavia, Peggy Pawlowski, Andy Pawsey, Alan Paxford, Chris Payne, Diana Payne, Douglas Payne, James Peach, Malcolm Peake, Carole Pearce, Christopher Pearson, Robert Pearson, Jan Pearson, Edward Peerless, Dave Peirson, Ben Peng, Natalie Pereech, Charlotte Pereira, Jean Pereira, Randolph Pereira, David Perkins, Jen Perkins, Matthew Perkins, Leslie Perrier, Nargis Persaud, Ann Persson, Tom Peters, Vivien Peters, Theresa Peterson, Kathy Petrakis, Katrina Pett, Philip Pettenuzzo, Rob Petty, Christopher Peugniez, Dominic Pflaum, Daniel Pharaoh, Ray Pheasant, Gary Phibbs, Stefano Philand-Maini, Stephon Phillip, Rachel Phillips, Will Phillips, Kirstin Phillipson, Aisha Phipps, Billy Picard, James Pickford, Leigh Piercy, Rebecca Pike, Tashia Pillay, Daniel Pilling, Rolando Pincay Macias, Jessica Pinho, Jonathan Fabian Pinho, Monica Piovesana, Sam Pitt, Angela Plah, Adrian Platt, Billy Plaw, Carol Plaw, Lindsey Plaw, Nikki Plaw, Toni Plaw, Milana Plecas, Andrew Plum, Tito Poblete, Jan Poklewski, Michael Poku, Lukian Poleschtschuk, Deborah Pollard, Glenn Pollard, Georgia Pollock, Mario Polo, Nicholas Poltorak, Anja Pomeroy, Sergei Ponomarjov, Jackie Pooley, Sarah Pope, Louise Port, Gerry Porter, Lucy Porter, Simon Porter, Anna Portosi, Vivienne Potter, Kevin Poulter, Seyedali Poursamar, Daniel Powell, Lee Powell, Zoe Prag, Raj Prasad, Kajann Prathapan, Alistair Prestidge, Paula Preston, Jess Price, Steve Price, Paula Prichard, Lynnette Prigmore, Neil Prior, Tiffany Pritchard, Tom Pritchard, Gavin Pritchard, Annette Probert, Loraine Prokopiou, Christine Prosser, Inderjit Puaar, Liva Puce, Timothy Purcell, Claire Purnell, Gill Purnell, Paul Nino Sunder Purswani, Gemma Putney, Sam Pye, Cornelia Pykett, Zhaoyu Qi, Junyan Qiu, Janeen Quentin, Hannah Quigley, Brendan Quinn, Jonathan Quinn, Noelle Quinn, Ash Qureshi, Sarah Radcliffe, Michel Radermecker, Sonia Rafferty, Sonal Raghwani, Anisah Rahman, Faizur Rahman, Avnish Raichura, Sonia Raichura, Thara Raj, Arti Raja, Louisa Rajakumari, Shamma Rajan, Andrew Raju, Rashmi Rajyaguru, Ruby Rall, Jess Ramasamy, John Ramchandani, Anil Ramdeen, Daniel Ramdeen, Maria Ramdeen, Danilo Ramos, Michelle Ramrachia, Clare Ramsaran, Lindsay Ramsbottom, Alok Rana, James Randall, Rachel Rankin , Wendell Raphael, David Rapp, Jeyakumar Rasaiah, Kabir Rashid, Sarah Ratford, Adrian Raven, Olivia Raven, Kumaran Ravendradas, Alan Rawlinson, James Rawstron, Darryl Rayner, Chris Read, Tim Reading, Kayley Redrup, Wendy Rees, David Rees, Luke Reeve, Michael Reeve, Olivia Reevell, Pier Reid, Lisiane Reis Moura, Ellen Reynolds, Cemi Rhule, Corinna Richards, Helen Richards, John Richards, Julie Richardson, Kate Richardson, Terence Richardson, Thomas Richardson, Tim Richardson, Jean Richmond, Cleo Ridgeway, David Risley, Angela Maxine Risner, Alistair Robbie, Elwyn Roberts, Helen Roberts, Stephen Robertson, Deborah Ann Robinson, Genevieve Robinson, Paul Robinson, Daniel Robson, Rob Rochette, Marek Rodgers, James Roditi, Donna Rodrigues, Paul Roebuck, Aurelia Rogalli, Xavier Roger, Nicholas Rogers, Oliver Rogers, Oliver Rogers, Tom Rogers, Stephen Rolle, Donald Romeo, Lauren Rooney, Chris Roots, Jose Rosa Diaz, Adam Rosbottom, Alan Rose, Joe Rose, Philippa Ross, André Rostant, Peter Rostron, Catherine Roulston, Amy Rowe, David Rowe, Richard Rowe, Scarlet Rowe, Mark Rowland, Christopher Rowland, Dave Rowlands, Tim Rudd, Cerian Rudd, Matthew Ruddick, Emile Ruddock, Ro Ruiz-Ochoa, Nick Rundall, Bridie Rushton, Pete Rusin, Adrienne Russell, Lin Russell, Megan Russell, Christopher Ryan, Carl Ryan, Chloe Ryan, Emma Ryan, Richard Sackey-Addo, Michael Sadan, Emily Sadler, Alex Sadowsky, Cleofe Sagun, Gogi Saini, Tom Sainsbury, Clarinda Salandy, Miranda Salter, Don Samkange, Eskandarian Samsudin, Prad Samtani, Julian Sanchez, Eduardo Sanchez-Seco, Zé Sandell, Ian Sanderson, Julee Sanderson, Simon Sandiford, Grishma Santosh, Ivan Sanz, Gaudi Sareno, Claire Sargent, Jasminder Kaur Satnam Singh, Christopher Savage, Tom Savage, Stuart Savill, Brandis Savizon, Farrida Sawh, Steven Saxby, Anya Sayadian, Katherine Sayce, Andrew Scarborough, Evan Schiff, Toby Schuster, Philippe Schwartz, James Sciberras, Joseph Sciberras Margrie, Albert Scott, Elle Scott, Elliott Scott, Helen Scott, John Scott, Sarah Scott, Sarah Scott, Charlie Seager, Martyn Seaholme, Ricky Seal, Lewis Searle, Maria Seale, Oliver Sears, Jenny Selden, Amy Sell, Lee Selvarajah, Viki Sena, Derek Senft, Luis Fernando Sepulveda Lopez, Felix Serkis, Jay Serrao, Yvonne Settle, Lis Seymour, Andreas Sfikouri, Carole Shackleton, Mohammed Shafi, Baldip Shah, Haroun Shah, Jatin Shah, Neil Shah, Priya Shah, Anisa Shahid, Melinda Shalet, Rahim Shamji, Kimberley Shamtally, Radhika Shanmuganathan, Colin Shannon, Sara Shao, Simon Sharkey, Jyoti Sharma, Ritu Sharma, Austin Shaun, Rachel Shaw, Neil Shaw-Smith, Phillip Sheahan, Tak Sheikh, Justin Shelley, Bright Shen, John Shepherd, Kitty Sheppard, Nigel Sheppard, Matthew Sherr, Amit Sheth, Andy Shirlaw, Damian Shirley, Jacqueline Shirley, Edward Short, Chris Shoubridge, Yagnesh Shukla, Alessandra Shurina, Siphosenkosi Sibindi, Andrey Sidelnikov, Emilie Silkoset, Victor Silva, Kimbo Silver, Emily Simon Thomas, Natasha Simpson, Thomas Simpson, Peter Sinclair, Grainne Sinclair, Anja Singer, Jaspal Singh, Minda Singh, Munjeet Singh, Paul Singh, Sulesh Singh, Robert Sira, Kasun Siriwardana, Katherine Sivieng, Ben Skelton, Alan Skewis, Mark Skinner, Philip Slade, Natasha Slaise, Alan Slee, Angela Slocumbe, Etan Smallman, Tom Smelovs, Adam Smith, Amanda Smith, Anthony Smith, Caroline Smith, Cedric Smith, Daniel Smith, David Smith, David Smith, Eve Smith, Graham Smith, Hannah Smith, Helen Smith, Janine Smith, Joanna Smith, Kay Smith, Neil Smith, Rob Smith, Russell Smith, Sam Smith, Sandy Smith, Susan Smith, James Smy, Barry Smyth, Marc Snell, Chris Snow, Bhavesh Solanki, Jay Kumar Solanki, Tim Sole, Desmond Solomon, Yading Song, Yuchen Song, Bola Sonola, Olly Soper, Marvin Soriano, Luisa Sotgiu, Jose Soto, Robert Sparrow, Todd Speakman, Ezra Spearpoint, Alec Spence, Dan Spence, Amy Spencer, Graham Spencer, Jill Spencer, Mark Spillane, Ruth Spokes, Justin Spray, Matt Squires, Nurinder Srao, Mark Stanborough, Kimberley Stanislas, Karen Stead, Roy Stead, Andrew Steavenson, Ashley Leanne Steed, Chloe Stephens, Richard Stephens, Simon Stephens, Katie Stephenson, Paul Stevens, Ted Stevens, Nigel Stevenson, Duncan Stewart, Michael Stickland, Andy Stillwell, Andrew Stimson, Emma Stoffer, Rhona Elva Stokes, Emma Stone, Peter Stone, Rodney Stone, Graham Stoner, Peter Stoyanov, Linda Strachan, Barbara Stryjak, Elena Sukhova, Sahil Suleman, John Sullivan, Mark Sullivan, Jack Summerfield, Richard Summers, Alan Sunny, Roberto Surace, Raman Suri, Simon Surtees, Carole Anne Sutcliffe, Chris Sutton, Chris Swain, Tommy Swale, Kate Swallow, Laurie Swan, Walter Swan, Dan Swann, Jake Swan-Walters, Elliott Swatton, Kelly Sweeney, Rebecca Sweeney, Susan Sweeney, Kathryn Sweetman, Matt Swinnerton, Bohus Sykora, Peter Szabo, Zsolt Szabo, Terrance Szulc, Taj Taak, Deepak Tailor, Motiur Taj, Toyomi Takeda, Paul Talman, Kai Yuan Tan, Aaron Tanice, Nicola Tanner, Martin Tatem, Jessica Tatnell, Regan Tauton, Isabelle Tawil, Joanne Tay, Alastair Taylor, David Taylor, Dougal Taylor, James Taylor, Julie Taylor, Kishore Taylor, Nadia Taylor, Siobhan Taylor, Tony Taylor, Victoria Taylor, Adele Teague, Herberto Tedaldi Di Tavasca, Roger Tedder, John Telfer, Roydon Temple, Sera Terry, Bharat Thakore, Lekh Raj Thaper, Thaya Thayaparan, Leslie Thelwall, Oliver Thelwall, Della Thielamay, Abraham Thomas, Alastair Thomas, David Thomas, John Thomas, Peter Thomas, Robert Thomas, Sophie Thomas, Steven Thomas, Alex Thompson, Andrew Thompson, David Thompson, Steve Thompson, Trevor Thomson, Richard Thornhill, Mary Thorogood, Joanne Thorpe, Helena Tidey, Wayne Tieken, Mark Tierney, Martin Tilling, Andreas Timm, Philippa Tipper, Gerry Tissier, Aileen Toal, Areta Toalima, Joshua Tomkins, Shirley Ann Tomlinson, Carlos Torres Torres Bujanda, Paul Torry, Frances Touch, Gary Tough, Liam Tracey, Jody Tranter, Carl Treddenick, Shyvonne Trench, Jamie Trentham, Fatima Tribak, Joanne Trim, Roderick Trim, Giulio Troccoli, Patricia Trott, Paul Trumble, Clare Tsangari, Shingo Tsuchiya, Stratos Ttofis, Joshua Tucker, Martin Tugwell, Saw Tun, Paul Tunnell, Susanne Tunnicliff, William Turnbull, Clare Turner, Jordan Turner, Mike Turner, Sam Turner, Shreena Turner, Yvonne Turner, Suzanne Turvey, Michael Tushaw, Alexandra Tutty, Kathleen Tutty, Laura Tutty, Jo Twyman, John Tyler, Mark Tyler, James Tyrell, Russell Tysoe, Agatha Uchendu, Mohammed Uddin, Nonyerem Udeh, Jonathan Underwood, Calum Upton, Umut Uysal, Nicoleta Uzorka Ion, Preeti Vadgama, Alex Vaks, Ella Vallely, Mia Vallely, Stewart Vallely, Vanessa Vallely, Sree Vallipuram Vallipuram, John Vallis, Ayanna van der Maten, Kimani van der Maten, Mario Van Poppel, Alice Van Sertima, Simon Vandepeer, Aisha Varachhia, Nicolas Vasseur, Jess Veale, Jan-Vincent Velazco, Thassiano Verissimo Bueno Pona, Andrew Verney, Rosemary Vidad, Marian Vidra, Elisenda Vila Basté, Sunny Virdee, Ella Virr, Rohan Vithlani, Brian Voakes, Arnie Voysey, Pierluigi Vullo, Mahesh Vyas, Karen Wainwright, Jacek Wajer, David Walach, Wendy Walach, Tasha Walden, Elijah Walker, Ann Walklet, Jason Wallace, Owen Wallage, Thomas Walmsley, Nikki Walpole, Adam Walsh, Deryl Walsh, Peter Walsh, Robert Walsh, David Walter, Mark Walters, Dawn Walton, Kim Wan, Yu Wang, Shukai Wang, Chris Ward, Harry Ward, Stephen Ward, Victoria Ward, Simon Wardley, Steve Ware, Roy Wareham, Lester Warwick, John Watkins, Rod Watson, Ewan Watson,

Volunteers
Bénévoles

Tom Watson, Chris Watt, Ray Watters, John Watterson, Richard Watts, Alfie Watts, Teresa Watts, Osy Waye, Thomas Wearne, Chris Weber, Lisa Webster, Roger Webster, David Weinstein-Linder, Christine Weir, Christopher Welch, Amber Wells, Andrew Wells, Lorraine Wells, Michael Wells, Andrew Welsh, Dionne West, Emma West, Leonard West, Melanie West, Katie Westgate, Dan Weymouth, Christopher Whalen, Stuart Whatmore, Stu Whatton, Ian Wheeler, Will Wheeler, Barbara Whilds, Kate Whitaker, Stephen Whitcroft, Christopher White, Ruth White, Sally White, Jonny Whitmore, Pamela Whitter Whitter, Chris Whyley, Sue Whyte, Keith Wickham, Elisabeth Wicksteed, Lettice Wigby, Lesley Wigham, Hemal Wijesuriya, Peter Wildman, Laura Wiles, Clifton Wilkinson, Linda Wilkinson, Roger Wilkinson, Dean Willars, Anthony Williams, Ben Williams, Cat Williams, Deren Williams, Gareth Archard Vaughan Williams, Jane Williams, Jonathan Williams, Joseph Williams, Peter Williams, Roger Williams, Spencer Williams, Tracey Williams, Nick Williamson, Georgette Wills, Pauline Willis, Robert Willis, Mitchell Willshire, Rudi Wilms, Dave Wilson, Hylda Wilson, Jane Wilson, Peter Wilson, Phi Wilson, Cecil Wimbridge, Gavin Winbanks, Deborah Winchester, Emma Winchester, Roger Winfield, Ellie Wingett, Jim Wingfield, Margaret Winniak, Luke Wisdom, David Wiseman, Lewis Withey, Neil Wolfson, Torsten Wolter, Ekie Wong, Andrew Wong, Tsz Wan Wong, Adam Wood, Bernard Wood, Henry Wood, Jeremy Wood, Natasha Wood, Paul Wood, Tim Woodhead, Annette Woods, David Woods, Patricia Woods, Joe Woodward, Peter Wooldridge, Joshua Woolery-Allen, Steve Woolmore, Mark Wootton, Robert Wormald, Michael Worthington, Jay Worthy, Tom Wotton, Gavin Wrangles, Becky Wright, Dave Wright, Derek Wright, Gillian Wright, Jason Wright, Noah Wright, Bian Wu, Gilbert Wu, Zhuoer Wu, Luke Wyeth, Emily Wynne, Wei Xiang, Zhiqiang Xiao, Siyao Xing, Chao Xu, Shengda Xu, Taylor Xu, Jing Yang, Tao Yang, Terry Yang, Xiaoqian Yang, Rukhsana Yaqoob, Ray Yates, Iris Yau, Mahmoud Yazdanpanah, Grafton Yearwood, Cheng Hiang Yeo, Ting Yeung, Hon Mo Yip, Wai-Lun Yip, Nava Yoganathan, Elaine Young, Nicholas Young, Paul Young, John Youngs, Vera Yu, Omolara Yusuff, Salik Zahid, Kamruz Zaman, Jose Zambrano-Navarro, Tomek Zarebski, Aivars Zarins, Mayur Zaveri, Rytis Zayancakauskas, Vakaris Zayancakauskas, Daniela Zebisch, Adriana Zermeno-Eternod, Chen Zhang, Lisa Zhang, Qingshan Zhang, Qinhan Zhang, Xinran Zhang, Yunqian Zhang, Tommi Zhou, Bo Zhu, Lucy Zidour Mcstravick, Preslav Zimnikov, George Zittis, Deborah Zrostlik **Happy & Glorious** Surah Ahmed, Juan Aimur, Mustafa Berk Ak, Oreoluwa Akinfemiwa, Androulla Andrews, Mariana Astudillo, Victoria Badcott, Frank Barber, Oliver Barron, Nicole Beattie, Molly Bloom, Migena Boda, Lillian Boothmam, Alice Brown, Sania Butt, Angela Cabey, Maisie Campling, Maimoon Chowdhury, Ella Clements, Susan Cole, Elizabeth Cooney, Ruby Cowan, Julia Coyne, Gemma Crossland-Lee, Sanam Dana, Grace Davey, Suzannah Davies, Alaine Demosthenous, Anwen Donlon, Selin Dursin, Shantae Elder, Shian Elder, Aidan Etchells, Cameron Etchells, Jenae Feisal, Katherine Finn, Richard Free, Rachel Glasstone, Ieaysha Goodridge, Sabaa Hamiyou-Alam, Carline Ikoroha, Joseph Jacobsen-Laws, Luka Jovanovic, Mohamed Khadar, Anna Kinsella, Matilde Leaver, Maria Lee, Den Levett, Isabel Levine, Walter Lomas, Lisamarie Mcdonagh, Eva Mcneill, Christine McNeill, Jacob Mellor, Marie Meyer, Catriona Minty, Isabel Minty, Martine Monksfield, Kalid Nasser, Daniel Noble, Efemona Omonoseh, Jack O'Neill, Alexandra Parrish, Christine Parrish, Aaliyah Perfect, Kiera Perfect, John Pickett, Lauren Pierce, Athena Pieri, Joseph Jean Rayapen, Joshua Ralph Rayapen, Liberty Reason, Sam Redfearn, Adina Reid, Ilana Reid, Teone Reid, Claire Reilly, Eleanor Reilly, Thalia Saber, Joseph Screene, Cassius Shanahan, Aleata Simpson, Claire Skinner, Anna Smith, Grace Spencer, Jane Spencer, Coco Sterr, Holly Strawson, Madeline Strawson, Lorna Stubbs Davies, Naomi Thomas, Tessa Thomas, Carys Thomas-Hargreaves, Rosa Thorlby, Zara Thorlby, Alice Tiernan, Elizabeth Tiernan, Georgia Timothy, Jessica Tolley, Nichola Tolley, Rebecca Tolley, Susan Tripp, Rayyan Uddin, Connor Vincent, Kathleen Waters, Florence Weston, Georgina Weston, Ella White, Alison Wood, David Wood **Second to the right, and straight on till morning** Zakariyya Abdul-Hannan, Shalom Abe, Rita Aboagye, Zubayr Absiye, Mommammad Abu Tahir, Jessica Adams, Toni Adams, Enkeleda Ademaj, Sahra Aden, Walter Adjei, Olayiwola Adunola, Hannae Afellad, Daisy Agidi, Tasneem Ahamed, Stephanie Ahern, Anas Ahmed, Ann Ahmed, Ayesha Ahmed, Chaudary Ahmed, Fabbiha Ahmed, Ilyas Ahmed, Isha Ahmed, Mujahid Ahmed, Nafisha Ahmed, Niyaz Ahmed, Rahma Ahmed, Rahul Ahmed, Sayeba Ahmed, Tanvir Ahmed, Wasif Ahmed, Oluwanifemi Ajayi, Alexander Ajilore, Mandip Ajimal, Johnson Akadiri, Adeola Akande, Tahira Aktar, Christalene Alaart, Ibrahim Alam, Nusrat Alam, Karin Albani, Liz Alderton-Ford, Christine Alexander, John Alexander, Jessica Ali, Mahfuz Ali, Sumayya Ali, Zahra Ali, Nkechi Aligbe, Hayley Allen, Lucy Allen, Kathryn Alley, Yasin Alom, Yunus Alom, Daniel Alvaro, Angela Amegadzi, Rebecca Amissah, Antonia Anderson, Deanne Anderson, Jemoria Anderson, Sally Anderson, Matt Andrews, Luke Anns, Sammy Junior Anwuzia, Ernesta Apanaviciute, Azel Appiah, Lisha Archer, Louise Archer, Sara Arenas-Lopez, Zehra Arkir, Ashvini Arulrajah, Anand Arya, Daniella Asante, Munira Asaria, Nikita Asher, Sara Ashlea, Asrress Asrress, Benedict Atkinson, Diane Atkinson, Ruth Atkinson-Wilks, Natalie Atmore, Sivakulan Atputhachelvam, Carolyn Avery, Margaret Avery, Toritse Awani, Wilbert Ayap, Muhammed Ayazi, Laura Aylett, Khadija Azad, Patrick Babb, Mawgen Baber, Joyce Babirye, Gustavo Bacchetti, Margaret Bacon, Annmarie Badchkam, Oluwatobiloba Badero, Alexis Badger, Khadijah Bah, Kristopher Bahadur, Harry Bailey, Dora Bakaity, Matt Baker, Nicola Baker, Nojus Balciunas, Allan Ballesteros, Alise Balode, Carys Bampoe, Mustari Bangladesh, Claire Bangs, Rachel Banham, Claire Banks, Jan Bannister, Harjit Bansal, Sharon Barbour, Abigail Barden, Karen Barkway, Cheryl Barlow, Kimberley Barnes, Stephanie Barnes, Lamin Barrow, Katy Barton, Alison Basa, Adila Bashir, Gillian Basnett, Maria Bassett, Jashandeep Bassi, Rosemary Bate, Emmeline Bathurst, Tanveer Batool, Rosemary Beale, Lucy Beasley, Catherine Beaton, Nicola Beattie, Ghislaine Beauce, Rashmi Becker, Joanne Beckett, Sharon Beckford, Gabrielle Bediako, Alex Beech, Fatima Begum, Jasmin Begum, Lana Begum, Rima Begum, Shupa Begum, Gintare Beinoraviciute, Nas Bello, Ella Bentin, Otilia Beres, Jerome Bernard, Andrea Best, Ronald Betco, Aaliyah Bevan, Lali Bhaga, Mandy Bhattal, Yousuf Bhatti, Kathryn Bhola, Shriya Bhudia, Muskaan Biban, Nicki Bickford, Justyna Bieniek, Craig Binch, Denise Bingham, Liya Bint Hussain, Theresa Bintoh, Kavirang Biswas, Charlotte Blyth, Nicole Bobb, Natalie Bodden, Callum Bonetti, Harrison Booth, David Boothey, Eliza Borek, Samuel Bourgein, Corinna Bourke, Cydney Bourne, Niamh Bowdler, Tan Bowen, Simone Boyd, Christine Boyle, Rachel Bradbear, Annabel Bradburn, Lisa Bradley, Tiago Bravo, Elyse Braysher, Teresa Bredl, Shirley Bridge, Beverley Brierley, Julia Briggs, Leanne Brisland, Rhonda Bristol, Tracey Brito, Aimee Broadbent, Ruth Brock, Ashley Brown, Darren Brown, Kate Brown, Kim Brown, Loretta Brown, Patricia Brown, Zachary Brown, Barbara Browning, Rebecca Bruce, Glen Bryan, Theresa Bull, Alex Bultitude, Katherine Bunch, Arune Buragaite, Carina Burgess, Michelle Burnett, Felitta Burney-Nicol, Jane Burnham, Rebecca Bygrave, Mary Caddies, Duncan Callis, Aisha Camara, Abigail Campbell, Angela Campbell, Eileen Campbell, Louella Campbell, Pauline Campbell, Lucinda Campbell-Jackson, Julie Cardwell, Sarah Carmichael, Stephanie Carolan, Ellen Carr, Simon Castle, Graeme Caul, Selin Celik, Aviva Cerner, Caroline Chambers, Fiona Chance-Larsen, Helen Chapman, Ruth Charles, Hana Charlesworth, Robert Charnley, Fong Chau, Scott Cheek, Yu Han Chen, Jing Chen, Katja Chessis, Lisa Chishaka, Sean Chitongo, Patricia Chiwapu, Whitney Chobbah, Olivia Choong Gregory, Nadia Choudhury, Athikur Rahman Choudhury, Arpita Chowdhury, Fawziya Chowdhury, Sahat Chowdhury, Christian Christian, Jake Christie, Nila Chudasama, Vivienne Chusney, Julia Clague, Althean Clarke, Janet Clarke, Monica Clarke, Rosemarie Clifton, Amanda Clotworthy, Gillian Cluckie, Claire Cohen, Sheila Cohring, Jenny Collier, Jeni Colton, Holly Conway, Yvonne Conway, Emily Cook, Chris Cooke, Lyn Cooke, Victoria Cooney, Tommy-Jack Coppin, Jan Cornish, Rebecca Corns, Joshua Costa, Rosemary Cowan, Maxine Cox, Trevor Cox, Louise Coyle, Tracey Coyne, Barry Crabtree, Kevin Crabtree, Jennifer Crane, Sarah Crocker, Meryn Crocker-London, Zoey Cross, Audrey Crossdale, Irene Crowley, Rebecca Cuffy-Oliver, Shuo Cui, Roweena Cummins, Faye Curley, Kyron Curtis, Eva Cyhlarova, Miguel Da Silva, Ibukunoluwa Dada, Elizabeth Dada, Tolula Dada, Marianna Dadejova, Jo Dafforn, Michael Daley, Emily Daniel, Sachin Daniels, Usman Fida Dar, Julie Darnell, Renu Daryanani, Priyam Das, Theresa Dauncey, Naomi Davie, Ayo Davies, Juliena Davies, Yvonne Davies, Alisha Davies-Reaz, George Davis, Nicole Davis, Sally-Ann Davis, Caroline Dawes, Leonie Dawson, Julia Day, Sarah Day, Lisa De Jonge, Bradley Deacon, Mandy Deer, Melinda Del Mundo, Edwin Dela Cruz, Linda Deleon, Merlyn Demaine, Mert Demiralay , Patricia Denhard Rae, Tanisha Dennett, Polly Denton, Shaheda Desai, Usha Desai, Lucia Devine, Nus Devon, Harman Dhesi, Sukie Dhesi, Adama Diallo, Anne Diamond, Laurie Diaz-Steptoe, Rayanna Dibs, Joyce Dimen, Alison Dines, Justine Dingli, Ria Diop, Sheryl Diprose, Naemma Diria, Rachel Dobbin, Jenna Dodd, William Doga, Lauren Domfe, Jade Dowie, Mollie Downing, Holly Drewett, Nicola Dryland, Drusilla Duke, Riley Dunmore, Jane Dunton, Anne Durell, Jasmine During, Uloma Duru, Sarah Duvigneau, Vakaris Dziugys, Pepper Eadie, Victoria Early, Charlotte Eccles, Kerina Edge, Kelly Edmead, Natascha Ehlert, Silvia Eiden, Anna Eka, Abitha Elangovan, Patricia Elcock, Idaho Eley, Sarah Elghady, Kathryn Elliott, Darnelle Elliston, Nabila El-Zanaty, Sue Emson, Tracey England, Victoria English, Taibat Enifeni, Jonathan Espie, Sara Essa, Mame-Esi Essilfie-Bondzie, Tyler Eugene, Fatima Evans, Jane Evans, Chloe Evans Purnell, Rachael Everitt, Kelly Evershed, Astrid Fadare, Phillip Fagcang, Bess Fairfax, Elena Falleti-Hill, Kirsty Fallow, Kate Faragher, Kelsey Farragher, Elaine Farrell, Shaun Farrell, Leonie Felici, Fiona Felix, Susan Fell, Katie Feltham, Olivia Fenton, Helen Ferber, Senith Ferdinand, Ada Ferenkeh-Koroma, Lois Fergusson, Sonny Ferrier, Olivia Festy, Adenamola Feyisetan, Richard Finley, Rose Fish, Joe Fisher, Bobby Fitzgerald, Rachael Fletcher, Sheila Fletcher, Glendelyn Flores, Niamh Flynn, Orla Flynn, Deborah Fofana, Venand Fonkon, Eve Forster, Janice Fortune, Anna Fortuny Torruella, Candice Foster, Fiona Fox, Greeta Franklin, Paula Fray, Gemma French, Deana Frost, Chinye Furner, Chris Gadney, Fainaan Gado, Anna Galasheva, Natalia Gallagher, Aoife Gannon, Alice Gardner, Pat Garner, Fatumata Gassama, Chantelle Gaston, Sulaja Gautam, Cymbeline Gaynor, Lisa Gee, Simone Gelinas, Ricky Gellissen, Kristina Gemkow, Jake Gibbons, Emma Gibson, Alexander Gifford, Nadia Gildeh, Freyja Gillard, Tegan Gilham, Kimberley Gilmour, Nicola Gilmour, Lauraine Gilson, Ilaria Giudiceandrea, Dawn Glover, Alison Goddard, Michelle Gollan, Claire Goodchild, Ryanne Goodman, Louise Gordon, Samantha Gore, Mary Gough, Janine Gower, Diane Gowers, Ann Granger, Annelise Grant, Elaine Gray, Joanne Gray, Doireann Greaney, Sophie Green, Marcus Greenslade, Melodie Greenwell, Hilda Greenwood, Evelyn Griffiths, Sophie Griffiths, Sergio Guimaraes, Lina Gulhane, Rita Gupta, Mariya Gurina, Valentina Hadome, Anthea Hall, Lesley Hall, Maisie Halls, Sarah Halton, Shifna Hameed, Linda Hammett, Katie Hammond, Naomi Hammond, M'Med Ali Hamza, Maria Hanna, Shenai Hannan, Emma Hannibal, Kerry Hanson, Hamza Haque, M'Mad Areeful Haque, Isma'Eel Haque, Shahida Haque, Victoria Harding, Trish Hardy, Claire Harries, Antoinette Harrison, Lorna Harrison, Toni Harrison, Vicky Harrison, Jack Hartland, Olivia Harty, Mustapha Haruna, Sarah Harvey, Sabrina Hasan, Yvonne Haskett, Elias Hassaini, Sumaya Hassan, Velda Hassan, Zara Hassan, Jerome Hassib - Allen, Janette Hawkridge, Theodosia Hayalidis, Emma Hayes, Nikki Haynes, Katharine Helps, Cas Hemelryk, Annie Henken, Patricia Henley, Sara Hennessy, Teneiyah Henry, Elle-Mae Hepworth, Harry Herbert, Catriona Heredia, Cemile Heseldene, Rebecca Hewitson, Anya Hewitt, Gemma Hicks, Andrew Higginbotham, Marina Hill, Jessica Hillicks, Edward Hillier, Leo Hillsden, Samantha Hinton, Tayvia Hippolyte, Joy Hjalmarsson, Gemma Hodgson, Natalie Hodgson, Elizabeth Holder, Hilda Holder, Emily Hollands, Sharon Hollingworth, Lavinia Holloway, Pam Hollyman, Janet Holmes, Issy-Trixy Hood, Mohammad Emdadul Hoque, Sam Horrocks, Katja Horsch, Gemma Hoskins, Rhea Houlker, Matthew House, Stacey Howard, Lucy Howes, Katy Hoxha, Linda Hudson, Catherine Hughes, Elle May Hughes, Kiyah Hull, Fiona Hulley, Ellie Hulme, Rebecca Hulme, Annette Hunter, Catherine Hunter, Iain Hunter, Paula Jane Hurrell, Angela Husband, Hafsa Hussain, Iarfat Hussain, Khadra Hussain, Lubna Hussain, Muhammad Hussain, Nasreen Hussain, Syeda Hussain, Thamid Hussain, Mohammed Hussain Jalal, Ihsan Hussain-Espinar, Jordan Hutchinson, Christopher Hyland-McCormack, Marina Iaverdino, Ebenezer Ibeneche, Muhammed Ibrahim, Sophia Ike, Anthony Ikemefuna, Gayathri Ilangairatnam, Elizabeth Ilesanmi, Liz Illman, Yusra Imam, Clare Inglis, Abdi Irad, Aaron Isaac-Hamm, Nazia Ishaq, Adam Ishaq, Jasmine Islam, Rejwana Islam, Suim Islam, Aaisha Islam Rakibul, Shuaib Mohamed Ismail, Galina Ivaciova, Wendy Ives, Katie Jackling, Keri-Louise Jackson, Lorna Jackson, Daud Jama, Drew James, Joan James, Heila Jansen Van Vuuren, Sharon Jarlett, Sabariya Javed, Lena Jawad, Zoe Jefferson, Susannah Jenner, Rickie Jennings, Emelie Jensert, Ceejay Jepson, Frances Jessie, Jennie Jethwani, Johan Tahaafe Johansson, Adele Johnson, Beverly Johnson, Donna Johnson, Lorraine Johnson, Penny Johnson, Alison Jones, Charlotte Jones, Christine Jones, Kelly Jones, Lizzie Jones, Nicholas Jones, Rosie Jones, Sarah Jones, Eveline Jonkute, Marsha Joseph, Nishka Joshi, Pushpsen Joshi, Jack Jugurnauth, Ayoola Kabara-Clarke, Shirleen Kadje Nguethe, Lyande Kai Kai, Elif Kalaycioglu, Nikhita Kalsi, Meeta Kalyanji, Michelle Kanalas, Kajipa Kandiah, Stephanie Kane, Jemi Kanjia, Rita Karaliene, Joseph Karanja, Tahirjan Karimov, Vidhyalakshmi Karthikeyan, Kayina Katalayi, Mandeep Kaur, Serender Kaur, Katherine Kay, Yelda Kaya, Junior Kazumba, Jillian Kee, Laura Kelland, Richard Kendall, Katy Kennedy, Hannah Kermeen, Agnieszka Kertynska, Eshal Khan, Hazera Khan, Rubina Khan, Tanvir Khan, Angelique Khan, Rahena Khanam, Rashida Khanom, Sawdha Khanom, Aklima Khatun, Ayshah Khatun, Jareen Khatun, Sumaiya Khatun, Christian Kimbugwe, Aimee Kimerling, Martina King, Keith King, Roland Kirkby, Frances Klemperer, Lizzie Klotz, Caroline Knight, Michelle Knight, Imelda Koch, Mojerioluwa Koleowo, Anja Konter, Ligia Kowalska, Gunta Kretova, Gabriele Kripaityte, Maithri Krishnan, Sabina Kurieniuviene, Adelina Labriola, Abelaine Ladinez, Meenu Lakhani, Anita Lalji, Poonam Lall, Dennis Lalusis, Sukwant Landa, Katherine Laporte, Fernanda Lara, Brandon Lasmel, Susan Lauder, Helene Laurent, Betsey Lau-Robinson, Mazeedat Lawal, Johanna Lawrence, Jenny Leach, Danielle Leacock, Laura Leadsford, Janet Lee, Katie Lee, Jo Lenchner, Rhielle Lerendu, Helen Leslie-Smith, Sharon Lester, Mandy Levy, Dominic Lewis, Lizzie Lewis, Stella Lewis, Chi Yan Lilian Li, Angela Lim, Chris Lincoln, Sarah Lindsay, Magda Ling, Christiane Link, Natalie Loader, Jane Lynne Logan, Humnaa Lokasher, Christine Lomas, Julie Loosley, Kathleen Theresa Lord, Asheley Lotter, Jackie Lowe, Estrella Luna Vera, Giuliano - Adrian Lupu, Sarah Luscombe, Alessandra Lustrati, Bach Luu, Diana Luu, Rachel Ly, Simeon Lynch-Prime, Ella Macaulay, Margaret Macdonald, Peigi Mackay, Elizabeth Mackie, Ella Macks, Margaret Macqueen, Neil Madden, Stella Mageto, Polly Maggs, Laura Maher, Teresa Mahoney-Bostridge, Manahil Malik, Asif Malik, Hakim Malone, Sam Malpass, Kudzai Mangwende, Avneet Manku, Ayesha Mannan, Emily Manning, Maja Manojlovic, Larissa Manyasi, Rajinder Marbay, Elizabeth Marchant, Wynford Marfo, Karen Marks, George Marshall-Childs, Harry Marshall-Childs, Bailey Martin, Carmen Martin, Chloe Martin, Linda Marulanda Beltran, Dipa Masud, Lizzie Mather, Sumiaya Matin, Denise Matthews, Holly Matthews, Judie Matthews, Linda Matthews, Mark Matthews, Matilda Maxwell, Robin Mayers, John Mayson, Ajay Mazumdar, Farhat Mazumder, Maggie Mbelo, Gladys Mbenga, Ariella Mbuyi, Sean Martin MC Ateer, Jacob Mcalinney, Courteney McCabe, Dylan Mccarroll, Jessica Mccarthy, Jenny Mcclure, Janet Mccormick, Claire Mcdonald, Keith Mcgee, Mark Mcglinchey, Joanna Mcglynn, Mark McGovern, Ryan Mcgowan, Kelly Mcintosh, Jade Mcintyre, Victoria Mckennell, Keanu Mckoy, Helen Mclean, Linda Mcleod, John Mcminn, Caroline Mcnamara, Jean Mcnamara, Marie Mcnulty, Laura Mcpartlan, Catherine Medcalf, Rory Mee, Isabella Mees, Tessa Mellow, Camelia Melody, Emiro Mendoza Enciso, Nannah Mends Buah, Abid Menezes, Lilian Janet Menezes, Trudi Mercer, Dominique Merlande, Samuel Metcalf, Katja Metz, Bana Mhaldien, Anib Mhamud, Hakim Miah, M'Med Mikdad Miah, Muhammad Miah, Nadirah Miah, Nasim Miah, Sameera Miah, Sophie Michael, Carita Middleton, Catherine Milabo, Lesley Miles, Derek Miller, Rebecca Mills, Tara Mills, Tim Milne, Abdur Minhaj, Esther Missengue, Sangeeta Mistry, Nadim Mobasser, Amin Mohamed, Halima Mohamed, Mahamood Mohamed, Mahir Mohamed, Shafina Mohamed Yousuff, Hamidah Mohammed, Jamal Mohammed, Sushmita Mohapatra, Cecilia Mojzes, Nneka Molokwu, Anisha Mondair, Patrizia Monteleone, Astrid Moore, Jutta Moore, Zoe Morey, Domas Morkunas, Gayle Morris, Lesley Morris, Sophie Morris, Noeleen Morritt, Natasha Louise Morrow, Denise Mortimer, Alicia Morton, Shazia Mowlabaccus, Ruth Mudiandambu, Krishna Mudra, Lizzy Muggeridge, Samirul Muhit, Cath Mummery, Gerry Munisteri, Fahin Muntasir, Beveline Mupata, Tari Muringai, Emma Murphy, Dana Murray, Laura Murray, Emily Muscatt, Robb Musgrave, Gemma Muskett, Sally Mussellwhite, Louise Must, Imran Naaji, Rachel Nabudde, Amina Nabukenya, Yusuf Naeem, Ashitha Nagesh, Bruntha Narendran, Sarah Naser, Nurani Nathoo, Rohan Nauth-Misir, Ana Navarro, Ammaarah Nazeer, Hilary Neal, Richie Neary, Kristijonas Nekrosevicius, Dante Nelson, Gamze Newell, Lucy Newman, Yasmin Newport, Helen Nicholson, Sue Nicholson, Christie Nixon, Suzannah Nobbs, Frankie Northfield, Abya Nouar, Kim Novak, Panayotis Ntourntoufis, Abian Nur, Afulenu Nwabuzo, Jonathan Nyong, Kasia Oberc, Caitlin O'Brien, Chris O'Connor, Niamh O'Connor, Jeremiah Odubade, Olusola Ogbajie, Miriam Ogbonnaya, Tola Ogidan, Tobi Ogumjimi, Solomon Ogundana, Leon Ojukwu, Fabian Okabe, Helen O'Kelly, Ugo Okonkwo, Florence Okorocha, Tina Okpodike, Ivie Okwuegbuna, Olusola Oladoyin, David Olajorin, Adaora Oli, Samuel Olley, Jamie Olney, Marvell Oluwaleye, Korlei Omaboe, Siobhan O'Neill, Michelle Onwusiri, Shanae Onyeka, Josie Oppong, Tase Oputu, Amanda O'Regan, Donna O'Reilly, Emanuela Orlandi, Chisolum Orliaku, Georgia Orunmuyi, Sarah Osborne-Fender, Victor Osei, Noirin O'Sullivan, Alice Outen, Anneke Outen, Sarah Owen, Deniz Ozdemir, Emma Page, Arun Pall, Christine Palmer, Hazel Palmer, Helen Palmer, Tyrone Palumbo, Ankit Pandey, Bina Pandya, Dharmana Pandya, Matthew Panter, Luca Paolone, Penelope Parisi, Katie Parks, Ellen Parnavelas, Azra Parveen, Iram Parvez, Maxine Passley, Stella Paszkiewicz, Afrin Patel, Deepa Patel, Minu Patel, Shreema Patel, Muhammed Patelia, Lynne Paterson, Sheliya Paul - Swaby, Rosalind Payne, Eve Pearson, Jessica Peek, Bruno Pereira, Tamasin Perkins, Terri Perrin, Anisha Pervin, Samantha Pescott-Frost, Julia Peters, Marcia Phillips, Maureen Philogene, Alex Philpott, Lesley Pick, Aaliyah Pierre, Amy Pieterse, Chris Pigram, Miloslava Pilatova, Faye Pincott, Nuno Pinheiro, Charlotte Pink, Aaliyah Pipe, Alexander Plank, Juanita Plaza, Janine Plummer, Angela Poku, Lanier Pole, Hugh Pomells, Sarah Porteous, Destiny Porter, Laura Porter, Victoria Porter, Aimee Porter-Smith, Clare Portman, Farzana Potter, Barbara Powell, Connor Power, William Power, Tracy Poyntz, Katherine Prees, Janine Prever, Alice Prevezer, Carlynne Preville, Michaela Prew, Callum Price, Lisa Price, Chris Prior, Judith Procter, Anjohleen Prozhmi, Amanda Pun, Deborah Purseglove, Samantha Purser, Muhammad Qadder, Paula Quigley, Mehrun Rabbani, Shagufta Rafiq, Abidur Rahman, Ali Awwal Rahman, Amanur Rahman, Anis Rahman, Fahmid Rahman, Mahdiur Rahman, Sadia Rahman, Abir Raj, Raghini Rajaram, Raquel Ramos Fraga, Paulina Ramos-Irele, Johannah Randall, Michael Ranft, Aysha Ranny, Alice Raper, Katie Raven, Bryce Raymond Da Silva, Kelly Read, Sue Reader, Helen Reed, Sarah Reeve, Yasmin Rehman, Sally Reichardt, Kiya Reid, Lisa Reid, Khepera Reid - Wynter, Grace Ren, Mignon Reynolds-Hall, Sandrine Ribeiro, Karen Richards, Matthew Richards, Melissa Richardson, Sarah Richardson, Linda Ridgwell, Daniel Robb, Carlene Roberts, Emma Roberts, Jasmine Roberts, Kaiya Roberts, Lorraine Roberts, Zoe Roberts, Vikki Robins, Hollie Robinson, Isobel Robinson, Elaine Rodrigues, David Rogalski, Constance Roger, Sheila Rogers, Helen Rogerson, Anna Rolfe, Brandon Rolle, Joanne Rooney, Ana Maria Rosales Hernandez, Amy Rose, Marina Rova, Rayhan Rumel, Denise Rushen, Chloe Russell, Jenny Rusyniak, Syed Ryhan, Lisa Sadler, Boothayna Sahnine, Emiko Saito, Anaar Sajoo, Samina Saleem, Danielle Salem-Tedj, Nakai Sambani, Genine Sambile, Catyah Samfat, Hanna Samueal, Justin Samuels, Beverley Samuels-Campbell, Regina San Juan, Lucy Sandford, Richa Sandill, Ayanfeoluma Sanusi, Sumayyah Sardar, Francoise Sargent, Charlotte Sarmiento, Ardchaya Satheskaran, Simona Sava, Nicola Savill, Leanne Saxon, Sinead Scanlon, Mirjam Schuke, Emily Scott, Gemma Scott, Lydia Scott, Lowri Seager, Janet Seeney, Samantha Selmes, Aaron Selvapandiraj, Jackie Serrano, Alecia Sesluk, Rashpal Seyan, Joanne Seymour, Danielle Shadbolt, Nayan Shah, Prisha Shah, Raima Shaheenul, Murshed Shahriyar, Isra Shahzad, Renee Sharkey, Grace Sharp, Hilary Sharpe, Pauline Shaw, Lesley Sheehan, Karen Shevlin, Rachel Shillito, Oly Shipp, Veena Shivnath, Ifaz Shohel, Victoria Shooter, Mehzabin Siddeka, Tia Siddiquee, Edmilson Silveira Neto Guilherme, Shaila Simon, Natalie Simpson, Amritraj Singh, Anas Sinole, Katherine Sissons, Nativel Siu Rodriguez, Tija Skvarciute, Emer Slattery, Aidan Slowie, Jamie Smart, Mia Smerdon, Bex Smith, Christine Smith, Graham Neil Smith, Janice Smith, Leonie Smith, Luke Smith, Michele Smith, Rashid Smith, Cathal Smyth, Nita Solanky, Irum Sorathiya, Shefa Sorathaiya, Jayson Sousa Vieira, Amandeep Spall, Wesley Spaull, Heather Spence, Alfie Spencer, Pauline Ssemubumbe, Reece St John-Commey, Sharon Stacey, Sinead Stack, Carolyn Stanley, Jacob Stanton, Kasia Stegienta-Toman, Melanie Stein Du Pre, Rosie Stewart, Ceyrone Stokes, Kat Stretch, Chun-Yiu Su, Valerie Suarez, Victoria Sugden, Moaiz Suletch, Humza Suliman, Keely Sunderland, Kashmira Sunni, Kadamban Suntharalingam, Marlo Surath, Katrina Swanston, Aoife Sweeney, Inaya Syeda, Tasnim Tabassum, Rachael Taiwo, Arshad Takun, Tina Tan, Donna Tang, Laiba Tanveer, Zoe Tasker, Gary Talor, Patricia Taylor, Anneliese Taylor, Amy Taylor, Brothers Taylor, Sheila Taylor, Juliet Taylor, Ciska Taylor-Reid, Bhavnita Tejura, Sandria Terrelonge, Linsee Tham, Gemma Thomas, Julie Thomas, Mecia Thomas, Mica Thomas, Dana Thompson, Dionne Thompson, Emma Thompson, Lorraine Thompson, Monica Thompson, Mia Thompson-Semackor, Emily Thomson, Amber Thorne, Andrew Thornton, Emma-Jane Thornton, Lauren Thorogood, Wanda Tiley, Darren Tippetts, Mary Todd, Jessica Tofan, Rachel Tompkinson, Satwinder Tooray, Carole Toth, Leona Tran, Nu Tran, Chitra Tripathi, Neeraj Tripathin, Konstantinos Tsormpatzidis, Orchid Tunaya, Chelsea Tunbridge, Emma Turtle, Anna May Ty, Suraiya Uddin, Nazifa Uddin, Victoria Ugbekile, Evie Ukairo Morris, Mara Ukairo Morris, Pearl Ukairo Morris, Eddie Uku, Zarin Ullah, Nuruzzaman Ummi Kulthoom, Sam Underdown, Verity Upton, Lisa Urbanski, Leah Vadher, Sheila Vanezis, Meera Varsani, Shambai Varsani, Oluwafunmilayo Vaughn, Chelsea Vaught, Laura Venegas, Jaden Victorin, Janina Villalta, Jenny Vincent, Kaitlin Vincent, Ieva Vinciarauskaite, Raquel Vives, Belinda Voos, Jessica Wade, Matthew Wade, Regina Wade, Claire Wadeley, Christine Walker, Gillian Walker, Erin Wallace, Julie Waller, Lauren Walsh, Janet Walter, Caroline Walton, Juliet Walton, Meimei Wang, Jin-Jin Ward, Hazel Ware, Michelle Warnes, Aleeza Wasim, Hannah Waters, Rosemarie Watley, Kayleigh Watson, Tina Watts, Sally Watts, Rebecca Weaver, Beattie Webber, Charlotte Webber, Doerte Weber, Ariadne Welby-Everard, Freda Wells, Rosamunde Wells, Sally Wetten, Hayley Weyman, Paige Wharton Stroud, James Whatley, Emily White, Emma White, Katie White, Shanae White, Wendy White, Jayne Whiteside, Ruth Whitfield, Ailsa Whyte, Josie Wicks, Jamie Wilcox, Jake Wilkes, Rebecca Wilkinson, Angela Williams, Danny Williams, Diane Williams, Indalasha Deer Williams, Jennifer Williams, Kate Williams, Katie Williams, Lindsey Williams, Muna Williams, Rhyanna Williams, Tim Williams, Luke Williamson, Kayleigh Williams-Stubbs, Claire Willis, Anna Wilson, Nicole Wilson, Paula Winter, Michelle Witheriff, Valentina Wong, Nicola Woodruff, Amanda Woods, Sarah Woods, Diana Woodward, Josephine Woolley, Janelle Wyke-Joseph, Julia Wykrota, Kai Yang, Heather Yates, Ezgisu Yilmaz, Karen Young, Fabbihah Ysmin Ali, Muhammed Yunus, J'Nae Zamore, Chenying Zang, Rebecca Zerkani, Zhuying Zhang, Angela Zhou, Marcel Zielonka, Darren Zingoula Dezo **frankie & june say... Thanks Tim** Harriet Abbiss, Kirstie Abbott, Madeline Adeane, Ayisat Adeniji, Elizabeth Adeyemi, Mauricio Affonso, Thelma Agbadze, Alexis Terry Aggett, Kurtis Agyekum, Nona Ahamat, Tahira Ahmed, Jordan Ajadi, Tomi Ajayi, Chim Akah, Sodiq Akanmu, Kenny Akindele-Eshinlokun, Precious Akpokodje, Vera Akuoko Akuoko, Taiba Al Bisher, Sarah Albano, Lorraine Albrow, Annabel Aldridge, Sophie Alexis, Shelina Ali, Motin Ali,

Glen Allan, Sophie Allan, Jenni Allen, Kim Allen, Kingsley Alleyne, Harriet Allum, Daniel Alvarez Gonzalez, Lucinda Al-Zoghbi, Daniela Amadio, Chloe Amankwah, Thalia Anagnostopoulou, Matt Anderson, Jessica Andrade, Coralina Andrews, Kate Andrews, Michael Annan, Iain Anstess, Francesca Antonyogarajah, Noel Antonyogarajah, Mehdi Aoustin-Sellami, Dekan Apajee, Katie Appleby, Lizzy Appleyard, Teeyana Araromi, Rafael Cristiam Araujo Ribeiro, Katie Arbuckle, Luke Armstrong, Laurence Arora, Adrian Arroyo, Gabriela Arthur, Ross Arthurs, Tabitha Ashby, Amber Ashby, Dorcas Asuming, Si Austin, Chloe Ayling, Kath Ayres, Patrick Azimi, Daphne Babalis, Jennifer Bacon, Ildiko Bagladi, Louise Bailey, Simon Bailey, Sarah Baily, Katherine Baines, Jennifer Baker, Lauren Baker, Miriam Baker, Rachel Baker, Ruth Baker, Dee Bakre, Francesca Balchin, Hemavli Bali, Marge Banes, Sabrina Bangladesh, Jerrica Bangura, Leonor Barbosa Gonçalves, Shay Barclay, Kimberly Barker, Michele Barker, Rhian Barker, Marc Barnes, Ruth Barr, Catherine Barritte, Keira Bartram, Erica Bartrum, Charlotte Barwick, Danielle Barwick, Lucy Basaba, Ethan Bascombe, Kirsty Bascombe, Zoe Basket, Julie Baskett, Sedudzi Basoah- Acolatse, Hannah Batchelor, Susie Bates, Katie Bayfield, Nigel Beard, Jennie Beeson, Rahana Begum, Catarina Beijôco, Aiste Beinoraviciute, Diane Bell, Lizzie Bell, Jane Bellamy, Holly Bellsham, Abena Bentum, Rachel Besley, Michael Bettell, Sej Bhabra, Tav Bhatia, Vipul Bhatti, Daria Bierla, Bryony Billingham, Tobias Bilton, Gina Birch, Emily Birleson, Charlene Bissessar, Laura Blaauw, Amy Joanne Blackburn, Katie Blackwell, Tyler Blackwood, Elena Blanco Alba, Stephanie Blandford, Claire Blatchford, Johanna Blight, Sarah Blow, Tessa Boakyewaa, Charlotte Bocarisa, Jan Bogdanowicz, Troy Bohn, Fiona Bolton, Zoe Bolton, Belinda Bonanno, Adam Bond, Anneka Bones, Katie Booth, Pam Borg, Gabriel Borozescu, Michelle Boswell, Diana Botey, Samantha Bottle, Jane Bourne, Regine Boutin, Elizabeth Bower, Daisy Bower, Robyn Bowers, David Bowers, Jessica Bowles, Kirstin Box, Fidelma Boyd, Courtney Boyle, Gillian Brady, Karen Braganza, Elaine Bramall, Helen Branton, Jasmine Breinburg, Katherine Brenchley, Claire Brennan, Sarah Brett, Claire Brewer, Joanna Bridge, Hannah Bridger, Emma Brigg, Matt Briggs, Samuel Brightman, Brian Brinkley, Matthew Brinkworth, Sophie Brockie, Heather Broderick, Chloe Brooks, Lara Brooks, Michael Brooks, Emma Broom, Laura Broome, Angela Broomes, Emma Broomfield, Amie Brotherton, Alexandra Brown, Katherine Ann Brown, Tyla Brown, Daniel Browne, Roseanne Browne, Richard Brownlie-Marshall, Ashley Bryant, Andrew Bryant-Chesworth, Angela Bucknor, Lucy Bugler, Corinne Bull, Daniel Bull, Ryan Bullman, Katie Bunting, Tamsin Bunyard, Samantha Burden, Alix Burhouse, Andrew Burke, Vicki Busfield, Georgina Bussell, Pauline Byles, Kirsty Byrne, Megan Byrne, Zhenjie Cai, Ria Cajee, Zaja Calder-Grant, Jenna Jay Cameron, Suzie Campbell, Cheryl Cannon, Min Cao, Louis John Capadosa, Chantelle Capstick, Christy Carey, Lauren Carne, Leonie Carpenter, Kyroe Carrington-Mckenzie, Nic Carter, Emma Carter, Josiah Carter, Kimi Carter, Eleanor Carwithen, Chez Cascarino, Maria Cascarino, Emma Casey, Elda Castillo Rivera, Natasha Cesco Gaspere, Deny Chacko, Jennifer Chadney, Laura Chan, Stephanie Chan, Weini Chan, Rachel Chance, Sebastien Chaneac, Angharad Chapman, Caroline Charles, Dikaia Chatziefstathiou, Dylan Chauhan, Leena Chauhan, Haixia Chen, Deborah Chernanko, Pinki Cheung, Rachel Chew, Ama Chin, Jane Chinery, Chris Chinnock, Claire Chin-Sue, Angelina Chudi, Josey Chukwuemeka, Mathurot Chuladul, Emily Churchill, Christina Churchman, Mark Civil, Brian Clark, Tim Clark, Andrew Clarke, Charlie Clarke, Marie Clarke, Victoria Clarke, Zara Clatworthy, Anna Clave Arderius, Becky Clayden, Emma Cleaver, Daniel Clegg, Penny Clements, Anne-Marie Clifford, Lyndsey Clifton, Paige Close, Declan Coates, Tessa Coates, Katie Cockburn-Smith, James Cogle, Sophie Colbourne, Daisy Cole, Nicholas Coley, Gaby Colotto Do Santos, Lauren Concannon, Wan Lu Cong, Sarah Conkling, Lis Cook, Lucy Cook, Kate Cooper, Nicola Cooper, Laura Corbett, Kate Corbett-Winder, Sam Cornelius-Jones, Henrique Costa, Emily Cotter, Laura Cottrell, Emma Cowan, Harriet Cowell, Kate Cowell, Emily Cowie, Farrell Cox, Peter Crawford, Jane Crawshaw, Andro Crespo, Karen Crookes, Jonathan Crowley, Raffaella Cuccia, Jakki Cummings, Tiffany Curtis, Tavy Cussinel, Ayodele Dada, Anna-Marie Dadd, Amish Dahyabhai, Laura Dajao, Joanne Cull Dalton, Cristina D'Andrea, Thuy Quynh Dang, Katie Daniels, Amy Darby, Zoe Darby, Sophie Darrington, Kismet Dauti, John Daveney, Landra Davidson, Katherine Davies, Mary Davies, Philip Davies, Sarah Davies, Sian Davies, Steph Davies, Andrea Davis, Beckie Davis, Leah Davis, Lewis Anthony Davis, Marcelle Davison, Alex Davy, Darrell Davy, Debbie Daws, Laura Day, Filipe De Barros, Jude De Bont, Sebastian De Verteuil, Lucy Deacon, Jody De'Ath, Natasha De-Freitas, Louise Dekker, Felino Antonio Dela Merced, Julia Delaney, Elena Dell'Acqua, Natalia Delmastro, Amanda Dempster, Charlotte Dengate, Amelia Dennehy, Himesh Depala, Camille Desmarest, Tyler Dew, Joseph Dewey, Sophie Dewing, Sonia Dham, Prabhjot Singh Dhami, Veena Dhulipala, Laura Diamond, Amy Dickens, Kate Dickety, Jennie Dickie, Helena Diffey, Kerry-Anne Dignam, Laura Dilloway, Matthew Dilworth, Iliana Dimoni, Xiaotong Ding, Tilini Dissanayake, Alka Dixit, Geeta Dixit, Jamila Dixon, Michala Dobiasova, James Dodsworth, Nathan Donaldson, Marcelo Dos Santos, Gurpreet Dosanjh, Sharan Dosanjh, James Douglas, Elizabeth Douglass, Holly Dover, Tess Dowdeswell, Megan Dowell, Samuel Doyle, Virginia Draper, Nicky Driscoll, Portia Dujon, Matt Dummigan, Rosie Duncan, John - Anton Dunn, Roanna Dunsford, Sruti Dupaguntla, Sultana Dyfan, Sophie Dymond, Katherine Eames, Tina Easteal, Gabriel Eaton, Angela Ebiner, Emma Edwards, Martin Edwards, Michael Edwards, Ryan Edwards, Sally Edwards, Clive Elkington, Catherine Ellis, Charlotte Ellis, Kieran Ellis, Amira El-Shafie, Ijeoma Emeruwa, Diana Endsor, Carly Enstone, Patricia Erdei, Beverley Erogun, Kylie Etherton, Jean Eu, John Evans, Morgan Evans, Rachel Evans, Zoe Evans, Nikita Eve, Karen Ewens, Alexandra Ewing, Femi Fagunwa, Savaughan Fairman-Campbell, Abi Fancourt, Rachel Fanshawe, Marcos Faquer Manhaes, Chantelle Farmer, Katie Farnsworth, Samantha Farnsworth, Emily Farrelly, Jumoké Fashola, Alexandra Feachem, Thomas Feeny, Charlie Fennell, Megan Ferreira Souto Jones, Cadi Fester, Rosa Firbank, Stephanie Firtt, Laura Fisher, Aston Fisher, Michelle Fisher, Rachel Flenley, Zoe Flight, Katie Floyd, Jo Foley, Kane Foley, Aiesha Fontaine, Angharad Forbes, Sam Ford, Mariella Fortune-Ely, Sarah Foster, Robyn Fox, Andrew Francalanza, Shynell Francis-Devaux, Joseph Francois, Audley Franklin, Chloe Franklin, Joshua Franklin, Maylee Fraser, Rupsha Fraser, Victoria Frayard-Smith, Stefanie Freeman, Angela Frost, Wendy Frost, Redz Fulgence, Ayaka Furukawa, Genevieve Fyfe, Megan Gadd, Alexa Gardner, Heidi Hovind Garwood Garwood, Valeria Gasparini, Isabella Gaupmann, Lanre Gbolade, Jazmine Genius, Robert Gentle, Daniel George, Elena Georgiou, Kiri Gibson, Laura Gilbert, Victoria Giles, Juliette Gilford, Lauren Gill, Rebecca Gillett, Monica Gimbernat Alemany, Nathalie Ginvert, Nicole Gipps, Matthew Glenn, Adam Glover, Emily Gloyens, Charlotte Godfrey, Katharine Godfrey, Ellie Goldsmith, Tracie Goldsmith, Anita Gomes, Ruth Gomez, Jennifer Gondola Bokoba, Caroline Gordon, Elizabeth Gordon, Sarah Gordon, Marcella Gordon-Chambers, Rahiem Gordon-Smith, Lucinda Gosling, Georgina Gould, Alistair Grant, Laura Grant, Serena Grant, Edwin Grappy, Maxwell Grappy, Andre Graver, Claudia Gray, Dinah Gray, Gemma Gray, Zoe Gray, Fabio Greco, Natasha Green, Sarah Green, Sue Green, Tanya Greig, Karina Grieco, Lauren Griffin, Jules Griffith, Claire Griffiths, Jessica Griffiths, Rowan Griffiths, Maya Gudka, Nicola Guenigault, Matilde Guerriero, Jo Gunston, Yulia Gusakova, Debbie Gustaffe, David Ha, Sally Hacking, Elena Haddad, Jessica Léa Haener, Hashma Haidar, Claire Haines, Jessica Hajdu, Afia Hale-Abusham, Phil Hall, Teresa Denise Hall, Zoe Haller, Victoria Hambling, Imogen Hamel, Dominic Hamilton, Kirsty Hamilton, Katie Hammond, Vicky Hampshire, Frances Hampson, Caroline Hampstead, Annie Hanafin, Alice Hancock, Lottie Hancock, Felicity Hand, Lisa Hann, Tsugumi Harada, Chloe Harcourt, Alexandra Hardman, Elaine Hargreaves, Elena Hargreaves, Michelle Ellen Harkes , Angelee Harris, Matt Harris, Natalie Harris, Rosemary Harris, Natasha Harrison, Ian Harrod, Ben Hart, Jayne Hartley, Philippa Harvey, Sarah Harvey, Maham Hashmi, Rouzie Hassanova, Gillian Hatherall, Suzy Haven, Sonia Hawkey, Clare Hawkins, Sam Hawkins, Sally Hawkridge, Mike Hawthorne, Harriett Hayden, Laura Hayman, Victoria Haynes, Anders Hayward, Sophie Hayzelden, Ellie Hazell, Kelly Head, Jo Heath, Catherine Hector, Bethany Hedges, Lindsey Hedges, Bal Heer, Kirsty-Ann Heggie, Tamsin Hellier-Hough, Mahalia Henry-Richards, Holly Heron, Claire Hetherington, Rebecca Hickey, Emalene Hickman, Amanda Higgins, Katie Hill, Sian Hill, Verity Hill, Emma Hixson, Chloe Ho, Sarah Ho, Philippa Hobbs, Giles Hockridge, Laura Hodges, Laura Hodgkins, Elaine Holbrook, Anna Holden, Pete Holland, Carrie Holman, Georgia Homewood, Jennie Hone, Louise Hooper, Jezz Hooton, Joanne Hooton, Samuel Hopkins, Rebecca Horgan, Katherine Horsham, Lauren Houlder, Jevan Howard-Jones, Eileen Hsieh, Yibai Hu, Iris Huang, Harriet Hughes, Sally Hughes, Ellen Hunter, Matthew Hunter, Steph Hunter, Stephen Huntley, Jake Hurlock, Alisdair Hurst, Amran Justin Matheo Hussain, Baber Hussain, Sayma Hussain, Kathryn Hyde, Ana Sol Ibanez Wilkinson, Catherine Ibbotson, Caroline Ienne, Luciana Ieno, Lara Inge, Victoria Innes, Anna Marie Iporac, Eshita Iqbal, Daniel Irvine, Louisa , Michelle Jackley, Amber Jackson, Natasha Jacobsen, Adam Jajbhay, Abdul Jalloh, Dean James, Sarah James, Claire Jared, Alex Jarrett, Paul Jarvis, Kevin Jarvis, Yvette Jarvis, Lasika Jayamaha, Annabel Jeffcoate, Trina Jeffers, Dora Jejey, Kelly Jenkins, Craig Jenner, Tom Jewett, Yu Jiang, Davinia Jimenez, Gwen JnoBaptiste, Savvanh John Leighton, Carrie Johnson, Chloe Johnson, Eleanor Johnson, Sian Johnson, Jonathan Johnston, Patrick Johnston, Alana Jones, Doreth Jones, Emma Jones, Nicola Jones, Nikki Jones, Rebecca Jones, Ruth Jones, Sion Jones, Wendy Jones, Mariem Joof, Jason Jordaan, Sophie Joyce, Paul Judd, Pauline Julian, Chloe Juste, Gemma Elisabeth Kalmakrian, Timea Kalmar, Isata Kamara, Rakeem Kamara, Kenneth Kangethe, Agni Kasparian Saraidari, Salimah Kassam, Irene Kavoura, Leanne Keatley, Sian Keauffling-Burns, Karen Keeley, Sarah Kelly, Clare Kendall, Karolina Kendall-Bush, Stephanie Kenny, Ruth Kent, Mary-Jane Kerr, Sarah-Ellen Kerr, Tristan Kerr, Georgina Ketteman, Lia Khan, Lauren Kidd, Rachael King, Michele Kingston, Amy Kippen, Jennifer Kipphut, Ella Kirby, Tom Kirby, Rhiannon Kirk, Hannah Kiss, Howard Klaasen, Adam Knight, Alison Knight, Phoebe Knight, Daniel Kok, David Kolundzija, Sammy Kong, Merin Kovoor, Maria Kramvi, Elmo Kuang, Madhura Kuduvalli Nagendra, Aaron Kumar, Akwasi Kwarteng, Loriane Laku, Claire Lambert, Siobhan Lambert, Susan Lambert, Audrey Lamptey, Tamsin Landells, Sarah Lane, Tom Langdale, Anneka Lange, Annabel Langley, Eve Langley, James Langridge, Lucy Lapham, Danielle Latimer, Kei Lau, Safiatou Lawson, Ellie Lawton, Paul Lazarus, Hannah Leach, Sinead Leahy, Alice Leake, Edward Lee, Jenny Lee, Rebecca Lee, Sammy Lee, Susannah Lee, Jennie Leggat, Kelly Legrange, Leigh Stevenson Leib, Jamilah Leigh, Amy Lennox, Chris Lewington, Caroline Lewis, Lisa Lewis, Michael Lewis, Kerri Leybourne, Linfei Li, Manyin Li, Marielle Li, Chen Liang, Helena Lima, Lindo Lindo, Christina Lindquist, Helen Line, Grazina Linkeviciute, Sian Lipscomb, Karen Lister, Lu Liu, Yang Liu, Amy Liversidge, Kenzo Liwasa, Lucy Llewellyn, Tahiia Lloyd-Evans, Paige Lockwood, Roberto Lonetti, Georgia Long, Alec Longair, Sarah Longley, Victoria Longmore, Melanie Loudonsack, Nuno Lourenco Rodrigues, Emma Lovell, Robert Lowe, Karolina Lubecka, Jack Ludwig, Stephen Lue, Angela Lurssen, Amelia Lynch, Kat Lynch, Tamira Lynskey, Janita Maaranen, Josephine Maccarthy, Ceilidh Macdonald, Sophie Macken, Eleanor Mackinder, Robert Macnamara, Leanne Mae Macphail, Liam Maddin, Emma Mageean, Holly May Magill, Izabele Maitusyte, Marta Maj, Alena Maksimuk, Anita Makwana, Emily Malcolm, Malina Malina, Pui-Tien Man, Jaini Mandoda, Margarita Maniati, Leanne Manning, Patricia Manning, Rosa Manning, Ibrahim Mansaray, Bethany Manser, Husnara Mansoor, Claudiu Marinescu, Kevin Marlow, Elodie Marques De Oliveira, Laura Marr, Alexander Marsden, Kayleigh Marsh Davis, Gracie Marshall, Claire-Monique Martin, Casey Martin, Georgina Martin, Joanna Martin, Leanne Martin, Rebekah Martin, Leslie Mason, Kevin Matadeen, Katharine Mathers, Kirstie Mathieson, Jermaine Matias, Sophie Matthews, Josh Mayhew, Anna-Louisa Mazzola, Karen Mc Walter, Francesca Mcarthur, Luke McCabe, Paul Mccarthy, Rachael Hannah Mccaul, Tamara Mccombe, Sally Mcconville, Katharine Mcculloch, Frazer Mcdonald, Scott Mcdonald, Lynne Mcdowell, Chloe Mcgregor, Clodagh Mcguirk, Phoebe McIntosh, Alicia Mckenzie, Jessica Mckenzie, Caitlin Mcstay, Kyle Meade, Neil Meads, David Meany, Palma Measho, Aliya Meghjee, Lucy Mellamphy, Precious Meyer, Laura Middleton, Brianna Middleton Macpherson, Inge Midl, Brian Mifsud, Kanna Mihara, Bobby Miklausic, Matt Miller, Nathalie Miller, Rachel Miller, Stephanie Miller, Desiree Mills, Nathan Mills, Remmie Milner, Stephanie Milton, Mila Mincheva, Roberta Miozzi, Sophia Mir, Hassan Mirza, Zee Misikonyte, Punam Mistry, Trusha Mistry, Dennis Mitakos, Will Mitchell, Charmaine Mitchell, Remel Mohammed, Shade Mohammed, Zi Hong Mok, Ingrid Molinos Torres, Joanne Molyneux, Victoria Monaghan, Victoria Moor, Miriam Moore, Elinor Moran, Chahna Morgan, Emma Morgan, Hannah Morgan, Kaneen Morgan, Keisha Morgan, Carlene Morlese, Amber Mortelman, Emily Moss, Olivia Motyer, Adam Moulder, Mareme Mufwoko, Fiez Mughal, Laura Marie Mulholland, Chloe-Louise Mullen, Abbie Munk, Klisman Murati, Steven Murphy, Amy Murray, Martina Murtas, Wendy Musson, Cigden Mustafa, Amanda Myers, Leanne Myers, Nic Myers, Danielle Nadal, Frieda Nakimbugwe, Lauren Nash, Rachel Nash, Samita Nathoo, Harriet Naylor, Ndenko Ndenko Manguntang, Katie Neal, Ciarra Nevitt, Gemma Newby, Karen Newby, Olivia Newey, Grace Nichols, Carla Nicholson, Yang Ning, Hannah Nixon, Kevin Noble, Teresa Noble, Sophie Northmore, Aicha Noui, Amanda Nyandoro Chiyangwa, Nicole Nyemi-Tei, Lise Nymoen, Martha Oakley, Emma O'Brien, Charley O'Dell, Emily O'Donnell, Afie O'Donovan, Gifty Oduro, Andy Officer, Andrea Ogden, Sam Oh, Kiichiro Okano, Brandon O'Keeffe, Joan Okere, Adaku Okoro, Christina Okorocha, Bomi Okuyiga, Tunde Olasupo, Cat Oldham, Diana Olishaba, Luciana Oliveira Sousa Pederzoli, Tolu Oluwadare, Amy O'Malley, Precious Omonuwa, Shreeya Ondhia, Matthew O'Neill, Adaora Onuora, Jia Wen Ooi, Anne-Marie Oreskovich, Rosie O'Rourke, Gem Orthner, Dana Osadebe, Ryan Osang, Brodie O'Shea, Helena O'Shea, Sheun Oshinbolu, Razak Osman, Emily O'Sullivan, Cheryl Oteng, Michael Othen, Amber Ould, Habib Ouro-Gnao, Amy Owen, Derya Ozbasmaci, Katie Page, Roxanne Page, Sarah Pagram, Samantha Pain, Michal Paker, Jo Palmer, Rebecca Palmer, Stephanie Palmer, Ieva Palujanskaite, Carolyn Panday, Demetriani Pandi, Eleni Papaioannou, Rianna Parchment, Hannah Parker, Rhoda Parker, Jennifer Parmenter, Natalie Parnell, Sam Parry, Lp Parsons, Freya Parsons, Deirdre Pascall, Darshna Patel, Meshali Patel, Mitesh Patel, Reshma Patel, Sanoobar Patel, Charisse Patton, John Paulsen, Anna-Joi Payawal, Steve Payne, Hannah Pearce, Emily Pearse, Victoria Peck, Lu Peng, Xavier Perez, Rachel Periam, Louise Perrin, Ambi Nick Name Phgura, Lee Phillips, Sarah Phillips, David Phillips-Peters, Balwant Phlora, Abigail Pickard Price, Persephone Pickering, Katie Pickford, Jennifer Pidgeon, Louise Piper, Charles Pitt, Delvene Pitt, Sasha Plache, Merriel Plummer, Karelle Plummer-Walrond, Henry Poh, Lindsey Pollard, Rose Pook, Kate Popham, Sarah Portou, Caroline Portsmouth, Charlie Pottle, Dillon Powlett, Verity Pownall, Charlotte Preko, Ben Preston, Jolyon Price, Natalie Prosser, Bright Pryde, Despo Pseftodiakou, Amber Pyott, Adriano Quieti, Kelly Quintyne, Sam Quy, Rebecca Radford, Mariam Rahman, Jai Raichura, Nahema Rajabali, Ziyana Rajabali, Iniya Rajendran, Sara Ranthe, Laura Rapley, Alison Ray, Charlotte Rebecca Read, Al Reburiano, Emma Reeder, Helen Reeve, Karen Registe, Magnus Reinvik, James Rene, Jo Restall, Christopher Reynolds, Nicky Reynolds, Charlie Richards, Nicholas Richards, Christi Richardson, Freya Richardson, Naomi Richardson, Hannah Richbell, Carissa Rickeard, Fran Ridge, Kelly-Marie Ridgers, Mel Ridley, Christopher Ridley, Jennifer Riley, Shaun Riley, James Roberts, Bola Roberts, T'Rell Robinson, Gemma Robinson, Victoria Robinson, Kate Roche, Catherine Rock, Francy Milena Rodriguez, William Javier Rodriguez Laverde, Francisco Rodriguez Weil, Consuela Rolle, Sara Roman De La Pena, Aaron Romano, Chloe Rooney, Nathalie Rosamont, Katie Roscoe, Alexis Rose, James Rose, Ella Ross, Claire Rowley, Zheng Ruan, Karen Ruddock, Dhruv Rupapara, Nicole Rush, Ruwodo Ruwodo, Hayley Ryan, Tamsin Ryder, Sarah Saba, Sejal Sachdev, Yvette Sackey-Addo, Noita Sadler, Chantal Sainsbury, Amanda Sallis, Nicole Sallis, Anna Salmon, Troy Salmon, Natalie Salmons, Chanel Sam, Aran Samaroo, Sami Samid, Jessica Samuels, Eleanor Sandars, Amar Sandhu, Harleen Sandhu, Ashley Sandsmith, Amber Sansom-English, Ben Sansum, Sara Sazan, Akosua Scantlebury, Shelley-Anne Scarff, Briony Scarlett, Marit Schep, Phillip Schone, Nichola Schwarz, Sandra Sciutto-Cook, Lauren Scott-Berry, Robert Searle, Carli Searson, Charlotte Selwyn, Stephanie Sen, Charlotte Series, Zarah Serrano, Sarah Serunjogi, Rebecca Sewell, Mahvish Shafi, Rakhee Shah, Kirstie Shand, Kapilan Shanmuganathan, Katie Shapiro, Sarah Sharkah, Ankur Sharma, Ruchit Sharma, Ellie Sharp, Rachel Sheahan, Natalie Shelton, Lucie Sheppard, Stella Shepherd, Kelsie Shingler, Faith Shires, Kirstin Shirling, Mark Short, Dominik Siedlecki, Adilson Silva Santos, Wilza Silva-Mendes, Rachel Silveria, Joseph Simmons, Paige Simmons, Claudia Simos-Dziewonska, Monique Simpson, Elaine Simpson, Rebecca Simpson, Sherene Skinner, Robert Skinner, Katy Slade, Sarah Smallbone, Susannah Smallman, Jack Smart, Adele Smith, Faye Smith, Gemma Smith, James Smith, Joanne Smith, Katherine Smith, Kirstie Smith, Lauren Smith, Mark Smith, Natalie Louise Smith, Russell Smith, Sophie Smith, Victoria Smith, Zenna Smith-Allen, Bailey Smith-Bailey, Nicola Smithers, Katrina Smith-Jackson, Cienna Smyth, Pritpal Sodhi, Sakhdeep Sohi, Matthew Solomon, Stephanie Sorum, Emma Soulby, Kate Sparling, Louise Spearing, Lizzy Spencer, Liz Spratt, Rochelle Squires, Bethan Stacey, Catherine Stambouzou, Lukas Stanczuk, Amy Standing, Lizi Stansfield, Nicole Starling, Catriona Statham, Laura Steedman, Gemma Steel, Grant Sterry, Jordon Stevens, Peter Stevens, Guy Stewart, Vicky Stickland, Susan Stickley, Bobbie Stone, Peter Stonnell, Jonathan Stringer, Lucy Strudwick, Jakiya Sultana, Xiangchen Sun, Mengdi Sun, Adithya Sureshkumar, Laya Suseelan, Amy Swalwell, Sophie Sweeney, Ben Sykes, Sandra Szadkowska, Eszter Szalma, Cat Szygula, Bhavin Tailor, Karinlolita Takacs, Emma Tallamy, Josaia Tamani, Johnny Tan, Ricky Tanna, Liliana Tavares, Caroline Taylor, David Taylor, Jaclyn Taylor, Stephanie Taylor, Theresa Taylor, Valeria Tello Giusti, Harriet Rose Temple, Gary Thatcher, Sarah Thayre, Asha Thomas, Geoffrey Thomas, Hannah Thomas, Louise Thomas, Mica Janet Thomas, Raewyn Thomas, Simon Thomas, Sita Thomas, Andy Thompson, Cherie Thompson, Eleanor Thompson, Felicity Thompson, Lisa Thomson, Eleanor Thurlow, Robin Thurlow, David Tihanyi, Damola Timeyin, Patricia Tobin, Steph Tollan, Blair Tookey, Husna Torabally, Naomi Trimble, Vanessa Trotter, Rebecca Trumble, Hoang Truong, Heloise Tsang, Aiston Tucker, Emma Tugman, Guzen Tuna, Hana Turkova, Andrea Turner, Beatrix Turny, Angela Turvey, Petia Tzanova, Matthew Ubogagu, Kenya Uchida, Marta Ucinska, Zafar Uddin, Francesca Florence Leatrice Ugwuegbulam-Condor, Mehreen Umar, Julie Unwin, Devanshi Upreti, Toby Urie, Ruth Uwadiale, Maudette Uzoh, Rachel Vallance, Daniella Varadi, Gabor Varga, Ben Vasey, Hannah Vaudin, Reanna Venn, Navadini , Emma-Louise Vincent, Hannah Vincent, Natasha Wade, Louise Wainwright, Sophie Wakefield, Clare Wakeling, David Waker, James Walker, Kay Walker, Kyle Walker, Shána Walker, Stuart Walker, Leah Jean Walker Murrain, Eliza Walkling, Rachel Wall, Carla Wallace, Jacqui Wallace, Abbie Waller, Nicole Walton, Wai-Mei Wan, Danlin Wang, Siwei Wang, Ivy Warari, Frankie Ward, Judith Ward, Julie Ward Ward, Kayleigh Ward, Rebecca Ward, Morgane Ware, Jess Warin, Laura Waringer, Michael Warrick-Gooding, Liz Waters, Daisy Watford, Sherryn Watkin, Watson Watson, Melanie Weatherhead, Katy Weaver, Lucie Weaver, Annalise Webb, Larissa Anna Webb, Amy Webster, Joseph Webster, Olivia Weeks, Basia W gorzewska, Holly Welham, Sophie Wells, Tony Weston, Kate Whalesby, Georgie Wharton, Milly Wheal, Peter Wheeler, Sharmaine Whilby-Brown, Alice White, Alyssia Symone White, Bria White, Hana White, Ian White, Jane White, Mary-Liz White, Natasha White, Samantha White, Denwin Whitebooi, Martin Whitehair, Katie Wignall, Rachel Wilcock, Laura Wilkes, Alison Wilkin, Jocelyn Wilkinson, Brooks Williams, Cheryl Williams, Dalanda Williams, Janette Williams, Jody Williams, Lisa-Ann Williams, Michell Williamson, Emily Willis, Maisie Wilson, Max Wilson, Sebastian Wilson, Bo Marcus Win, Becky Wingham, Susanne Winkler, Laura Winnan, Rochelle Wisdom, Paige Wise, Avital Wittenberg, Thais Wizenberg, Adam Wojcik, Max Wolf, Russell Woo, Clare Wood, Jemma Wood, Jamie Woods, Mark Worthington, Carina Wrapson, Katherine Wrench, Ayesha Wright, Keeley Wright, Lucy Wright, Nikki Wright, Victoria Wright, Thomas Wynn, Alicia Wynton, Bethan Wynton, Shannen Xenofontos, Rui Xi, Yaz Yahya Alahdal, Mu Yang, Tiffany Yarde, Kimberley Yarde, Selina Yasmine, Emily Yau, Gabriel Yau, Mona Yeganegi, Juliet York, Shereen Young, Grace Yusuf, Mohsin Zaidi, Omer Zakaria, Ao Zhang, Louisa Ziane, Sylvia Zsigmond **Welcome** Salim Abdulwasie, Yewande Abiodun, Adejoke Abudu, Nell Adams, Elizabeth Adediran, Oluwafoyinsayo Adekusibe, Naseem Adeniran, Elizabeth Adlington, Cintea Ahamefule, Saber Ahmed, Shuel Ahmed, Tanyel Ahmet, Oluwatosin Ajibade, Nazia Aktar, Kalsuma Akthar, Blessing Aladetoun, Camille Alleyne, Samantha Alleyne, Sayequl Ambia, Lisa Anderson, Emily Anderson, Marija Andrulyte, Shannon Antoine, Amy Anzel, Danielle Apakoh, Charlotte Appleby, Eylul Arif, Natasha Armitage, Ismael Arratte, Mandy Ashmore, Sonny Athey, Lola Atkins-Omojola, Niha Bajpai, Perter Bakarr, Nichola Baker, Tinashe Balayi, Chantelle Ball, Olivia Ball, Dumitru Bandol, Eva Banik, Laura Baranik, Laquisha Barden-Simpson, Guna Bareika, Brooke Barker, Alana Barnard, Natalie Barrett, Samsrithaa Baskaran, Mikaela Bates, Rayyan Bawazir, Pamela Beattie, Khiltee Beeharry, Amita Begum, Poppy Begum, Rima Begum, Cathryn Bell, Imogen Bell, Ugne Bendikaite, Lauryn Bennett, Conrad Bernard, Alice Bird, Briony Black, Harry Blake-Herbert, Christine Blayney, Mary Boateng, Fatima Boudafcha, Charlotte Boundy, Adriana Braz, Callum Brierley, Hollie Brill, Katherine Brown, Eimear Browne, Larissa Bulla, Alice Bullard, Fiona Bullard, Adam Burman, Gypsy Bushaway, Kellie Butcher, Marie Calvert, Megan Campbell, Huy Cao, Jhean Capitan, Sara Carter, Rebecca Carver, Darryl Causon, Lun Chai, Miguel Chamorro Correa, Joey Chapman, Peter Chong-Yen Gebrian, Afser Choudhury, Eshaan Choudhury, Jamal Choudhury, Maria Choudhury, Lennox Christie, Caroline Cobby, Siobhan Cockfield, Mariatu Cole, Lucas Coleman, Courtney Connolly, Roseanna Connolly, Samuel Connolly, Emily Cornuaud, Jamie Cornuaud, Amy Jane Cotter, Nerys Coventry, Rebecca Coxon, Julia Crawley-Boevey, Rhona Crewe, Ashleigh Crowhurst, Emma Curzon, Wendy Dang, Irina Danilova, Klesha Darroux, Zaynab Daudo, Catherine Davies, Tilly-Rose Day, Clare De Jode, Ellis De Stefano, Thomas Dear, Elizabeth Demetriou, Danielle Deveney, Parveen Dhanda, Kristen Dintino, Hannah Diribe, Isobel Dobson, Nazeem Doherty, Xianhui Dong, Liza Dos Santos, Rayner Dougan, Meilan Duong, Maria Emilia Dutto, Nicola Dykes, Emeke Ejimadu, Leila Elbahy, Ayorinde Elegbe, Molly Eley, Selina Elliott, Blessing Emenike, Erica Emm, Crystal Emmanuel, Gokay Emre, Ellyse Essel, Simone Etienne, Katie Evans, Lewis Evans, Chidnma Ezeabasili, Melanie Farquharson, Adele Fash, Martine Faulkner, Rocio Fernandez Fresquet, Ellen Fife, Syra Flaxman-Ali, Morgan Forlan, Morgan Forrester, Georgie Foster, Jennifer Franich, Shea French-Gibbens, Sophie Fuller, Kristina Gadalin, Fei Gao, Patrisha Garlang, Clooniy Gaspar, Marissa Geldenhuys, Monique Geraghty, Joy Grace Gilbert, Alice Gilkes, Jennifer Gilkes, Nathan Giraudel, Cherelle Gogar, Charlotte Goodhew, Olivia Gooding, Joanie Goss, Aimee Goyette, Amber Grange, Natalie Gray, Sophie Greaves, Charlotte Green, Jordan Green, Jack Grimwood, Kacper Grochocki, Hiruni Gunasekara, Lisa Ha, Millie Hagland, Nicola Haji-Antonis, Clare Halifax, Maria Hamalainen, Christopher Hancock, Paul Hansen, Ornella Hardie, Mersyl Harding, Yonis Hashi, Amina Hassam, Aoife Hawe, Victoria Hawkes, Amanda Hawthorne, Caryn Haynes, Nathan Haynes, Nathan Hayward, Patsy Hayward, Leticia Alejandra Herrera Perez, Ryan Heselden, Ailsa Hewitt, Sara Hill, Elias Hmaimou, Wendy Ho, Emma Hobbs, Juliet Hogarth, Alice Holt, Christine Hopson, Wan-Ting Hsieh, Carrie Hua, Huarui Huang, Albert Hughes, Polly Hunt, Jakeya Hussain, Rahinoor Hussain, Lufton Hyseni, Arbaaz Ifzal, Inemesit Imoh, Victoria Irving, Sayka Islam, Claire Jackson, Felicity Jackson, Tiffany Jackson, Ramazan Jakupi, Mahroof Jalil, Joely Johnson, Sheree Johnson, Jessica Johns-Parsons, Georgia Johnston, Bradley Jones, Ezgi Kahraman, Adelina Kalanyos, Phoebe Kane, Miriam Karanja, Millie Karn, Viktoria Kasetaite, Balwinder Kaur, Paul Keating, Hana Kelblova, Kase Keogh, Frances Keyton, Hakim Khan, Fateha Khanam, Shorifa Khanam, Thameda Khanam, Liudmila Khvan, Ahsan Kibria, Lyndsey Kilkenny, Ceara King, Ellie King, Eboni Kirton, Harry Kitchener-Trevillion, Thomas Knight, Yvonne Kumi, Ergys Kurtulaj, Selda Kurtuldu, Margaret Labongo, George Lagalle, Clare Lane, Constance Lawton, Bethan

Volunteers
Bénévoles

Lee, Danyang Lei, Viktoria Lengyel, Kristina Lewis, Tia Lewis, Zhen Lim, Hannah Lloyd-Jones, Sophia Loi Shaw, Diane Longmuir, Musa-Eiggie Luba, Emmanuelson Luizi, Flo Lunt, Xiaomin Luo, Michaela Lupton, Morgan Lyons, Leon Mabiala, Robert Macdonald, Magdalena Maciejewska, Nida Mahmud, Corinne Maillet, Danilson Malungu, Benedicty Mambi, Zachary Manamella-Chwalek, Mary Ann Mangano, Kayleigh Mann, Cheryl Manning, Jessica Manuel, Japera Marshall-Mcdavid, Cristina Mascia, Daisy Mayhew, Ana-Paula Mazarini, Aiden Mccarney, April Mccarthy, Natalie Mcgrath, Megan Mckenna, James Meikle, Tanya Melia, Caesar Mendee, Forhad Miah, Zoe Middleton, Anna Miles, Caroline Mistry, Aye Moe, Angela Moran, Rebecca Morgan, Sonia Morjaria, Michael Morris, Reanne Morris, Rachel Morton, Sarah Mujinya-Motima, Shirley Mukisa, Luke Munro, Liam Murphy, Lis Mustafa, Christina Myers, Nila Natkunan, Beverley Nderu, Caroline Nembharde, Wein Ng, Annine Ngesang, Sabine Nguini, Susan Nguyen, John Nguyen, Charlotte Nice, Danica Noh, Adil Noor, Holly Norman, Thea North, Tabassum Nusiba, Alexander Nutt, Owen Nwanebu, Kariba Nwodo, Cindy Obasa, Mirian Obiozo, Mary Obrien, Olivia O'Callaghan, Caroline Odogwu Odogwu, Fajila Oguz, Michael Okosie, Anike Okusanya, Suliet Oladokun, Olamide Olaiya, Diana Olloova, Samson Oludemi, Charlton Omo-Edoh, Rugile Oraite, Elsie O'Rourke, Jonathan Ortavikiabakufi, Karl Osei Kwateng, Mercy Osinlaru, Kima Otung, Willaim Palaganas, Caitlin Parr, Rupal Patel, Ibrahim Patel, Nimish Patel, Daniel Pearson, Sam Pellicci, Hanna Peltonen, My-Linh Phan, Sunanta Phattanavibul, Kye Plakhtienko, Monblanc Pondani, Tabitha Porter, Hannah Powell, Janette Powell, Rasheed Powell, Spencer Prichard, Katie Proctor, Michele Puliti, George-Martin Purssord, Jacob Radford, Izzie Radley, Peter Rafferty, Mahjabin Rahman, Tahmidur Rahman, Firdausi Rahman, Vanessa Ralte, Sinead Rampat, Preeti Rana, Anya Reevell, Jo Regis, Charlotte Reilly, Charlotte Riche, Veronica Ripo, Marisa Robinson, Natasha Robinson, Stephen Robinson, Ilaria Rovera, Agnieszka Rudnik, Shannon Rule, Karim Saber, Hardeep Sahota, Arafat Said, Fahad Said, Jacob Said, Esat Saiti, Danielle Sampson, Dominique Sapsin, Berry Saunders, Lucy Scotchmer, Charlotte Scott, Kathrin Selbmann, Dilara Sert, Rita Sexious, Nishtah Sian, Leah Simmons, Rachel Simmons, Isobel Slater, Hayley Smith, Janesia Smith, Pippa Smith, Hilary Smith, Daria Solovyeva, Deidre Sorensen, Vaishnavee Sreeharan, Kimani St. Hill, Amanda Stewart, Ellie Stringer, Lilith Sumesar-Rai, Hayley Syme, Kerry Tabb, Elba Tapia Montes, Olivia Taviani, Archie Taylor, Morgan Taylor, Julie Taylor, Liam Taylor, George Thompson, Soriah Thompson-Dunkley, Cat Thrower, Eleanor Thrower, Justine Thrower, Anthony To, Hannah Tobin, Anna Tomlinson, Monique Toussaint, Frances Tresadern, Isabella Tresadern, Yulia Tskhay, Yvana Tuladhar Lorenzo, Aisha Tunio, Bonny Turner, Lorna Turner, Michael Tyler, Oliver Tyzack, Adam Uddin, Amirul Uddin, Chantelle Ullah, Ilayda Uludag, Sarah Usuanlele, Amanda Vacianna, Laura Viander, Vivien Vinning, Katie Vorontsova, Scott Wallis, Joshua Walsh, Wenjing Wang, Emily Ward, Jodie Watson, Susannah Wells, Ryan West, Sarah Westergaard, Aimee White, Nyome Whitfield, Gemma Whyley, Amy Wicks, Jennifer Wilkins, Bethan Williams, Samantha Jane C Williams, Tahirah Williams Espinosa, Tommy Wills, Avenell Winston, Katey Wood, Thomas Wray, Josh Wright, Louise Wright, Aliki Zachariadi, Aliza Zafar, Oscar Zebala, Violeta Zepinic, Linda Zeqja, Chen Zhang, Jia Zhao **Bike a.m.** Maryam Amatullah, Benjamin Askin, Ian Barrow, Scott Baxter, Martina Ben-Shaul, Paul Bird, Peter Bowers, Joanne Bradley, James Brooke Turner, Andrew Caldwell, Damian Cannon, Adam Capes, Zoe Capstick, Christopher Carter, Geoffrey Castello, Michael Coles, Anthony Collier, Wayne Crombie, Orlando Cubitt, Ian Curran, Jacob Dean, Andrew Dowden, Tracy Farrell, Wendy Flicker, Barry Garnham, Darius Garnham, Paul Gathercole, Peter Gottlieb, Martha Grekos, Matt Griffin, Adrian Harrison, Peter Harvey, Tony Harvey, Jeff Hathaway, Richard Herbert, Rory Huston, Gareth Jones, Joseph Kamau, Dean Keable, Fraser Kennedy, Richard Kerslake, Sandra Levet, William Mcavock, Julian Mccarthy, Alex Milne, Vincent Mullen, Stuart Newman, Geoff Nutter, Simon Oxley, Rob Parry, Debbie Patel, Leo Perez, Anthony Price, Mark Reader, Adrian Robinson, James Robinson, Steph Robinson, Victor Romsom, Louis Sargent, Matthew Shaw, James Shore, David Taylor, David Tiplady, Peter Tyler, Arlen Vartazarian, Charles Whelan, Tony White, Alex Whiting, Joe Willis, Tim Worboys **There is a Light That Never Goes Out** Alex Adams, Joseph Adams, Andrew Ainscough, Patrick Aiyeola, Paloma Algarra, Niall Allen, Anthony Anderson, David Ansell, Julian Ansell, Paul Ansell, Megan Ashfield, Sabah Ashiq, Simon Atherton, Cecilia Bagenholm, Anna Baker, Gareth Baker, Steven Baldry, Lesley Barratt, Roger Barratt, Rastislav Bartek, Alexander Beck, Daniel Beck, Robert Bedford, Stephen Berry, Zak Bickerstaffe, David Birchall, Matthew Birchall, Anthony Birkbeck, Tony Blackmore, Gary Blakemore, Mark Blunnie, Catherine Bocken, Simon Borg, Julie Bowerman, Mark Bragg, Richard Breslin, David Brewer, Owen Brewster, Emma Bridges, Nicholas Bristow, Julian Britnell, Keith Brown, Kelly Brown, Stephen Brown, Stephen Burley, Andrew Burns, Cheryl Burpitt, Gillian Butcher, Royston Butcher, Roger Button, Sean Byrne, Colin Caddy, John Calland, Jason Calvert, Juan Canada, Nichola Chambers, Karl Chaplow, Mustapha Charki, Sarah Chimes, Suzanne Clark, Samuel Cocker, Dafydd Coe, David Coffey, Andrew Collins, Edward Collis, Catherine Colman, Charles Cooke, Colin Cooper, Zac Cornish, Charlotte Cox, Kevin Crean, Christine Crosby, Ian Crosby, Oonagh Crotty, Robert Crouch, Tomothy Culverhouse, Stephen Daly, Scott Dark, Colin Davies, Kevin Davies, Malcolm Davies, Richard Davies, Wyn Davies, Andrew Davison, Jeffrey Denehan, John Dennis, Ryan Derbyshire, Mykola Derevinskyy, Dexter Dest, Daniel Devonport, Brian Ditchburn, Craig Ditchfield, Adam Doak, Phillip Dodd, Neil Doherty, Andrew Downes, Dr. Florian Block, David Dropkin, Robert Druce, Michael Duncan, Martin Eastham, Stuart Eastmead, Matthew Eastwood, Victoria Eddins, Christine Edwards, Derek Egan, Roy Elliott, Scott Ellis, John Ellision, Soraya Elwin, Lucas Epp, David Evans, John Evans, Nicholas Evans, Timothy Evans, Keith Farthing, Michael Fee, Adam Feeney, Neil Fernee, Warren Few, Christine Fielding, Lauren Finch, John Fisher, Stephen Fogg, Timothy Forbes, Billy Ford-Langan, David Fortey, Paul Foskett, Gary Francis, Robert Frost, Kevin Fryer, Siegmar Gabler, Constantin Gainat, David Galavan, Joe Gallagher, Elsa Garcia Lopez, Paul Gare, Robert Garland, Patrick Gavin, Arthur Gelling, Samuel Gilston, Marcus Ginns, Kandiah Gnaneswaran, Belinda Goh, Alv Gomez, Javier Gonzalez Hernandez, Robert Goodall, Clifford Gordon, Peter Gordon, John Gradwell, John Graham, Michael Green, Paul Green, Andrew Grice, Malcolm Gulvin, Lotay Gurmeet, Stephen Hackney, Christopher Hall, Edwin Hamilton, Stephen Hamnett, David Harley, Jeremy Harmsworth, Graham Harvey, Jonathan Hawes, Jamie Hay, Andrew Hayward, Lisa Hearse, Juergen Helmer, Darren Henderson, Joby Henderson, Michael Hewlett, Gaynor Hill, Clive Hills, Mark Hindle, David Hines, Gerald Hogben, Craig Hooper, Kevin Houlihan, Shaun Hoyle, Daniel Hudson, Jarrod Hulme, Akbar Hussain, Naveed Hussain, Joanna Hyland, John Hyland, Patrick Hyland, Susan Hyland, Francesca Ibrahim, Eloise Irving, Soaad Islam, Heiko Jaap, Antony Jackson, Stephanie Jackson, Colin Jacob, Anthony Jameson, Daniel Jarvis, Paul Jearum, Kingsley Jenkins, Richard Jenkins, Dale Jennins, Gwenael Jerrett, Martin Johnson, Philip Johnson, Antony Jones, Huw Jones, Matthew Jordan, Darren Joyce, Stanislav Kamburov, Andreas Karaiskos, Benet Kaser, David Kay, Tony Keane, Keith Kearton, Christopher Keenan, Andrew Kelly, Manus Kelly, John Kennedy, Alena Kereshun, Michael Keverne, Eamon Kilgannon, Freddy Kinavuidi, David King, Nicola King, David Kirkland, Barry Knight, Joanna Kuzelewska, David Langley, Damon Lavelle, Susan Leach, Mark Leeming, Darren Lever, Scott Lewis, Michael Line, Paul Lloyd, Samuel Longley, Adam Lucas, Daniel Lucas, Katie Lucas, Annette Macauley, Roderick Macauley, Thomas Maccarron, Anil Mahey, David Mahoney, Tim Mak, Thomas Mann, Elvet Mantle, Richard Marsh, Clifford Martin, Mark Maynard, Neil Mccallum, Hugh Mccann, John Mclafferty, Fergus Mccormick, Donald Mcdade, Daniel Mcdermott, Michael Mcdonald, Martin Mcevoy, Sean Mcgranaghan, Paul Mcgrath, Martin Mcguire, Patrick Mcmanus, Paul Mcsloy, Ray Mcspadden, Paul Mead, Mark Melnick, Laura Menzies, Henry Miller, Caroline Mills, Victoria Milnes, Paul Mitchell, Rhett Monahan, Brian Moone, Carly Moore, Brodie Moran, Virginia Morris, Kenneth Mulholland, Andrew Mulligan, Declan Murphy, Hensley Murray, Laurence Murray, Sean Neary, James Neill, Bruce Nixon, Brian O Brien, James O'Dwyer, Joshua O'Hagan, Denis O'Leary, Mark O'Neill, Kendal O'Reilly, Dean Orr, James Owens, Gordon Park, Abdul Kadir Parkar, Robyn Parton, Bhogilal Patel, Pirathapan Perayeravar, Saverimuthu Phillips, Daniel Phillips, Daniel Pilling, David Pitchford, Henning Plschke, Claudia Poller, Stuart Potts, Matthew Preston, Philip Quedou, Michael Quinn, Jacqueline Radford, Christopher Randall, Somkiat Rangkla, Stephen Raw, Philip Rayment, Matthew Razzell, Garry Reeves, Gary Reeves, Lindsay Reid, John Rhodes, Ceri Richards, Alan Richardson, Robin Rix, Jacqueline Roberts, Sophie Roberts, Jack Robinson, Bryn Rodgers, Anke Rollenhagen, Phillip Rosby, Scott Roscoe, Paul Rothwell, James Rowe, Charlotte Rowell, Christopher Rowell, Jean-Baptiste Ruat, Roshantha Rupesinghe, Andrew Russell, Mark Russell, David Ryan, Gurminder Saron, James Saunders, Judith Schulz, Russell Scrase, Alfie Scully, Megan Seal, Michael Searle, Sophie Severs, Prabjit Shehri, Kieron Shepherd, Michael Simmons, Russel Simmons, Dave Simpson, Janine Sjoblom, Stig Sjoblom, Christopher Slater, Mark Slater, Sara Slaytor, Ben Smith, Christine Smith, Derek Smith, Howard Smith, Joanne Smith, Paul Smith, Raymond Smith, Scott Smith, Trevor Snell, Neil Snow, Kar-Paik Soon, Gary Soutan, Robert Sperring, Marc Spinner, Anthony Stanford, Elvira Stathatou, Jacob Steele, Michael Stephens, Barry Stone, Lee Stones, Hugh Strathern, Ashokkumar Subbiah, Hamish Sutherland, George Sweeney, Rafiuddin Syed, Jonathan Tague, Brian Tapp, Isobel Tapp, Derek Taylor, Gary Taylor, George Taylor, Susan Taylor, Tom Taylor, Martin Teasdale, Matthew Teasdale, Benjamin Thomas, Dean Thomas, Jeffrey Thompson, Robert Thompson, Andrew Timbers, Van Tran, John Travers, Nadia Trepkowska, Kenneth Trippick, Clare Tubman, David Tull, Keith Turnbull, Joseph Turner, Badar Uddin, Richard Unwin, Vadims Unzakovs, Maria De Jesus Villar Canovas, Akash Wadhawan, Jamie Walker, Thomas Walker, Stephen Wallace, Daniel Walls, John Walton, James Ward, Jeffrey Warner, James Warren, Joanna Waterfield, Tracy Waters, Kay Watson, Anthony Welsh, Karen Welsh, Robert Wesoly, Aisling Whelan, Joseph White, Paul White, Richard White, Lee Whiteaker, Robert Wildman, Peter Wilkinson, David Wilks, Lara Williams, Roger Willicott, Amy Wilson, Richard Wilson, Michelle Winstone, Andrew Wintle, Louisa Wood, Sharon Wood, Nicholas Woolley, Frank Worsley, Craig Yates, Scott Youlds, Michael Young, Hernando Zambrano, Yanev Zlatko, Andreas Zoch **Creative Team** Makayla Abraham, Ash Sohyun Ahn, Caroline Akselson, Jessica Albon, Tanya Alexander, Fatima Ali, Nazia Ali, Jahir Ali, Louise Allberry, Jennifer Allen, Justin Allin, Josephine Allitt, Shaimaa Alruwaished, Hana Amer, Katherine Anderson, Ashley Andrews, Maria Anning, Alicia Apaloo-Edwards, Jack Appleyard, Helene Arnesen, Isabella Asimadi, Storm Athill, Sophia Austen-Meek, Sian Ayres, Yvonne Bailey, Mathura Balanadarasan, Sophie Bann, Claire Bannister, Rebecca Barclay, Penelope Bardoni, Lyndsey Barnewell, Matej Barszcz, Tonia Bastyan, Dean Batte, Natalie Beales, Daisy Beattie, Anna Beckett, Apia Begum, Shahania Begum, Shamama Begum, Katie Bell, Eki Belo-Osagie, Carol Belston, Charlotte Bentham, Piotr Berkowicz, Agathe Bernardon, Deepti Bhalla, Sobia Bhatti, Grant Bigland, Jennifer Bigland, Gemma Bishop, Poppy Biswell, Chloe Blake, Matthew Blount, Kathleen Boland, Anna Bonomi, Natasha Bott, Charlotte Boulton, E Boussekson, Katie-May Boyd, Eve Bradshaw, Geno Brantley, Molly Bray, Eve Brayshaw, Bernadette Brennan, Eleanor Brereton, Amy Brian, Ross Britten, Charlotte Brook, Gregory Brown, Claire Bunyard, Tazmin Burr, Lily Burrows, Eleanor Butcher, Sarah-Jane Caddock, Luman Cai, Fabianne Calitri, Grace Cameron, Charlotte Campbell, Stuart Campbell, Lisa Carracedo, Rachel Carter, Danielle Casey, Bridget Cass, Amy Cassell, Ella Chadwick, Bonnie Chai, Kit Shuen Chan, Yu Hui Chan, Ying Tung Chan, Rosie Chaplin, Nadine Chapman, Jason Charles, Grace Cheetham, Szu-Jung Chen, Viviane Chen, Eponone Chen, Dong Hoon Choi, Joanna Christou, Lidia Cimule, Loren Clark, Emma Connor, Victoria Conte, Alison Convery, Adam Cookson, Eleanor Coole-Green, Anne Cooper, Shaun Corcoran, Helga Cory-Wright, Florence Court, Chloe Cowan, Zac Coyle, Alex Crawford, Alexandra Cresswell, Amy Cresswell, Emma Cresswell, Connie Croasdale, Mary Cuffe, Mary Cuffe, Danielle Cullen, Henrietta Curtis, Anna Czerniavska, David Daglish, Miriam Damanhuri, Alice Dan, Sharna David, Gabrielle Davies, Frances Davies, Holly Davies, Lucy Davis, Julia Day, Amy De Rees, Daniel Defreitas, Amy DeRees, Amanda Derrick, Joana Dias, Claire Docherty, Rebecca Doidge, Tatiana Dolmatovskaya, Blake Douglas, Harriet Dyson, Danielle Eagles, Anthony Earles, Harriette Earp, Samantha Easey, Joanna East, Carolyn Ebanks, Katie Eden, Georgina Edwards, Bryony Edwards, Maja Ehliar, Charlotte England, Gemma Evans, Constantina Evriviadou, Tobias Fairclough, Josie Falconer, Aileen Faller, Jonathan Fensom, Sophie Finch, Wendy Foggin, Charley Fone, Edwin Ford, Rebecca Forknall, Luca Formica, Jessica Fournier D'Albe, Samantha Fox, Melissa Francis, Christabel Franklin, Chloe French, Marjorie Frick, Gemma Friel, Momoko Fujiwara, Katie Garden, Ruby Gaskell, Suchen Ge, Lauren Gee, Noella Geoghegan, Eleanor Gibson, Enka Gill, Caroline Gladwin, Beata Goaszweska, Joanna Goodman, Danielle Grant, Elizabeth Grant, Jessica Green, Elaine Guillon, Tharanga Gunawardena, Karen Gurney, Sandra Gustafsson, Zlatka Halkova, Melissa Hall, Jessica Halsey, Holly Hamblin, Kim Hamilton, Meng Hao, Alissa Harger, Iyo Hasegawa, Geraldine Hawkins, Alison Haworth, Jemma Haywood, Florence Hazard, Celestine Healy, Emma Heard, Audrey Elizabeth Hedgecock, Chloe Henderson, Holly Rose Henshaw, Clare Hepburn, Abigail Hernon, Francesca Hey, Amy Hickie, George Hims, Lysette Hodgson, Ruby Hodgson, Alix Holdaway-Salmon, Scarlett Hooper, Rachel Hopper, Sarah Hosein, Tina Hsu, Shuyi Huang, Chanel Huang, Jessica Hughes, Rosina Humphrey, Joanna Hunnisett, Toria Hunt, Jamila Hussain, Michelle Huynh, Silje Isaksen, Nur Ismail, Annan Jaggernauth, Gillian Jarvis, Rebecca Jempson, Madeleine Jenkins, Laura Jenkins, Katie Jenkinson, Laura Jenkinson, Charlotte Jepson, Amy Job, Bob Johnson, Margaret Johnson, Natasha Johnson, Georgia Jones, Lucy Jones, Rebecca Jones, Sophia Joseph, Eleanor Joyce, Holly Judd, Elizabeth Kane, Abul Kasam, Abul Kasam, Megan Keegan, Holly Keen, Tanya Keen, Muireann Kelly, Charlotte Kelly, Kristine Kenmochi, Ahhyun Kim, Joseph Kim-Suzuki, Harriet Kings, Leanne Kinnie, Osnat Koblenz, Veronika Kovacikova, Igli Kroqi, Georgina Lamb, Darren Lancett, Alexandra Langman, Sophie Langsford, Sara Laratro, Josie Lee, Tom Leggat, Demelza Leng, Caroline Lewis, Ge LI, Yangyang Li, Ruoxuan Li, Shuang Liang, Kate Lithgow, Roberta Lockett, Narash Lohia, Sue Lowe, Antonia Lynch, Eilidh Lyons, Amy Macpherson, Emma Madray, Sara Maggi, Beverley Magtibay, Saad Mahmood, Rebecca Mahoney, Maria Mantilla, Ivan Manzella, Kathryn Marooney, Joanna Marshall, Freya Martin, Sierra Martin, Anna Martin, Tasha Marvell, John May, Ann-Marie Mays, Tansy McCluskie, Pete McDonagh, Jo McDonald, Sammi McGuigan, Michelle McHale, Letitia McLaughlin, Dorothy McLennan, Amy McPherson, Laura Meichtry, Olivia Catherine Mellowes, Cheramour Meoquanne, Florence Meredith, Gabrielle Milanese, Stephanie Miles, Jennifer Millen, Darci Miller, Dan Miller, Bo-Kyung Min, Clodagh Miskelly, Jasumati Mistry, Hannah Mitchell, Connor Mitchell, Sabrina Mohamed, Abigail Moller, Paula Gonzalez Montecino, Rosey Morling, Ronan Morrow, Madalaine Mould, Jillian Murray, Yuki Nakamura, Kamal Natt, Chloe Newman, Candice Newton, Billy Yu Lok Ng, Mandy Ngo, Fern Nolan, Jo Noon, Tanya Noor, Bianca Nugent, Michael Offei, Tosin Ogunsanya, Rebecca O'Higgins, Christina Omideyi, Zanna Orage, Zeanab Oshinbolu, Rainelle Osuji, Priscilla Otema, Lucy Packham-O'Brien, Sharon Page, Georgia Paget, Samuella Palmer, Natasha Payne, Donna Pendarvis, J. Childe Pendergast, Manavi Perera, Cathy Perkins, Fong Perry, Shamaela Perwiz, Louise Phelan, Gloria Enechojo Philip, Sabina Piccini, Hannah Pick, Patrick Pintaske, Lucy Pittard, Richard Pledge, Alice Pocock, Fiona Pollard, Claire Pompili, Lucy Ponting, Lara Prentice, Natasha Prynne, Faye Pulleyn, Anna Radecka, Syd Rae, Samantha Ranaweera, Kernisha Ransome, Nadia Rasheed, Harriet Reed, Megan Reidy, Natasha Ridley, Barbora Rimkova, Reenell Roach-Williams, Mark Roberts, Pamela Roberts, Elizabeth Roberts, Emma Robinson, Katherine Rogers, Madeleine Ross-Masson, Calista Ross-Peterson, Sophie Rowatt, Megan Rowlands, Sunita Sagoo, Nassima Saidani, Rachel Salenius, Clara Samuel, Kaylee Sanford, Billie Sanger, Marcio Santarosa, Pranav Sarin, Gerda Satunaite, Anna Saunders, Kate Seckington, Wamika Sehgal, Mai Seida, Rabeeah Shah, Melissa Sharpe, Sobia Shatti, Mengqin Shen, Deric Shen, Emma Sheppard, Poonam Shukla, Monika Sievers, Yana Simakova, Rachael Simpson, Gurfateh James Singh, Charlotte Slade, Mark Smith, Charlotte Smith, Lucia Smith, Olivia Broadbent Smith, Rosanna Smith, Chris Smith, Emme Sparre-Slater, Angela Spink, Lorna Stimson, Camelia Sule, Kemi Sulola, Tamanna Sultana, Emma Sutcliffe, Philippa Sutcliffe, Hannah Sutherland, Sarah Sweet, Kazusa Takamura, Angel Tam, Nicola Tattersfield, Poppy Taylor, Matthew Taylor, Molly Taylor, Nicola Teale, Helena Tegeder, Marina Tegeder, Helen Thomas, PK Thummukgool, Kathryn Tickle, Mai Tieu, Beth Tilly, Charlie Todman, Bryony Tofton, Isabelle Tollitt, Billie Towers, Katherine Towerton, Julia Townend, Sekou Traore, Cecile Tremolieres, Louisa Trickett, Gina Trinchese, Anastasia Tsangarides, Melanie Tse, Alice Tucker, Beca Tuffnell, Jonathan Turner, Lisa Valde, Wendy Castano Vega, Sophie Venes, Ruby Vestey, Paul Vincent, Daniel Vincenze, Kalpani Vitharana, Tom Voller, Jana Vrabelova, Angela Wade, Angela Wade, Caroline Walotka, Xiaoyun Wang, Victoria Watson, Jordan Watson, Elizabeth Webb, Jamey-Leigh Weber, Lianna Weidle, Jess Wheelband, Leanne White, Gianne Williams, Naomi Williams, Anna Witcombe, Finola Woolgar, Stephanie Woolven, Ying Wu, Lixiaoxue Xia, Jing Yang, Lanxiubo Yang, Yang Yang, Farhana Yeasmien, Amanda Yuan, Jovana Zarubica, Mona Zaw, Ruth Zewge, Xinyu Zhang, Yiyi Zhao, Min Zhou **Technical Team** Tracy Abercombie, David Adkin, James Adkins, Mauricio Affonso, Ash Ahn, Christopher Amaning, Keren Amroussi, Eleanor Andrews, Nick Ashby, Theo Athanasopoulos, Miles Baldwin, Charlotte Banner, Jonathan Barlow, Andrea Bennett, Paul Bond, Nikki Boone, Bekki Boot, Alastair Borland, Matt Boswood, Rachel Bottomley, Charlotte Boulton, Heather Bourne, Alex Braithwaite, Alex Bratza, Natalie Braune, Simon Brockwell, Chris Brown, Claudia Bryan-Joyce, Jess Buckley, Jarrett Bulat, Mike Burke, Rowan Burton, Elliot Carmichael, Becky Carolan, Kriss Carr, Laura Carus, Pamela Casasa, Danielle Casey, Claire Charlesworth, Tania Clarke, Peter Clerkin, Matthew Compton, Matt Compton, Itziar Coteron, Megan Courage, Lesley Covington, Roz Creusson, Reece Crisp, Moira Cross, Holly Curtis, Anna Czerniawska, Adam Dallman, Merlin Dass, Lee Davies, Christian Davies, Tom Davis, Amanda Derrick, Hannah Dimelow, Stuart Dingley, Ian Dixon-Wilkinson, Ben Donoghue, Grace Douetil, Myfanwy Dowding, Katie Ducarreaux, Alex Durrell, Sasja Ekenberg, Sandra Elsom, Susan Entwistle, Ilse Euser, Gabriella Fewster, Holly Fitch, Nathalie Fitzgerald, Luke Flint, Hazel Frame, Gemma French, Juno Frewing, Laizan Fung, Sean Gallacher, Jimmy Garner-Currie, Jayne Gibson, Sam Gilham, Abi Gill, Lesley Gill, Caroline Gladwin, Phil Gomme, Linda Gray, Adam Gray, Erin Green, Simeon Green, Jamie Grossman, Charlie Hain, Laura Hammond, Kate Harries, Rachel Harris, Iain Harvey, Iyo Hasegawa, Joyce Hastings, Ceri Hazelden, Anthony Holme, Abby Holmes, Chris Howard, Emily Howie, Emma Hughes, Rebecca Humphreys, Hilary Hunt, Amy Insole, Sarah Jackson, Rory Jakeman, Piran Jeffcock, Charlie Johnson, Lisa Juergensen, Maria Kalamara, Helena Kanoute, Jessica Kelley, Francesca Kelly, Marie Kristine Kenmochi, Reese Kirsh, Olivia Alice Knight, Eleftherios Kotsis, Katie Kozlowska, Kemey Lafond, Jennie Leach, Nigel Letheren, Charlotte Levy, Qiming Liu, Tink Lloyd, Chris Lloyd, Edward Locke, Daisy Long, Sam Mannis, Theodora Marlas, Elisabetta Massimi, Hannah McArdle, Jo McDonald, Danielle McNiven, Marta Micallef, Hannah Moore, Josh Moore, Joe Morgan, Rikhil Morjaria, Luke Morton, Luisa Mota, Valerie Munday, Sophie Naisbitt, William Newman, Anna Newton, Anh Hoang Nguyen, James Nicholson, Katy Nixon, Sam Ohlsson, Connaire Packeer, Christina Palaiologou, Amelia Palmer-Johnston, Hannah Pardon, Joe Park, Heather Passmore, Ryan Penny, Alex Peters, Philip Peters, Theresa Pine, Patrick Pintaske, Ellie Pitt, Gareth Prentice, Beth Price Williams, Alison Prior, Will Purton, David Putman, Alex Randall, Joe Ratcliffe, Sonia Razi, Caroline Rechter, Greg Reekie, Yuan Ren, Daisy Rigley, Daniel Roach-Williams, Jonathan Roberts, Thomas Robinson, Tom Robson, Seth Rook Williams, Jack Ryan, Alison Rycroft, Alison Rycroft, Venetia Samuel, Priti Shah, Caroline Sheard, Kathryn Shooter, Jeremy Silverstone, Elliot Sinclair, Sophie Skelton, George Smith, Ollie Smith, Damien Stanton, Hannah Stewart, Sharna Stockdale, Sam Stuart, David Tague, Sabina Tajbhai, Karl Taylor, Ann Taylor, Richard Thurlow, Charlie Todman, George Townsend, Dave Train, Michael Trasmundi, Lucy Vann, James Wakerell, Luke Wallace, Paul Walmsley, Caroline Walotka, Becca Walters, George Walters, Louisa Ward, Shirley Ann Waterhouse, Gina Watson, Amy Watts, Ben Watts, Jenny Webster, Tara Wells, Laura Whitley, Amy Whittle, Paul Williams, Anthony Willis-Osborne, Liz Wimms, Jon Wing, Jonathan Wright, Ben Yager, Noemi Zajzon **Operations Team** Temitope Adetunji, Tryvell Allen-Charles, James Angel, Nabeel Arshad, Becki Austin, Dandan Bai, Loudmar Bento Portilho, Chris Blackledge, Cormac Bonar, Reece Bourne, Mary Boyes, Jenna Brailey, Doyin Brown, Delphie Callender-Foster, Laura Cantegreil, Jody Chappell, Meng Chen, Tianran Chen, Cheng Cheng, Amy Christie, Lea Clark, Sue Clarke, Christal Clashing O'Reilly, Alexandra Clipa, Nicholas Columbo, Joshua Connolly, Scott Crowhurst, Andrew Davidson, Gemma Davis, Li Ding, Andrea Donigan, Efi Doron, Farid Dudha, Laurene Duret, Katy Earth, Rowanne Eeles, Toby Erskine Crum, Rhea Foy, Mary Furlong, Vanda Galazka, Rosie Gamble, Gus Garcia Lopez, Charmaine Nicole Griffith-McCann, Emma Gyasi, Julie Haggar, Hannah Hand, Emma Hannibal, Coretta Hart, Suchita Hathiramani, Philomena Hayward, Jay Heard, Sophie Heath, Sze Lok Ho, Barbara Hochrath, Danielle Holland, Shan Howes, Minghan Hu, Chen Huang, Jessica Ibeh, Susan Johansson, Akshata Kamath, Tijana Kasic, Ambrosia KejingZhu, Michelle Lacey, Holly Laws, Martina Lee, William Leung, Yee Row Liew, Mei Chern Lim, Henry Lin, Sasha-Louise Lopez, Richard Lorde, Mark Luggar, Laura Macrae, Rob Madeley, Tanisha Malkki, Peter Marley, Shayesteh Mazloumian, Rachel McDermott, Sharon McElhinney, Ambre McGee, Peter McGuinness, Alexander McKinven, Danni Mehta, King Mensah, Saira Mirza, Kirsty Moss, Hollie Munford, Carol Nascimento, Laura Nastase, Selena Ng, Sian Nicholas, Laura Oakley, Sarah-Jane O'Brien, Dawn O'Brien, Sevda Onder, Luis Ortega Contreras, Hilary Osei-Asibey, Julia Ouzia, Jonny Paim, Viktorija Panfilova, Wai Yee Pang, Louise A Panteli, Franklin Pate, Vaneshaben Patel, Kathy Peacock, Amanda Peck, Zoe Pickburn, Olivia Pole-Evans, Elizabeth Redpath, Alexandra Redpath, Tammy Rennie, Tim Reynolds, Olivia Roach, Niel Robbins, Joanna Rockliff, Sue Rowland, Jack Rule, Lena Ruprai, Nathan Ryan, Kimberley Sayers, Shreeya Shah, Mark Shannon, Bing Sheahan, Matilde Silva, Bhupinder Jit Singh, Aga Spiewak, James Stock, Yuka Tanaka, Kath Tatlock, Jack Tattersall, Alex Taylor, Carol-Ann Tennant, Ruth Tesfai, Emma Thompstone, Vuong Tong, Jeff Tong, Kate Tucker, Edson Sydney Tucker, Andrew van Blommestein, Nancy Vigrass, Benjamin Walker, Gavin Walsh, Charlie Welch, Toni Wong, Jing Zhao, Ji Zhu **Thank you to the following groups who appeared in the Ceremony.** The BRIT School, Grimethorpe Colliery Band, Howard Goodall Choir, The London Pearly Kings & Queens Society, Mahogany Carnival, Nostalgia Steel Band, Only Men Aloud, The Original Pearly Kings and Queens Association, staff and In-Pensioners of the Royal Hospital Chelsea.**Thank you to the east London Host Borough schools whose pupils appeared in the Ceremony.** All Saints Catholic School, Barking and Dagenham College, Brook Community Primary School, Colegrave School, Crown Woods College, Cumberland Secondary School, Essex Primary School, Gainsborough Primary School, Grafton Junior School, Hackney Community College, Hallsville Primary School, Heathcote School, Henry Maynard Junior School, Heronsgate Primary School, Hunters Hall Primary School, Jenny Hammond Primary School, Langdon Park School, Leyton Sixth Form College, Lister Community School, Manorfield Primary School, Marian Richardson Primary School, Marner Primary School, Newham College of Further Education, Newham Sixth Form College, Nightingale Primary School, Sherington Primary School, Sir Thomas Abney Primary School, Skinners' Academy, St Angela's and St Bonaventure's Sixth Form, St Josephs RC Junior School, Waltham Forest College, Warren Junior School. **Thank you to all the Games-time role volunteers who contributed to the delivery of the Ceremony. And thank you to all the drama, dance, music and sports groups, societies, centres, organisations and clubs throughout the UK for all their help and support and for publicising our call for volunteers. We couldn't have done it without you.**

Delivering a memorable Olympic Games to inspire a generation with the support of our Partners

Worldwide Olympic Partners

London 2012 Olympic Partners

London 2012 Olympic Supporters

London 2012 Olympic Suppliers and Providers

Aggreko, Airwave, Atkins, The Boston Consulting Group, CBS Outdoor, Crystal CG, Eurostar, Freshfields Bruckhaus Deringer LLP, G4S, GlaxoSmithKline, Gymnova, Heathrow Airport, Heineken UK, Holiday Inn, John Lewis, McCann Worldgroup, Mondo, NATURE VALLEY, Next, Nielsen, Populous, Rapiscan Systems, Rio Tinto, Technogym, Thames Water, Ticketmaster, Trebor, Westfield.